Into
the
Eyes
of
Lions

Into
the
Eyes
of
Lions

GRAHAM MERCER

Matador
9 Priory Business Park,
Wistow Road, Kibworth Beauchamp,
Leicestershire, LE8 0RX
Tel: 0116 279 2299
Email: books@troubador.co.uk
Web: www.troubador.co.uk/matador
Twitter: @matadorbooks

ISBN 978 1838592 295

British Library Cataloguing in Publication Data.
A catalogue record for this book is available from the British Library.

Printed and bound in Great Britain by 4edge Limited
Typeset in 11pt Minion Pro by Troubador Publishing Ltd, Leicester, UK

Matador is an imprint of Troubador Publishing Ltd

This book is dedicated to Anjum, my wife, best friend, soulmate and safari partner. Were I to be granted one final day on Earth to spend as I chose, it would be with her. On safari. In the East Africa that we loved and where we enjoyed some of the most wonderful and exciting times of our lives.

"I have looked into the eyes of lions and slept under the Southern Cross. I have seen the grass of the great plains ablaze and covered with delicate green after the rains"

Karen Blixen – *Letters from Africa*

INTRODUCTION

"Into the Eyes of Lions"

I got out of the car and started walking towards the lions. Three adult females and one sub-adult. All four sprang up and the three adults loped off in alarm. The sub-adult stayed put. She sank into a crouch, ears back, teeth bared, uttering a low, rolling growl, the tip of her tail twitching. I walked a little closer, more slowly now, knowing how quickly a charging lion can cover ground. I clapped my hands as if shooing a neighbour's cat out of the back garden. She was not a neighbour's cat. She sank lower, muscles tensing.

Nothing was lost in translation. The essence of her body language seemed distilled into her eyes. They burned as if with some internal brightness, not mere reflection. It was they that stopped me in my tracks. The eyes of a lion, when you are unarmed and on foot and when they dare you not to take one more step leave no room for misunderstanding. Slowly I backed off, my eyes on hers. With every step backwards I half-expected her to charge. It took about two minutes before I saw the bonnet of my car out of the corner of one eye. Those two minutes seemed like twenty. And then I was back. The car door was half-open. I slid inside and sat down.

Walking towards wild lions on foot and unarmed is not the wisest thing I have ever done. I cannot even blame the impulsiveness of youth; I was 37 at the time. All I can say is that it was part of a sincere but half-baked attempt to prove a theory that wasn't even mine. The famous conservationist Dr. Bernhard Grzimek once alleged that "Plains lions still show a distinctive flight reaction when approached by a tall Maasai carrying a spear". Henry Fosbrooke, first conservator of Ngorongoro, agreed that "as a scientific observation this statement is faultless but it doesn't go far enough". Lions, Henry insisted, would also run away "if approached by Dr. Grzimek carrying an umbrella, or a Klu Klux Klansman carrying a fiery cross…"

The debate had intrigued me. I had long been fascinated by big cats and wanted to learn as much as I could about them. Over a period of several months, whenever I encountered lions on safari and with no one else around (often the case in those days), I would stop my car some distance away and walk towards them. At no time brandishing an umbrella or fiery cross. I relied only on a few handclaps to encourage the lions to race off should any of them prove stubborn. It worked surprisingly well. Until I encountered the young lioness in Mikumi.

There was nothing admirable about these escapades; they were essentially self-indulgent. I was as much interested in my own reactions as I was in those of the lions. Happily that phase of my life on safari was short-lived (as I might have been), and I finally started to grow up. But they did help to satisfy a genuine, if misguided, yearning for adventure. And adventure, after all, is largely what life on safari is all about.

CHAPTER I

"The Child is Father of the Man"

My yearning for adventure was not unusual. Many of the lads that I grew up with, in the terraced streets at the edge of a south Lancashire industrial town in the 1940s and 50s, must have had similar longings. Our heroes, other than famous footballers and cricketers, were Spitfire and Hurricane pilots, the crews of the Lancaster bombers, the men who had served on the Atlantic and Russian convoys or who had fought on the battlefields of Europe and North Africa. And of course we had lived under the leadership of our greatest ever statesman, Winston Churchill, himself an adventurer. Meanwhile, in school, we were encouraged to admire the achievements of other, less militant heroes, such as Florence Nightingale, Grace Darling, David Livingstone and "Scott of the Antarctic".

We never thought of emulating them; they were as remote as the pantheon of Roman Gods. Our day-dreams were restricted to playing football or cricket for England or winning a VC as an Army private or Naval rating in the next war (officer status and service with the R.A.F. being beyond our expectations). National Service, almost entirely with the Army, provided some of the older boys in our area with a more adventurous lifestyle, if only for two years, though more than one spent the two years peeling potatoes in Aldershot.

I had other dreams. Thanks to my father I had been fascinated by wildlife, and in particular by what is now known as the "mega-fauna" since early childhood. The so-called "big game" animals of Africa and India and elsewhere featured in the frieze that Dad had pasted around my bedroom. They encircled my mind as well as my room. I must often have fallen to sleep whilst looking at their pictures on the wall. Maybe that is where my fascination for the large mammals – and in particular the big cats – began…

But the creatures in the frieze, like those I saw in books, were no more than symbols. I wanted to see the real things. And when I did, probably in Manchester's Belle View Zoo when I was six or seven, it was the big cats that would have excited me most. My first real lion would almost certainly have been sleeping, or at least lying around looking as bored as a teenager at a funeral tea. Yet I would have been transfixed. A few years later I saw lions in a circus and these were the real deal, jogging through the tunnel that led to the ring in single file and in ominous silence before taking up their positions on respective stands. To snarl, just like their Metro Goldwyn Mayer cousin that I sometimes saw "at the pictures", at the lion tamer, armed only with his inevitable whip. It was like watching a Hollywood version of "Daniel in the Lions' Den".

The next advancement would have been to see such animals in the wild. But this, when I was a teenager, was unimaginable. A thing of dreams. All that was open to me, and as far as I knew all that would ever be, was the wildlife in the wastelands and fields a short walk away from our tiny terraced house, at the edge of a heavily industrial town.

It was, for a while, more than enough. From the doorstep of that house, on a fine spring day, we could hear the skylarks singing above the adjacent wasteland that we called "the fields". And within a hundred yards of where the lower stone setts of our street ended, Red Admirals, Orange Tips, Meadow Browns and other beautiful butterflies, as well as Cabbage Whites and several species of bees, could be seen as they fluttered or buzzed among the dandelions, daisies, "Tom Thumbs" and clovers.

A little further afield could be found water voles, dragon-flies, great crested newts, fish such as roach, perch and even pike and a host of bird species. As well as ancient woodlands of oak, beech, sycamore, ash and hazel, their banks, sloping down to a stream, seasonally carpeted with bluebells, or, along the stream itself, white clouds of wild garlic. To me it was bewitching. A wonderland not only to be explored but to become entwined, like bindweed, throughout the double helix of my DNA.

Sometimes, on his weekly "48-offs" from the glass factory, Dad would take me for walks, or rides on the cross-bar of his second-hand bicycle, through these fields and woods or along the towpath of the Sankey Canal, established in 1757. He taught me the names of birds, fishes, insects, trees and flowers. He taught me things that are illegal now and that were probably illegal then; how to find birds' nests and blow eggs for my collection; how to catch butterflies or dragon-flies or bees; where to find certain wild flowers to take home for my mother. And he taught me to wander at will around the local countryside, ignoring notices declaring that "Trespassers will be prosecuted" by climbing through fences or squeezing through railings.

He respected the land, if not its private ownership, and like many working class men and women of his time had a deep-seated affinity with nature, a compatibility now greatly diminished. Through him I learned to appreciate the intricate beauty of a dunnock's nest, the blue fragility of a song thrush's eggs, to follow the soaring flight of the lark, to marvel at the magnificence of a red admiral's wings or the spotted orange belly of a crested newt, to breathe in the fragrance of hawthorn blossom or bluebells or new-mown hay as if they were as vital as oxygen itself. And in those northern waste-lands and woods, among these fields and by the canal and colliery flashes, I learned to love adventure. Nothing death-defying but adventure nonetheless.

My interest extended far beyond these local haunts. Inspired by my father's stories of tigers and other "big game" that he had seen as a private soldier in India during the Second World War, I began to read books about the jungle and the bush. The expression "big game", though still widely used, has obvious hunting associations but at the time hunting was regarded, by many (including myself), as a reputable and "manly" profession. Certainly my new heroes included Jim Corbett, the Anglo-Indian hunter who was often called upon to track and kill man-eating tigers and leopards in and around the present-day tiger sanctuary named after him, and J.A. Hunter who lived up to his name in colonial Kenya.

"The child" became "father of the man". At the age of 20, longing for a more adventurous life than that of a postal counter clerk, I ran away to sea. Or to be precise took a train down to the Navy's basic training establishment *HMS Raleigh* in Cornwall. From there, after technical training at *HMS Collingwood* near Portsmouth I was posted to Pitreavie Castle, just north of the Forth Bridge in south-east Scotland. The castle, built in 1615 on land once owned by a sister of Robert the Bruce, was then the headquarters of the NATO North Atlantic Area.

I enjoyed Scotland and my time at Pitreavie but I hadn't joined the Navy to live there. Eventually I was required to complete a drafting preference form and more in hope than expectation asked to be posted to the survey vessel *H.M.S. Owen*, operating in the Antarctic. That, I felt sure, would provide me with the excitement that I craved whilst satisfying my love for wildlife, in particular the "mega-fauna" that fascinated me. No fauna, after all, is more "mega" than the great whales of the southern ocean.

Life, let alone the Royal Navy, rarely grants our dearest wishes, but to my delight I was assigned to the *Owen*. Well aware of the rigours of the Antarctic (after all, Robert Falcon Scott and Ernest Shackleton were both members of the Senior Service) the Navy kitted me out with a heavy white sea-jersey and thick white stockings. Not exactly transforming me into an Antarctic explorer overnight but a step in the right direction. The weather-proof anoraks and trousers, the snow boots, balaclavas, anti-glare goggles and a team of huskies would, I imagined, follow once I joined the ship.

Meanwhile it was thought prudent (it was mid-winter at the time) to pack me off from time to time to the nearby Ochil Hills or the more distant Cairngorms, to master the art of skiing. Or more probably (to borrow a Naval expression) to learn to "fall arse over tit" without losing too much face or too many bodily extremities. I was just about learning to stay upright when Pitreavie's Master at Arms, a short and stocky Glaswegian, summoned me to his office. To tell me that the *Owen* had been transferred from the Antarctic to the tropics. She was to take part in the 1962-64 International Indian Ocean Expedition. "That'll fickin' teach ye!" he added.

It did. It taught me that when one door closes, another one really does sometimes open…

CHAPTER II

Safaris on a Shoestring

—

A Dream Come True

As the *Owen* approached Mombasa just before Christmas in 1962, after six weeks spent charting the mid-ocean Carlsberg Ridge, we were informed that official Christmas cards were being issued from the ship's office. The cards, left-overs from the previous year, showed *H.M.S. Owen* standing off the steep, snow-chequered cliffs of South Georgia. Soon after we had docked I sent one home. I suspect that my dear mother, never having left the UK and conditioned to think of the equatorial African coast in terms of swaying palms, coffee-creamer white sands and turquoise shallows, never quite got over this shock to her system.

There is, of course, one place within a 6 hour or so drive of Mombasa where snow and ice *are* to be found, and three days after our arrival I was heading for it, on my first East African safari. Two friends and I had booked the trip through "Jimmy's Tours", as low-budget as it sounds (£12 each, including an overnight stay at the Kibo Hotel at Marangu, on Kilimanjaro's lower slopes). We travelled, with a Kenyan driver, Mohammed, via Tsavo East National Park, where we saw, among many other things, red elephants (covered in laterite dust) and a black rhino, standing in the shade of an acacia close to Aruba Lodge.

And for the first time I saw giraffes quite unlike those in their high concrete compounds at the zoo. Elegant now in movement as well as appearance, as they lolloped languidly away from our Peugot 404, like creatures in a seamless, slow-motion dream. Women in particular love them, and it is easy to see why, for giraffes seem to embrace the most feminine of qualities, especially when cantering away and then stopping to turn and look at their admirers. Arguably through the most beautiful eyes in the animal kingdom.

I also saw zebras in a very different light (literally as well as figuratively), for although the light in East Africa is not always as clear and sharp as is often said to be, it usually is. And there is more of it. In such clarity zebras stand out like figures penned upon the vellum of an illuminated manuscript, defying us not to notice, acknowledge and photograph them. Their stripes – never mind what the biologists say – having evolved with photographers in mind, to help with focusing before the invention of the auto-focus lens. And in so doing commit the Zebra to posterity with the precision it deserves and demands.

What we did not see on that first safari were lions. It didn't matter – yet. I was giddy with infatuation.

I didn't see the snows of Kilimanjaro either until we were well on the way back, despite having slept on its lower slopes overnight. On the outward journey the upper slopes of the mountain had been hidden in cloud and on the morning of our departure we had left Marangu before daybreak. Soon after re-entering the Tsavo at Mbuyuni we were distracted by the first of many breakdowns that I was to experience on safari – and take my first walk in the African bush. Some distance from Mbuyuni Gate the radiator of our Peugot 404 erupted in a sibilant spout of steam and Mohammed braked. The water pump had sprung a leak. The radiator was now empty and foolishly, neither we nor "Jimmy's Tours" had thought to carry extra water in case of emergencies; it was that kind of safari.

In those days that corner of the Tsavo was practically deserted so we couldn't expect help, but long experience of working for companies like "Jimmy's" has advantages. Mohammed was nothing if not inventive. With an old screwdriver and no doubt a silent appeal to Allah he somehow patched up the water pump. And then led us off, with a city dweller's distrust of the wilderness, to look for a waterhole. He was carrying a *debe*, a large tin can that had once held cooking oil, and an old tin mug. These, together with the screwdriver, comprised the complete "Jimmy's Tours" emergency tool-kit.

The red-brown track was scarred, here and there, by the hoofmarks of zebras, various antelopes and the huge, unmistakable prints of a giraffe. Like us, the animals must have been desperate to find water, for despite the rains further east this region of the Tsavo was dry. When we finally found a waterhole it was little more than a shallow depression, dark with churned up mud and pitted with hoof-marks. I was relieved, and disappointed at the same time, to see no evidence of lions. But the only water was that which had seeped into the deeper hoofmarks at the centre of the depression, discoloured and foetid.

Mohammed, murmuring gloomily in Swahili, squatted in this muddy central patch. Mechanically he began to scoop up what water he could with the tin mug, transferring it to the *debe* as we looked on. Eventually, with the debe only three-quarters full, he stood upright and said, without enthusiasm, "*Twende!*" ("Let's go"). We followed him back down the track in silence.

He poured the water carefully into the radiator, stopping when the flow became thick with sediment. "Not enough" he said. One of my companions, a young, pragmatic engine room artificer, suggested that we all "piss into the tin" to help make up the shortfall. Leading by example he took the *debe*, turned his back and donated his contribution. Fortunately, in a Moshi dance hall and bar the previous evening, we had all drunk more lager than was good for us and one by one we followed Martin's lead. Mohammed emptied the makeshift chamber pot into the radiator but looked less than optimistic about the outcome. "Give it a try" said Martin, "at least it might get us back to the gate". "*In shaa Allah*" murmured Mohammed.

And by the grace of Allah or good luck we reached the gate though the liquid in the radiator (I can hardly call it water) was bubbling furiously. We climbed out of the car and Mohammed lifted the bonnet. The duty ranger, who had earlier welcomed us, emerged from his hut. "*Pole sana!*" ("Very sorry!") he said gravely. Mohammed brought out the *debe* and addressed the ranger quietly in Swahili. He was obviously asking for water but in this lonely, drought-dessicated outpost it was like asking for a magnum of chilled Dom Perignon. The ranger's head shook slightly, not in refusal but to emphasise the seriousness of the request. But this was Africa, and this was the bush, and we were strangers in need of help. In those days that was enough. Taking the *debe* the ranger disappeared while Mohammed drained the radiator of its foul-smelling contents.

Returning with the *debe*, now full of water, the ranger handed it to Mohammed. Once the radiator had cooled he looked on despairingly as Mohammed poured the water in, remonstrating at the smallest wasteful dribble. And then Mohammed pleaded for a top-up. Which was reluctantly granted. As a token – we had little else to offer – I gave the ranger my naval working shirt and cap, complete with its *H.M.S. Owen* tally, which for some reason I had brought with me. He immediately put them on, standing to attention and saluting (albeit army-style) as we drove away. I have often wondered how many travellers entered or left this fairly remote gate in Tsavo to encounter a black Kenyan ranger in Royal Navy working uniform, 200 kilometres from the sea.

We had no more problems with the water pump but some time later, close to the Teita Hills, we were all in need of another pee. Mohammed stopped and we got out to relieve ourselves by the roadside. In the midst of this distraction I happened to look up and around, at some risk to my new Bata safari boots. Away to the west I saw, high amidst the grey-white clouds, a whiter patch of cloud, its upper edge improbably straight. As the German missionary Johannes Rebmann had done in May 1848, and by coincidence from almost the same spot. And like him I suddenly became aware that the dazzling white cloud was in fact snow. And that I was looking, for the first time, at Mount Kilimanjaro.

The following year, this time with three officers and two lower deck friends, and with the ship's medical officer driving, I returned to Marangu and the Kibo Hotel, again via the Tsavo. We spent a day on "Kili", as the mountain is affectionately known, climbing through the rainforest to the first hut, Mandara, at almost 9,000 feet (2,743 metres). Just beyond Mandara, where the forest phases into heath, we saw Kibo peak in the distance. So immediate in the thin, cloudless air that I felt like running across the rolling upland moors to scoop up the snow, to prove that it existed.

We also drove to Ngurdoto (now Arusha) National Park. We spent only two hours or so there, as time was short and steady rain was falling. We must have seen elephants, buffaloes, hippos and giraffes, among others, but all I remember, apart from the rain and the lake and the dripping green forests, is a rhino seen from a distance, through binoculars, wallowing in the mud at the southern end of Small Momela Lake. By the time we reached the spot it had gone.

But our little trip had been far from disappointing. By the time we left Ngurdoto it had, like the Tsavo, imposed a lasting impression upon me. Years before it had been described by Sir Julian Huxley, English evolutionary biologist and much else, as "a gem". His unoriginal though sincere remark has been quoted, ever since, in just about every guide-book and website that mentions the park, as if there is nothing else to add. It was, of course, intended as a great compliment though I would like to think that Arusha National Park is far more precious than a small stone, however attractive.

Soon afterwards I spent time ashore on the Kenya coast, operating, in those pre-satellite days, transportable navigational beacons to pin-point the ship's position as she surveyed the offshore waters. Initially I was in Malindi, before it became a popular tourist resort. Later I was transferred to Kipini, on the remote Tana estuary, with two different shipmates. We lived in the old District Commissioner's house, deserted and reputedly haunted after two D.Cs had died there, one after going mad and shooting himself in 1919. His mother, after visiting his grave to pay her respects, had also committed suicide. The two DCs were buried in a small grove between the house and the sea. A third grave contains the body of the former manager of a rice and rubber estate who had also ended his own life, by "throwing himself into the Tana River".

Little wonder that the superstitious locals gave the house and the grave site a very wide berth; I recently read that they still do, even though the house is now in ruins. They were not alone in their fears, it seems. From the 1930s a "ghost book" was kept at the house, presumably so that the D.Cs of the time could record any spectral shenanegans. One of my two colleagues, a normally carefree "stoker", would never spend time alone in the house, and refused to keep night watches in the small uniport hut that housed our transmitter-receiver equipment. The hut was situated in the bush between the old house and the sea, close to the little grove and its three graves, and spending the night there, with no one for company and only a paraffin lamp for illumination, was a lonely business.

I myself often felt a sense of eeriness, especially when, during the night, I was obliged to walk over to a second uniport hut some distance away in the bush, to top up the generator that was housed there. The unglazed window by the generator looked out towards the little grove of trees, and sometimes the moonlight would reflect from one arm of the marble cross at the head of one of the graves, as if someone was standing there, holding a lamp. When I first witnessed this illusion it was quite frightening. But the living are far more threatening than the dead and whenever I walked between our two huts after dark I was more worried about bumping into a wandering hippo or elephant, or treading on a puff adder, than coming face to face with a ghost.

Not that I ever encountered any large mammals or snakes on my nocturnal excursions, though there were certainly hippos and crocodiles in the nearby river and plenty of snakes in the bush, and elephants were certainly present in the locality. Just south of the river, in the Tana Delta, big game was common. Members of my ship's inshore surveying party, put ashore to erect a radar beacon, had once been chased out of the bush there by a rhino. One of them, an ageing, overweight seaman later told me that he had looked over his shoulder whilst running and seen "the whites of its eyes". I envied him. I wanted to tell stories like that. Providing, of course, that I, like him, had lived to tell the tale.

The land beyond the river fascinated me. A triangular expanse of palm savannah, seasonally flooded grassland, forest fragments, lakes, mangroves, sand dunes and deserted beaches, it posed an ever-growing challenge. One morning, on a rare off-duty day when the ship was re-provisioning in Mombasa, I decided to go there, and persuaded one of my colleagues, Jan, to join me. At 33 he was almost elderly by Naval standards; he even had false teeth. He was also a quiet, educated man for someone on the Lower Deck, and though not particularly interested in wildlife was always ready for a bit of excitement. Not that we were attempting anything too daring but with the exception of our brief walk to find water in the Tsavo, it was my first experience of being on foot in the African bush. A very different prospect to being in a vehicle.

We hired a local fisherman to take us across the river in his dug-out canoe and hopefully pick us up again in the late afternoon. Once across the river the presence of wild animals – and big ones at that – soon became evident. The beach above the tide-line was block-printed, in places, by the petal-patterned prints of hippos and scattered, here and there, with their dung. Less frequently we saw the platter-like footprints of elephants, with their filigree of fine wrinkles as if the soles of their owners' feet were in need of ironing. Their owners' droppings, large as children's footballs and obviously fairly recent, lay nearby.

Some distance from the beach, beyond the intervening thorn-bush, rose a long, low ridge. If we could find a way to get to it, through the dense bush, I told Jan, we would be able to look out over the delta and plan a way forward. But the only access to the ridge proved to be by way of game trails, at best no more than narrow tunnels through the thick embranglement of thorns. I decided to take a chance and with Jan close behind began to make my way through one of them. With not even a stick to protect us the sharp demarcation between bright, breezy beach and the gloomily enclosed stillness was more than a physical challenge. The tunnel, no broader than an elephant and little higher, didn't just lead to the ridge but into a different, more dangerous, world.

In such a world, when you are on foot and unarmed, one quickly becomes reliant on senses normally taken for granted. And with a much greater intensity. In our day-to-day life these senses are mostly on standby or at least subdued. In big game country, especially in thick bush, they are constantly on red alert. You revert quickly to your ancestral hunter-gatherer type, begin to see and hear and smell things that you would normally have overlooked. Johnny Johnson, the Battle of Britain fighter pilot ace, owed his success rate and survival to such heightened awareness. He taught himself to look *into*, rather than at, particular patches of sky. Similar skills are essential in the bush.

Not that walking in wild Africa, even without a gun, is anything like as dangerous as flying a Spitfire in the Battle of Britain. But fatalities and serious injuries do occur and to minimize the risks you have to learn to read the bush as Johnson read the sky. Like him you rely mainly on sight, but in the bush you also learn to rely on hearing and on smell. You learn to listen to silence as he looked at apparently empty skies. Your ears strain, as if with a little more effort they might pick out the sound of the heat rising from the hard-baked earth.

We could certainly smell the rising heat, pungent in places with the urine and droppings of large pachyderms. I could even taste the sharp sourness of the dust upon my tongue. I felt vulnerable, like a hermit crab between shells. But excited and alive, my brain striving to filter out the less meaningful sensations, the insistent cooing of a dove, the perfume of acacia blossoms, the patternless monotony of dessicated leaves and entwined branches. In order to concentrate on the potentially threatening; the sights and sounds and smells that I didn't want to see or hear or smell at all. An irregular, darker patch of shadow, buffalo-black amid the anarchy of thorns; the almost inaudible, hollow thud of a hoof as some large animal, asleep on its feet in the thick, hot air, shifted it weight; the smell of warm dung or drying urine, the tom-cat smell where a lion or leopard has sprayed its signature.

Your brain and the senses that inform it undergo a crash course in bush-craft, the neuro-electric impulses between it and them flashing back and forth at the speed of light. In the urban world it is said that information is power. In the bush and unarmed, all power is stripped away. The only advantage you can hope for, however efficient the cerebral information-gathering, is in the form of an early warning system. "Proceed with caution!", "Beware!" "Back off while you still can!"

My own powerlessness was impressed upon me with every step. It was obvious that the game-trail was frequently used by large animals. And just as obvious that the savage maze of thorn on either side was impenetrable to a human being. I wondered, pointlessly, what would happen if I rounded a bend to find a rhino or elephant or buffalo confronting me. I was high on adrenalin, more excited than afraid, not fully aware of the tension until I felt it draining away later. By the time we reached the relative safety of the ridge I was a different man from the one that had left the beach half-an-hour before, a change that went deeper than my sweat-soaked shirt and the lacerations on my arms.

Once on the ridge, revelling in relief, the rediscovered breeze and the much greater visibility, I scanned, through my binoculars, the landscape below, a flat mosaic of grey-green thornbush and palm groves and small slades of coarse grassland. Almost at once I saw the sway-backed upper bodies of several elephants. They were some distance away in single file, shouldering through the thickets. I was thrilled. And a little concerned, for they were heading in our direction. One by one they began to emerge from the bush, coming to a stop amid a small expanse of grass. I counted four adults and three or four young, including a tiny calf. Soon afterwards I saw what seemed to be a large bull, some way behind and still partly hidden.

The leading elephant curled a querulous trunk to test the air. Other trunks were raised, like a small colony of long, tubular sea-plants waving in a slow current. The breeze was blowing in from the shore, carrying our scent towards them.

After some hesitancy, however, the matriarch resumed her leisurely advance. The others followed in single file. As the ground dipped into a shallow declivity they broke into the head-swinging, ear-flapping jog-trot that elephants often adopt when travelling down a gentle slope. As the grassland levelled out they slowed to a stately march, advancing in that deceptively ground-covering way that would become familiar – and at times disturbing – to me in the years ahead. Purposeful and sure, as if they not only sought some elephantine Holy Grail but knew exactly where it was. "I think", said Jan, "that we'd better get out of here."

The elephants had now vanished into the bush that separated us and them, no more than about ten minutes away. The landward slopes of the ridge were gentle, they would not slow them down for long, if at all. We quickly retreated, hurrying back down the game trail before the elephants reached it. The thought of coinciding with them in that confusion of natural razor wire was not pleasant. When we finally emerged on to the beach, sweaty with heat and adrenalin, we spontaneously stripped off and, elated by our adventure, raced across the sands to fling ourselves naked into the sea.

Our little jaunt had been foolish. I would never enter bush like that now, even with a rifle. But it had been exciting, my first encounter with big game whilst on foot. Many more such encounters lay ahead but sadly I would never again set foot in what was then one of Kenya's least-explored and most wonderful wildlife regions, the Tana Delta. Soon afterwards Somali bandits, known as the *Shifta*, fore-runners of today's Al Shabab terrorists, were reported to be active in Tana District. They knew about our little station on the coast and we were warned that they had threatened to kill us. After they had shot two villagers in Witu, some eight miles inland, we were quickly evacuated one night, by sea.

Not so long afterwards, however, I returned to my first love, the Tsavo, and yet again to the Kibo Hotel in Marangu. Our skipper David Haslam, (later Rear Admiral Sir David Haslam K.B.E, C.B, Hydrographer of the Navy and President of Derbyshire Cricket Club) was as distinguished as he sounds. A friend of Noel Coward, he could easily, with his wartime record, his rugged good looks and his ever-present pipe, have played a leading part in Coward's film *In Which We Serve*. Possessed of "the Nelson touch", that sureness and self-belief that can turn a blind eye to officialdom, he was, like Nelson himself (though much less warlike or vain), as popular with the men on the lower deck as those in the wardroom. As our two-year participation in the International Indian Ocean Expedition came to a close he organized an overnight "jolly" (Naval slang for an enjoyable run ashore) to Marangu, open to any of the ship's company not on duty.

We went via the Tsavo in an old Kenyan bus, presumably hired from Mombasa Council. It was one of those long-distance monsters with a huge roof rack and once we arrived at Tsavo East's Buchuma Gate most of us, including the skipper, climbed up there and made ourselves as comfortable as we could, almost certainly breaking national park regulations. If so we soon found out why when we were mock-charged by a bull elephant. It pulled up just a few metres from the bus, screaming blue murder. Its trunk and tusks, from our elevated and exposed situation, looked particularly menacing and the screams cut through us like the screech of flying shrapnel. But the lads, in their spirited innocence, let out a lusty cheer and the elephant backed off, as it would have done anyway. Commander Haslam, teeth clenched on his pipe, calmly watched it go, like a senior officer at Trafalgar watching the retreat of a French man o'war.

That evening, after some serious drinking around the circular open fire in the "Kibo Hotel's" lounge, the ships' company, with a few exceptions including the skipper, stripped naked in the hotel's back garden and dived recklessly into the tiny unheated swimming pool, which at 5,000 feet above sea level was cold enough to impose a sudden, if temporary, sobriety. We re-entered the Tsavo next day suitably chastised and hung-over, but still piled eagerly out of the bus and on to the roof again for the last phase of the final "jolly" of the *Owen's* two-year commission. And for what I assumed would be my last East African safari.

"Right", announced the skipper as he made himself comfortable in our midst and sat puffing at his pipe, "This morning I want to see *lions!*". He had recently read *Born Free*, the story of Elsa the lioness that had captured the imagination of people around the world. We all wanted to see lions, no one more eagerly than me. Everyone new to safari wants to see lions.

The Lion, after all, is embedded in our psyche. Like so many others, I had seen them in books and photographs, on pub signs and postage stamps, on national flags and on the white sweaters of my national cricketing heroes, on tins of syrup and packets of envelopes and of course I saw one, and heard it snarl, whenever I watched a Metro Goldwyn Mayer film. I read about them at home, and in school I heard stories such as "Androcles and the Lion" or "Daniel in the Lions' Den".

I never dared to dream that one day I would see one in the wild. And yet, in only my 23rd year, here I was, on the luggage rack of a bus in Tsavo East National Park, with a sizeable portion of my ship's company. And here was Commander Haslam sitting next to me saying "Now I want to see lions". And when the skipper wanted something he usually got his wish.

Time was running out when we suddenly came across a herd of impalas in the semi-arid wastes close to Aruba. We had seen hundreds of impalas already but these were bunched together in the middle of a small area of parched grass and red laterite soil, half-encircled by dense thorn-bush. They were facing away from us, still as the subjects of a snapshot, the black and white "alarm" striping on their rumps distinct, their ears poised like a flock of tick-birds about to take wing. Their eyes were fixed on one particular area among the nearby thorns.

We all realised that we had interrupted a hunt. That somewhere in that grey-brown confusion of bush and straw-coloured grass was a predator. Almost certainly a lion. Instinctively we all fell silent. Watching... Waiting... Hoping... Through my binoculars I scanned the bush, striving to see a meaningful pattern in the chaos. But seeing none. We seemed to have interrupted the passage of time as well as the hunt. No one spoke and none of the impalas, except for the flicker of an ear or the twitch of a fly-bitten hide, moved a muscle.

And then the spell was broken. "Sorry lads", said the skipper eventually, "looks as if we've had it. We need to get back." Even as he spoke he was still, like us, peering hopefully into the bush. For a few moments more we all looked and waited in silence. Then the skipper called down to the driver and the bus's engine soon stuttered into a steady throb, causing the impalas, momentarily, to turn their heads. I remember feeling dreadfully disappointed, eyes still on that patch of bush as the bus began to pull away. I had been so close to seeing my first – and probably my last – lion in the wild.

CHAPTER III

A Good Man in Africa

Amazingly my next chance came only three years later, quite out of the blue as chances sometimes do. At the time I was serving on the minesweeper *HMS Wiston* in the Persian Gulf. The Gulf was considered, not without reason, as a hardship post and perhaps to deflect mutinous thoughts or the possibility of us all losing our marbles the Navy had come up with a wonderful compromise. After a certain length of time, circumstances permitting, any one of us could apply for two weeks "rest and recuperation" leave, to be spent in either Beirut or Nairobi.

For most young sailors who had spent a year or more in the Gulf, not known for its bucolic pleasures or fleshpots, the choice would nowadays be known as "a non-brainer". Beirut was still known as "the Paris of the East", with all that this implies. So when a shipmate and I opted to fly to Nairobi more than a few eyebrows were raised. Not least because the shipmate in question would normally have lolloped off to the Lebanon *tout de suite*. His name was Peter but like almost everyone on the lower deck he was known by a nickname, in his case "Lofty". He must have been about six foot two but looked even taller because of his beanpole figure. With his chin-strap beard and semi-permanent broad grin he looked like a garden gnome that had been stretched on the rack.

Lofty was a star performer at the occasional "sod's opera", an impromptu concert, characterised by much drinking and bawdy singing, through which "Jack" lets off steam after weeks at sea. A fortnight's bar-hopping in the less salubrious streets off Beirut's Corniche would have been his cup of tea, or more appropriately his glass of *arak*. But I had persuaded him, against his better judgement, to accompany me to East Africa. He was an adventurous as well a jolly soul and by one of those strokes of luck that seem heaven sent we had been presented with an opportunity that no young man of spirit could ignore.

With the fortnight's "r and r" in mind I had written a speculative letter to John Owen, Director of Tanzania's National Parks, whose name I had seen in a book and whose official address I had somehow tracked down. I told him of my passion for East Africa and the bush and that my friend and I were hoping to camp in one of East Africa's national parks. We could not afford the normal tourist rates but we were not, I assured him, looking for "freebies". We would live as simply as we could to cut costs and as independently as circumstances allowed. All we asked was the required permission and to hire a small tent and a few pots and pans. Everything else we would arrange ourselves, and pay for.

Lofty and I were only one rung above the lowest of the low in the naval hierarchy. And completely unknown to John Owen. But he responded at once and said he had been in touch, on our behalf, with a man called Desmond Vesey Fitzgerald. Vesey, as he called him, was "one of the best field scientists in East Africa", an authority on grasses and much else, and honorary warden of Ngurdoto National Park (later incorporated into present-day Arusha National Park). He was, John told us, happy to let us camp in Ngurdoto. All we had to do was to write to him to co-ordinate things.

Thrilled, I immediately wrote to Vesey and he too replied promptly. I still have the airmail letter, kept out of respect for a very special man. "You are most welcome," Vesey wrote, "to come here any time you like and stay as long as you like… There is usually plenty of variety as I am also occupied in exploring Meru Mountain and in work at Lake Manyara. You can quite easily, if rather uncomfortably, come down by bus from Nairobi."

The bus journey was as uncomfortable as he had predicted but for us utterly absorbing. It took us past the rolling grasslands of Nairobi National Park, scattered with wildebeest and zebras and gazelles, and as we travelled south several Maasai "warriors" joined us, laying their spears in the aisle and smelling, not unpleasantly, of rancid butter. As we approached the border post at Namanga we saw Kilimanjaro in the distance, and closer at hand, Mount Meru.

In Arusha we stayed overnight at the "New Arusha Hotel" (in fact 73 years old). It had seen more illustrious guests than Lofty and me, including Edward, Prince of Wales, Baron von Blixen (Karen Blixen's ex-husband) and even "Big John" Wayne. None of them could have appreciated it more than we did, though we only stayed overnight. After breakfast in the beautiful gardens the next morning we persuaded a reluctant taxi driver to take us to Vesey's bungalow in the heart of Ngurdoto National Park.

His reluctance soon made sense. Ngurdoto was only about 30 miles away but the track leading up to the park from the main Arusha – Moshi road was fairly steep in places and studded with rocks. At its upper end we had to ford at least one stream, the driver scanning the luxuriant banks lugubriously for large, ill-disposed animals. In a Land Rover it would have been a doddle but in a 2WD saloon car held together, like most Tanzanian taxis of the time, by faith and friction, every jolt and clang had dolorous implications.

We emerged unscathed at the park's Ngurdoto gate and from there drove on without incident and much joy through the forest to the low hills overlooking Small Momela Lake, where

Vesey's little thatched bungalow was situated. He was away on safari as he had said he might be but we were greeted by his houseboy, Chilufyia. I have since read that the name means "absent-minded" in his native Zambia; if so Vesey would have found it appropriate as he often chided the young man, usually good-humouredly, for forgetting to do or to pack or to remember something of importance.

Chilufyia was probably in his late-twenties but had the face of a man who had opted, in the interests of gravitas, to bypass the frivolities of youth in favour of early and self-imposed middle age. There hung about him an air of seriousness and melancholy rarely seen outside funeral parlours. My mother would have said that "He looks as if he's lost a pound and found a penny". But he welcomed us with quiet, if unsmiling, good manners. We were expecting to camp but Chilufiya would have none of it. "Mr. Vesey say you stay here", he insisted, showing us into the bungalow's cosy guest room and ignoring our protests. "Now", he announced as he left us to it "I go make dinner".

We learned later that Vesey's cook, Benson, was with him on safari. Chilufiya had been detailed as a temporary stand-in. Not, I suspect, with Chilufiya's wholehearted approval or with great confidence on Vesey's part. But if nothing else Chilufiya had a chef's matter-of-fact attitude towards murder and soon afterwards we heard the alarm squawks of *Gallus gallus domesticus* as one of its representatives upon Earth legged around the bungalow in a vain attempt to avoid a violent and untimely end. Life for a chicken in the midst of an African national park must have been perilous enough without having Chilufyia hot on its tail with a kitchen knife. "Poor bugger", murmured Lofty.

To distance ourselves from an atrocity committed on our behalf we made our way outdoors, averting our eyes as we passed the adjacent kitchen. Soon we were sitting on a log on the crest of the hills overlooking the Momela Lakes. It was like being parachuted into Paradise. Away to the east, beyond the lakes, Kilimanjaro was hidden in cloud, waiting to knock us for six the next morning when we saw it through the bungalow's picture window. To westward the sharply castellated peaks of Meru, the "Black Mountain", combed the light of the lowering sun into strands of silver. Below us, amid the down-sweep of bush between us and Small Momela, we saw through binoculars two widely separated pairs of black rhinos, their upper contours and horns sharp in the evening light.

As the shadow of Meru fell across us we were called in by Chilufiya and sat down to plates of stringy but tasty chicken, with fried onions and steaming mounds of rice and a couple of cans of beer, before retiring to bed, dazed by the circumstances in which we found ourselves. The next morning we sat down to a typical "white East African" breakfast of sliced paw-paw and fresh lime followed by fried eggs and buttered toast and large mugs of Africafe, the instant arabica coffee from Tanzania's southern Highlands.

Whoever had planned the building of the bungalow had been inspired. And sensitive, for despite the extraordinary view that it commanded it was virtually invisible from any of the regular park tracks. Each morning as we sat down to breakfast in the living room Kilimanjaro would be stretched across the picture window in cinemascopic grandeur, blue-grey and white and ethereal. Sometimes an elephant or giraffe, passing by the window, would lend its imposing presence to the view. The elephants also provided Vesey with fuel, for at that altitude, in the dry season, the evenings were cold and Vesey burned balls of elephant dung in his open fireplace, as people in Ireland and the Western Isles of Scotland burn peat.

Vesey returned later that first day in a battered old Land Rover. He looked exactly what he was, an educated man of action in his late fifties who had spent much time in the Arabian desert and in the African bush. Shortish, robust, bespectacled and genial-looking, with grey hair, he was wearing the kind of neutral-coloured clothing that one associates with safari, his trousers tucked into the knee-high brown boots that he always wore and that gave him his popular nickname among the Africans, "*Bwana Mungozi*" ("Mr Leather Boots").

He was immediately welcoming, his eyes, twinkling behind the circular lenses of his glasses, hinting at a mischievous sense of humour, his cheeks aglow with good health. Despite the fact that we were strangers – and not very accomplished ones at that – he was to treat us with great generosity and goodwill. Which considering that recent guests had included Prince Bernhardt of the Netherlands and Charles Lindbergh, the reclusive pioneer aviator who in 1927 had become famous for his solo, record-breaking Transatlantic flight in *The Spirit of St. Louis*, was something of an honour.

He soon excused himself and, not wishing to "get under his feet", we spent much of the rest of the day out on the crest of the ridge looking down upon the lakes and scanning the bush through binoculars. We saw the same four rhinos, a family of elephants and a single bull, a herd of buffaloes and a good many giraffes. As well as waterbuck, warthogs and various birds, including flamingos. Plus pods of hippos in the lake. At dinner that evening we enthused about all this but Vesey, sensing that we were looking for something a little more adventurous, promised to let us walk around Small Momela the next day, accompanied by an armed ranger.

The following morning, after a breakfast served by a beaming Benson, we set off with Vesey's blessings and with one of his rangers, Godfrey, who carried a large-bore rifle. The walk was exciting enough but relatively uneventful. The next morning we went again, though this time Godfrey, for some reason, was armed only with a *panga* (machete). What he was expected to do with it, should we be charged by an elephant, buffalo or rhino, was unclear. Fortunately we were not to find out, as the walk was no more dramatic than that of the previous day.

I was quickly learning that the East African bush is characterized not by constant tension, as so many wildlife documentaries imply, but by a predominant tranquility. A tranquility that can, however, be dangerously deceptive. For it is essentially the poise between finely balanced, opposing natural forces; the calm stability of the tightrope walker. Except that in the bush anything falling from the high wire rarely climbs back.

Vesey, happy to take risks, was doing all he could to provide us with the adventure we craved. On the third morning he allowed us to go walking alone and unarmed. I cannot imagine a Chief Park Warden today doing this, especially for the benefit of two young, inexperienced men that he hardly knew. It is, in any case, against national park regulations, as it was then. And if anything had gone badly wrong Vesey would have been in serious trouble. But he, like my old skipper Captain Haslam, was near-Nelsonian. Turning a blind eye was part of his make-up.

Even before we began our walk that morning Lofty and I discovered how misleading the tranquility of the bush can be, and this within fifty metres of the bungalow. With our foot safari in mind we had gone to scan the lie of the land through binoculars, from the log at the edge of the ridge. We saw, yet again, the two pairs of rhinos in their accustomed places, neither of them far from the track that we would soon be taking. Seeing nothing else of any concern we stood up and started walking back to breakfast. Suddenly a buffalo bull charged out from behind a bush that we had passed only fifteen minutes earlier. We froze, hearts thudding in apparent synchrony with the buffalo's hoof-beats as it crashed across the path a few metres from us and into the undergrowth beyond.

Vesey smiled when we told him over breakfast, though the smile was a little tight-lipped. "Yes", he said, "They can take you by surprise at times. And", he continued, his smile broadening, "if you come across any elephants, don't stop to feed them oranges!" He elaborated by recounting a little story that did nothing for our self-confidence. "Not so long ago", he said, "four young British nurses came on a day trip from Arusha. In a Volkswagen Beetle. "Elephant smashed it into scrap", he continued, "Just down the track, between here and the lake. Silly popsies stopped to feed the damn thing oranges, apparently".

"Just what we wanted to hear, Vesey", muttered Lofty as the older man smiled again and reached for his pipe. The four girls, it seemed, had leaped from the car and astonishingly escaped with their lives. "The elephant", Vesey explained, "was only after the oranges."

With this anecdote still in mind Lofty and I set off soon afterwards. The last sight of Vesey's cosy and secure little bungalow was a little like the last sight of land before a spell at sea. As we strode down the slope towards Small Momela I began to feel a heightened sense of awareness about the things around me. Godfrey, who even when armed only with a *panga* had represented a placid, experienced presence, was no longer with us.

I saw things that I had previously seen; the tunnel nests of the White-headed Bee-eaters in the track-side bank, as if some ship-of-the-line had fired a 12-pounder broadside into the low cliffs; a tree topiarised into conformity by browsing giraffes; a large rock alongside the place where the elephant had tusked the nurses' V.W. Beetle into scrap. But now, dependent entirely on my own faculties, I noticed much more. I saw the sway of seed-heads in the lightest swirl of wind, heard things other than the "Coco-Pops!" call of the Boubou Shrike and the coo of doves, smelt the aromatic fragrance of wild sage, crushed by the passing of some large animal. It was like being born again. Every little thing mattered.

Sooner or later, if you spend much time on foot in the bush, close encounters with large and sometimes truculent animals are inevitable. As we were about to discover. Having reached the lakeshore and relaxed for a while, watching hippos in the distance, we moved on. Now we were even more alert, for here the track swung away from the lake to pass through dense bush. Somewhere in the midst of that bush, as we had seen from our vantage point by Vesey's bungalow just an hour-and-a-half or so earlier, were two rhinos. As we walked on, eyes and ears alert for any suspicious movement or sound, I wondered how often rhino tended to roam, and at what time of day they came to the lake to drink or wallow.

Africa has an engaging habit of distracting you from one crisis by presenting you with another. Suddenly we saw, a little way ahead, not a rhino but a group of elephants. We stopped and watched as they crossed the track. They had recently waded across the lake, their bodies pale grey above and dark grey below, where the water had wetted them. There were seven, about a hundred metres ahead. And two invisible rhinos a little way to our right. And who knows how many buffaloes nosing short-sightedly through the grey-green sprawl.

The elephants were in no hurry and had fanned out to feed, alongside the track. Thinking to detour behind them I moved into the bush to our left, between track and lake. Lofty followed. If he thought that I knew what I was doing he was soon disabused, for a little further on, engulfed by vegetation, we were stopped by sounds that would become familiar to me over the years; the rustle of leaves, the snap of branches, the gurgling rumble of elephants' digestive systems and their low frequency growls of communication.

We were now between two sections of the same family, one closing on us by the minute. Both groups were browsing contentedly, unaware that we existed. Thinking that we might just have time to squeeze through the gap I moved forward, only to see, dead ahead and no more than twenty metres away, the sway-backed upper body of a large elephant showing above the bush. I half-turned to retreat but Lofty, like me maintaining an instinctive silence, gestured with a thumb towards our rear, where two inquisitive trunks were curled above the intervening bush. We were surrounded.

Concerned and yet strangely calm (helplessness can act like an anaesthetic) we hurried off to our right, away from the approaching group but towards the other, which we could now see, feeding calmly just beyond the track where the bush sloped up towards the ridge. There was now a rising commotion among the nearer group as its leading members coincided with our scent-trail. Fearful that they were about to panic and rush to join the others, with us in their path, I clapped my hands several times. The claps smacked through the near-silence with the impact of gunshots.

The bush surged into pandemonium. The elephants on the slopes hurried off in panic as I had hoped. The ones we could not see, and who could not see us, just panicked, screaming and splintering and crashing. Expecting to be trodden into the earth at any moment, we discovered how the expression "rooted to the spot" came into being. There was no point in running or moving at all and for several long seconds we stood helplessly, listening to the cacophony. And then the bush fell silent. Fifteen or more elephants had vanished in half as many seconds. "Bloody 'ell!" muttered Lofty, before breaking into a broad grin.

The act of grinning exaggerated rather than reduced his permanent frown, which seemed to have gained a few more furrows. "Fuck that for a lark", he muttered, still grinning, as we regained some composure and the specious safety of the track. The Caesars of imperial Rome, it is said, kept a slave whose job it was to remind them, when vanity and hubris seemed about to overtake them (an occupational hazard among the Caesars); "Caesar, thou art mortal". No such slaves are needed in the African bush.

The rest of our walk was as uneventful as our previous two walks had been, but our encounter with the elephants had taught me an important lesson; that large, potentially life-threatening animals, even elephants that make no attempt to hide, can often remain unseen. And unaware of human presence. It had also taught me something about myself, and about human nature. The experience had been nerve-racking but exhilarating. I wanted more. Though not, perhaps, just yet.

The next morning Vesey, still doing his utmost to please us, decided to show us another facet of his beloved national park by driving us up to the rim of the volcanic crater after which Ngurdoto was named. "We'll take a little picnic", he said, and make a day of it". It was the first time we had been out with him and as we drove to the foot of the crater some miles away he slowed down or stopped off along the way to share, rather than show off, his deep and wide-ranging knowledge. In the words of his friend (and another outstanding naturalist) Leslie Brown, Vesey "could look at any tract of country and read it like a book". And with quiet authority Vesey read paragraphs of that book to us now.

His expertise was devoid of conceit, for Vesey, as Leslie Brown has also said, "was the quietest and most modest of men". And like children enraptured by exotic names and fascinating new words we listened as he introduced us to the places that punctuated our journey, with their soft-sounding Swahili and Maasai names. Lake Kusari, where the yellow-barked acacias grow; Lake El Kekhotoito where rhino and other game were wont to come and drink; Losokonoi, with its fine view of Mount Meru, at almost 15,000 feet (4,562 metres) Tanzania's second-highest mountain; Kambi ya Fisi, "The Camp of the Hyena"; Lake Longil with its islands of papyrus and mace reed and the nearby Longil Glades where star grass (*Cynodon dactylon)* and Kikuyu grass (*Pennisetum clandestinum*) remain green throughout the year. The classical names flowed as easily from his tongue as the smoke from his pipe, untainted by intellectual snobbery.

But the best was yet to come, for a little way up the track to the crater rim he brought the Land Rover to a stop by a gap in the forest. The track and its grassy verge were scuffed and hammer-marked by generations of hooves. "Ancient buffalo trail down to the crater floor", said Vesey. "Mainly used at night. By elephant and rhino as well as buffalo". The crater floor itself was out of sight but Vesey was staring down the game trail to where it dipped and disappeared into the greenery, with that dreamy kind of look that you sometimes see in the face of children, lost "in another world". "Beautiful place, the crater floor" he murmured. His voice had the reverential softness that guides adopt in the hush of some great, much-loved cathedral. I asked if he ever went down there. "Very infrequently", he answered, in another murmur. "We try to keep it untouched..."

"Untouched", "unblemished", "sacrosanct", "inviolate". The floor of Ngurdoto Crater, we could see, was a hallowed place to Vesey. Soon, from the crater rim, we would see why. Meanwhile, as he emerged from his temporary trance and we resumed our drive towards the misted upper slopes, he said "Maybe we'll go walking down there one day". It was a promise, I knew, that he rarely made. And one, perhaps, that he never intended to keep. Not through insincerity but because he himself would not want to go, not want to force himself upon a place he venerated.

We drove up into the wreaths of mist to Leitong, at nearly 2,000 metres (6,000 feet) the highest point of the rim. Soon afterwards the cold mists cleared and the sun soaked into the absorbent white wool of our naval sea-jerseys, its light turning the caldera floor,

1,250 feet below, into an enchanting pastiche of emerald-green grassland, darker patches of woodland, brown reed-beds and pools that shone silver in the sun, the lawn-like grassland patterned with a tracery of game trails and dappled with cloud.

Leitong, like most place names in what is now Arusha National Park, is Maasai in origin. In the late nineteenth century Maasai clans had fought each other in the Momela area but "Leitong" has a peaceful derivation. It means "Prospect pleases". The Maasai are not a mountain people but some of the *ilmurran*, the warriors, had perhaps made their way, out of curiosity, into these same mists, and looked down from this same point. And been silenced by the view that greeted them. As we were.

Few prospects are more pleasing to the pastoralist mind than the sight of good grazing and the Maasai would have been as delighted as we were, though for different reasons. For the grassland on the caldera floor was being grazed as we watched, by a small herd of buffalo, two sounders of warthogs and two bush-buck. And combed by a foraging troop of olive baboons for whatever seeds, roots, tubers or insects they could find. A rhino browsed by the forest fringes and later, as we sat with Vesey on the wooden bench overlooking the caldera we saw a single elephant bull stride across the arena and disappear into the forest with the self-importance of a successful C.E.O, late for his company's A.G.M.

Vesey, seeing that we were captivated, had started up his pipe, contentedly puffing fragrance into the still air. Before contriving to make everything even more pleasurable by opening the picnic hamper that Benson had prepared. He took out thick corned beef and onion sandwiches and slices of cake, wrapped in tinfoil. And a huge flask of coffee fortified with rum. "For medicinal purposes," he smiled, eyes twinkling. "Thought you Naval types would appreciate it. And besides, it's bloody cold up here…"

After the picnic he led us a little way around the rim. He pointed out the nests of Black Roughwing Swallows in a bank alongside the grassy track and the darting, swooping birds themselves; a pair of Cinnamon-chested Bee-eaters perched high in a nearby tree; and in the canopy of other trees a troop of black-and-white colobus monkeys, leaping from branch to branch in protest at our presence, their flowing capes and tails showing snowy-white. And leaping too, I suspect, in sheer acrobatic abandon, as if they lived at the edge of space itself, not a mere two thousand feet above the crater floor.

In the late afternoon, after coming down from Ngurdoto rim, we coincided with another troop of colobus. We had been making our slow way home but close to the Lokie Swamp Vesey stopped and led us off yet again, this time deep into the lower forests, where he had erected a viewing platform by a forest glade. As we stood in the silence and fading light of the glade a sudden thump of hooves and crash of leaves caused us to rush for the safety of the platform. I was pleased to see that Vesey, for all his experience, had joined us in our headlong dash. The three of us stood by the rail of the platform, expecting a rhino to pound from the forest, puffing into the glade like a runaway locomotive. To our embarrassment and Vesey's spluttering amusement a male bushbuck, no bigger or more threatening than a fallow deer, shot into the open and came to a standstill, as frightened as we were. "Well", said Vesey in self-defence, "Better safe then sorry..."

Just then, as if to confirm that being safe is indeed preferable to being sorry, we heard a rhythmic, gutteral sound in the middle distance. Like that of a heavy saw tearing easily and slowly through wood. "Leopard", said Vesey. The ensuing silence, as dusk began to enclose us, was broken by another, more haunting sound. "Colobus monkeys!" whispered Vesey. Their calls seemed to come from two distinct troops, emanating in chorus from the forest canopy beyond the glade, perhaps alarmed by the leopard and our presence. Their croaking roars reminded me more of giant bull-frogs than monkeys but that sound, rising and falling and echoing through the forest in the fading light, was one of the most enthralling I have ever heard.

The next day Vesey had been asked to host an important benefactor of the Tanzanian National Parks, an American multi-millionaire who was passing through Arusha with his two daughters. Vesey had decided to take him and the girls up to the collapsed crater of Mount Meru, 8,000 feet (2,400 metres) up the mountain. And being Vesey he invited Lofty and I along, possibly in the hope of us providing welcome company for the girls, Laura and Karen, both in their late teens and quite attractive. His hopes, if such they were, proved stillborn. The girls, stuck in the back of Vesey's Land Rover with two impoverished, less-than-charismatic matelots and one of Vesey's rangers, Frank, did little but exchange meaningful looks and half-suppressed giggles.

After fording the rocky Ngare Nanyuki River that formed the western boundary of the park we passed through the attractive open country at the foot of Meru and pressed on up the mountain track to the now well-known, much-photographed "Fig Tree Arch". Here, Vesey treated us to one of his little lectures, a man in his element, talking plants to a captive, admiring audience. The track up Meru passes through the arch that was formed, Vesey told us, by two different trees, now united in the embrace of a strangler fig. Charles, the American businessman, remarked on the relative neatness of the arch and Vesey explained that the gardeners responsible were wandering elephants, which find the fig's aerial roots appetizing, thus keeping it trimmed. These days – a sign of the times – the arch is probably kept trimmed by rangers, as elephant populations in Arusha National Park, as elsewhere, are much diminished.

Acknowledging our appreciation of his lecture with a smile, Vesey asked if we were ready to move on, but in his doomed role as match-maker suggested that Lofty and I, and the two girls, might want to continue the journey on foot through the forest, accompanied by Frank. We would meet him and Charles at Njeku, he said, where he had built a log cabin by the caldera. The girls, communicating as women often do through sidelong glances rather than words, left us all in little doubt that trekking through buffalo and elephant-inhabited forests with Lofty and me was not high on their wish list. "Guess they're still tired from the flight, guys", said Charles diplomatically.

His daughters, visibly relieved and with no obvious signs of jet-lag, climbed quickly back into the pick-up before anyone could stop them. "Right", said Vesey with the air of a would-be Cupid allowing his bowstring to slacken, "The boys want to walk, I'm sure". He didn't expect or need an answer. "Keep your eyes open for giant forest hogs", he told us, "We think they are found on Meru but we've had no official sightings. Very big and dark, can't mistake them. Anyway – see you at Njeku!" "Have a nice walk, guys!" called Charles, heading for the Land Rover. Laura and Karen, as it drove by soon afterwards, waved at us before easing thankfully back into their seats.

"Toffee-nosed buggers" growled Lofty as we followed Frank into the forest. The ranger was carrying a Greener 12-bore under one arm, like a gamekeeper on a grouse shoot. "His badge of office", Vesey told us later. "Totally useless against elephant and buffalo but it makes a big bang. If it's loaded, which I doubt..." Knowing a little about guns I was aware of the Greener's limitations but the thought of encountering elephants and buffaloes was exciting rather than worrying. Frank, a solemn, good-looking young man, and like most rangers extremely fit, wasn't out to break any records, content to set a plodding but tireless African pace. There were no tracks, nothing but trees and their under-storey and the slope itself. But Frank moved confidently upwards through the maze in his green uniform and crumpled bush hat, at home and at ease in forests so relatively unexplored that a huge species of wild pig might wander there unknown to science.

We saw no game and few birds until we emerged from the forest, after an hour or so, to rejoin the dirt road to the caldera. Within minutes, at the top of a steep bend, Frank held out a stiff arm, at right angles, like a policeman holding back traffic. We stopped at once. Seven or eight metres away to our left we saw the head of a buffalo bull, framed by the trackside greenery, glowering at us with a buffalo's baleful, glassy-eyed stare. Its higher position, on the banking, made him seem even bigger than he was, his great, dark head, wet nose and shining horns defined, in a shaft of sunlight, as clearly and precisely as a pen and ink drawing. Frank, more out of instinct than intent, had half-raised the Greener.

The buffalo broke the tension with a snort, turning and galloping back into the forest. Frank lowered the 12-bore but stood watchfully, listening as the sound of the buffalo diminished and died. After a while we moved on, though Frank's gaze was fixed on our forested left flank. Rangers and game scouts, who sometimes treat lions almost with disdain, are rarely casual when it comes to buffaloes or elephants. His caution was soon justified. From the forest came a steadily escalating rumble, like the beginning of a landslide. Then a living black rock-fall came streaming from the trees. A horde of buffaloes thundering down the banking and across the track, reckless and wild-eyed, pouring down the steep slopes beyond in a jostling, apparently suicidal panic.

We stood in stupefied silence, hearts walloping blood and adrenalin around until the clamour ceased. Then grinned at Frank to show him that we had not been frightened. Unimpressed,

Frank picked up a couple of rocks, and tossed them, one after the other, into the forest from where the buffaloes had broken out. The rocks clattered through the foliage then again there was silence. Frank, knowing how full of guile the Cape Buffalo can be, watched and waited, wary of the herd's back-markers, the halt and the lame and the crochety, arthritic old bulls. When none charged out he motioned us on, eyes still on the forest to our left. We followed, just as warily, crossing the broad trail that the living landslide had so recently left, heavy with its lingering, cowshed smell and scarified by a thousand hooves.

Once well away from the scene Frank, as if to show us that not everything in the bush is life-threatening, stopped to point out, with the barrel of the Greener, a clump of flowers by the flared buttresses of a tall tree. "Black-eyed Susan", he said. Vesey had already introduced us to the species but to please Frank we stood admiring the flowers, with their orange day-glow colours and the black centres that give them their name. Encouraged, he sought out and pointed to some other flowers, pink and white and pretty. "Balsam", he said. Vesey, devoted as a priest, would have been pleased at his acolyte's knowledge, however basic. In his quiet way Frank was also pleased. Even the poorest Africans, like many poor people, have a respect for learning, aware of its power to change lives.

We moved back into the shade of the forest. Whilst crossing a clearing Frank stopped again, still as the trees, and my heart again began to thud. I looked beyond Frank's statuesque pose, expecting more buffaloes, or an elephant. I saw nothing. Then I noticed a movement, the flick of an ear in the shadows at the far side of the glade. The ear became a head and then a neck and then a complete bushbuck. It had appeared in installments, like a picture in one of those early children's computer graphic programmes that would emerge with each movement of the mouse. The bushbuck, a female, was unaware of us, another rebuttal of the myth that wild animals always know that you, the lumbering human intruder, are around.

In fact it began to move towards us, raising each slender foreleg in turn with dainty, exaggerated caution, a living definition of the phrase "walking on eggshells". As it stepped into the centre of the glade its bright chestnut coat, with its cryptic white markings, became dappled with extra spots by sunbeams as slender as spears . Still it came on, until no more than fifteen metres away, when it stopped, looking towards us for what seemed like minutes, its beautiful eyes shining, its coat shivering off a persistent fly. Then, with a snap of its head, sideways and back again like a tango dancer, it bolted.

At last we left the forest for a second time and soon saw "Vesey's" Land Rover parked in the shade where the track ended. From here it was just a short, steep walk to Njeku through a "ghost forest" of contorted old junipers and cedars, still and silent and hoary with "old man's beard", like trees in some arboreal catacomb. Emerging from this "forest of the dead" we found ourselves by the caldera. Beyond it towered the precipitous remnants of the original wall, rising almost 5,000 feet (1,500 metres) to Meru Peak, now re-named "Socialist Peak" by the left-leaning Tanzanian government. The wall's eastern sector, Vesey explained later, had been blasted away in the distant past by a series of explosive eruptions, flooding the Momela area with mud and rubble. Depressions in this "lahar", as the geologists call it, eventually became the Momela Lakes that Lofty and I had walked around.

Thanking Frank, the two of us hurried on to the caldera edge, where Vesey was standing, waving and smiling, with Charles alongside him. The girls were sitting nearby on the short grass, legs dangling over the edge of the low, clean-cut cliffs that border, at this point, the caldera floor. Vesey asked about our walk and we told them about the buffaloes, at which the girls looked obligingly open-mouthed, the younger one, Karen, gasping "My! Pretty scary, yeah?", a little too sincerely. Charles shook our hands as if we were Burton and Speke and said "Must have been exciting! Did you see the forest hogs?". Anticipating our answer, Vesey announced that it was "Time to eat like hogs – are we all hungry?"

It was a rhetorical question. In Swahili Vesey called out to Frank, who was standing by the log cabin that Vesey had had built a year or two earlier, asking him to bring the picnic hampers over. "Much nicer to eat out here, don't you think?" and again we all agreed. Charles went further, looking out yet again across the caldera and saying "You know, Vesey, this place has a real kind of spiritual feel about it – reminds me of some of the old Indian hangouts in the Black Hills back in South Dakota". "Funny you should mention the Black Hills", said Vesey "– the Maasai call Meru *Ol Doinyo Narok*, the Black Mountain. And your instincts about the spirituality are spot on. After we've eaten I'll show you the rain tree. The mountain, and this place in particular, are sacred to the Meru people. In times of drought they come up here to sacrifice a sheep or bull under the tree, to bring rain".

The "spiritual feel" was almost palpable. The caldera, like its adjacent "ghost forest", had an aura of petrified mysticism. Looking down I saw the floor of the collapsed crater, flat and grey-brown and bare but for scattered volcanic debris and patches sprung with young cedars. The shallow headwaters of the Ngare Nanyuki flow through this wasteland, debouching over a waterfall below the Njeku Viewpoint. But the prominent feature of the caldera, half-shielded by the wings of the shattered crater wall, is the volcano's ash cone, formed by relatively recent eruptions and classically conical. The whole place exudes an air of brooding, blasted desolation. Made more preternatural by its vacuous, silent stillness. Not for nothing did the Maasai name the mountain "Meru", meaning "that which does not make a sound".

Benson had excelled himself with the picnic lunch. Like all good cooks he could transform the simplest ingredients into something memorable. We didn't tear into our lunch boxes like wolves but I think we all wanted to. What the roasted chicken legs lacked in plumpness they made up for in palatability. Or perhaps, in the cool mountain air, we were all too ravenous to notice. We were thankful that they had flesh at all. And grateful too for the chickens' libidinous immoderation, for our lunch boxes also contained the inevitable hard-boiled eggs that feature, quite rightly, in every East African packed lunch. And there were thickly cut sandwiches made from freshly baked bread and thickened further by generous slices of ham or cheese, and carrot cake that Vesey introduced as "Benson's piece de resistance".

Vesey, almost as happy as when talking of grasses or trees, his round cheeks reddened by sun and wind and an Anglo-Irish zest for life, opened the cool box that Frank had carried over from the Land Rover and invited orders. Laura and Karen opted for soft drinks while we men chose cans of lager, their bloom of condensation promising ecstasy in the strengthening sun. The food seemed to make the girls more friendly, or perhaps the lagers made Lofty and I less tongue-tied and judgmental. When I found a single red lily growing right by the edge of the caldera, a beautiful, poignantly fragile, drooping thing ("Minor variation of *Gladiolus watsoniodies* – highland species. Lovely, isn't it?" said Vesey) the girls came over to look, and we got talking hesitantly. They curious about life at sea and we about life in the US. When the time came to go, we drove down together, six very different people united briefly and by chance.

CHAPTER IV

The "Mad-cap" of Manyara

Soon after we got back to "Vesey's bungalow Charles and the girls left for Arusha. That evening after dinner, warmed by the embers of the elephant dung fire in the living room, Vesey, who had been sitting in his armchair puffing dreamily at his pipe, suddenly stirred himself. "Now that you've seen Ngurdoto and Meru", he said, "I thought you might like a change of scene. Tomorrow morning when we're all ready we'll drive down to Lake Manyara. I need to check some plots there. And I'll introduce you to young Iain and get him to show you his elephants. You'll enjoy that" – adding, tongue-in-cheek, "if you survive, that is… Ian's a bit of a mad-cap. We'll stay in the park hostel – rather basic but it's OK. Chilufyia will come with us to do the cooking and keep him out of mischief. How does that sound?"

It sounded pretty good. Only the chance of going to the Serengeti or Ngorongoro could have excited me more. Who the madcap "young Iain" was, or why his elephants might threaten our survival, I had no idea, and Vesey didn't elaborate. But I went to bed as I had as a child on Christmas Eve, impatient with the night and for the morning. And grateful for our Fairy Godfather. Looking back I realise that Vesey was pulling rabbits out of hats to give us the experiences of a lifetime. The trip to Manyara, I feel sure, was for our sake, not his.

When the time came to leave Lofty and I, raring to go and indoctrinated with the Navy's insistence on punctuality, had been waiting by the Land Rover for half-an-hour before Vesey bustled out. "You two jump in the back", he said, "Chilufiya can sit in front with me. When he deigns to turn up…" And with that he bellowed out "Chilufiya!" towards the bungalow door and muttered a despairing comment about the servant's disregard for time. The subject of this grumble eventually appeared, to be treated to a good-natured ticking off and verbally frog-marched into the front passenger seat. With a shrug and a stagy sigh Vesey hauled himself into the cab and soon afterwards we pulled away.

We bounced down the rocky track to Usa River and the main Moshi – Arusha road, on through Arusha itself to the tiny settlement of Makuyuni at the eastern edge of the Rift, crossing the intervening Ardai Plains that rolled away on every hand like the easy swells of a spell-bound sea. The plains were sparsely settled then by the Maasai and Arusha, their *enkang-iti*, or extended family homesteads, studding the grasslands here and there like "fairy circles". Out on the sun-dried pastures, on their way to or from the few watering places, lines of humped cattle trailed streamers of dust, attended by herdsmen in billowing, bright-red *shukas* or boys in drabber browns or greys. Other Maasai, young *il-morani* with gleaming spears or shaven-headed women bedecked with beads and driving laden donkeys, strode or trailed across the landscapes, looking, in the enormity of the plains and the deceptiveness of distance, like columns of coloured ants.

Vesey pulled over and stopped at one point and jumping down from his cab called for us to join him. Following him back along the road we saw him stop by a dead animal. "Aardwolf", he said as we joined him, "You don't see them very often". Chilufyia, with the widespread African disinterest towards inedible animals, remained in the cab, wondering, no doubt, how a dead hyena (as he would have seen it) could possibly cause anyone, least of all a man of standing, to break his journey. Some time later Vesey stopped again to let us see some Thomson's gazelles, pale and petite with designer-logo side-flashes and tails that seemed to be suffering from some hyperactivity disorder, among some scraggy whistling thorn. Chilufyia surveyed them through the eyes of a newly promoted cook, a man who had tasted "Tommy" chops and would welcome more.

Vesey, whilst we were stopped, pointed out the volcanoes that stretched across the skyline to the north, reciting the blank verse of their Maasai names in east-to-west progression; Kilimanjaro (*Ol doiny' oibor*, the "White Mountain), already hidden in the clouds beyond Meru (*Ol doiny'orok*, the "Black Mountain")", the base of which was visible way behind us. "Monduli – don't know the meaning – *Oldoinyo Purko*, named after at a Maasai clan and *Essimingor*, the Wild Cat".

As we moved on the road rose, curving south-westerly before falling gradually, through feathery young *Acacia tortilis*, to Makuyuni, "The Place of the Fig Tree". The fig tree had long gone, and not much had taken its place. Makuyuni was little more than a dusty crossroads with a filling station, a clutter of dilapidated *dukas* and wooden huts. And a hapless collection of people, mostly Maasai, half-heartedly touting cheap souvenirs or sitting in whatever shade they could find with trance-like resignation, waiting for lifts that might never come.

Makuyuni had its eccentricities. Years later, on my first personal safari to the north, my companion John drew my attention to a sign placed in the midst of the wastelands beyond the settlement's filling station. On the rough wooden board was painted the injunction: "PLEASE DO NOT URINATE ON THE OTHER SIDE OF THIS NOTICE". We never worked that one out for beyond the notice the Makayuni wilderness stretched "boundless and bare" like the "lone and level sands" in Shelley's *Ozymandias*. On another occasion, following a dehydrating crossing of the Rift with a different companion, I rolled thankfully into the filling station and saw, in the station's little store, a large new chest freezer, emblazoned with the logos of popular soft drinks. We could not believe our good luck, for petrol and diesel were often unattainable at the filling station, let alone cold drinks. Before the mirage faded I yanked open the fridge's lid. To find it stuffed with the severed heads of several dozen goats, complete with horns.

But the worst thing about Makayuni was the road that connected it to the village of Mto wa Mbu on the far side of the Rift. My first experience was better than later ones, for Vesey was driving and we were in a Land Rover, but it was bad enough. After topping up with fuel we drove to the crossroads, watched listlessly by the would-be hitch-hikers. As we said goodbye to the tarmac Vesey called back "Here we go, boys – hang on for dear life! Just imagine you're at sea in a Force Ten!" I have been at sea in a Force Ten and it wasn't much fun but the road across the Rift was worse. It had the power to change personalities – not for the better. That which we fear we come to hate, as Shakespeare said, and I came to fear and hate that road. Why anyone had bothered building it was a mystery, for the underlying basalt bedrock could hardly have been worse.

Land Rover Defenders were known for ruggedness (the prototypes were tested in Tanzania) rather than comfort. We were shaken to the core. It was as if the shifting tectonic plates that had caused the Great Rift were still shifting as we bounced and rolled and shuddered towards Manyara. The track, though only thirty-six kilometres long, was constructed of ribbed red murram, hard as bone and, towards Manyara, scattered with white quartz chips. Here and there the bedrock, camouflaged by dust, protruded in sump-threatening hummocks. A road capable of reducing strong men to despair and of inspiring premature births among pregnant women.

The most hateful of its features were the corrugations. They are presumably created by predominant winds, funneling along natural irregularities or the tread-marks of graders and gouging them into a series of transverse ruts. Driving across them jars spines from coccyx to cranium and shakes vehicles into disintegration, whilst in the midst of the juddering bedlam other vehicles suddenly appear in your driving mirror as they materialize out of your dust-trail, blinding you with their own dust and squirting chunks of gravel from beneath their tyres like deadly tiddley-winks, shattering windscreens and nerves with African impartiality.

Old Africa hands will advise you to drive across such corrugations at speed. The advice is scientifically sound, for at a critical speed the tyres skim relatively smoothly over the ruts. The problem comes if you suddenly have to brake, when your vehicle will skitter sideways in an out-of-control skid. And the need to brake suddenly, on rural African roads where a stray cow, goat or child might burst out of the bush at any moment, is a fairly common occurrence. If you opted for driving slowly the crossing of the Rift could take well over two hours and the constant jarring and jolting could at times be almost unbearable. But with luck you arrived at the other side with all your limbs, most of your sanity and your vehicle's component parts intact. As I always owned my own cars, and paid heavily for the privilege, I was of the "slow but sure" persuasion.

Vesey, driving his old National Parks Land Rover, was a graduate of the "faster" school of thought. Some way along the road he risked his life and ours by taking one hand off the shuddering steering wheel to point out what Hemingway, who hunted in this area, called "the shine of Lake Manyara" in the distant haze. Fortunately Vesey didn't have to brake, either then or later, and as the western wall of the Rift grew more distinct with every minute our spirits lifted and we rolled relieved into

Mto wa Mbu ("River of the Mosquito"), the little settlement by Manyara.

Vesey dropped us off in the village to "look around" while he and Chilufyia went up the road to the national park headquarters to confirm that our accommodation had been prepared. In 1967 Mto wa Mbu was a very small frontier town, reminding me of a film set for a low-budget western. "Not exactly Las Vegas", as Lofty put it. But its location, on the road to Ngorongoro and the Serengeti and within a lion's roar of Manyara, would eventually ensure its future as a "stop-over" and provisioning depot at the lower end of the tourist spectrum, a place to pick up vegetables, fruit, rice, eggs and cheap souvenirs, or enjoy a welcome beer.

Even in the late sixties "Mto" was slowly swelling as typical frontier town pioneers moved in. Small-time entrepreneurs and drifters from across northern Tanzania and beyond and of many different tribes, attracted by the prospect of making a little money as the tourist trade increased. Mto also catered to the local peoples, the Maasai or Arusha from the hot, dusty Rift and the Iraqw from the cold, misty plateau above the escarpment. For the Iraqw the journey on foot, via the rocky road that slalomed steeply down from the plateau, must have been punishing enough in the heat of the day. But the walk back, often after dark and a tankard or two of *mbege* (banana beer), had its own hazards. Not long before that first visit with Vesey, at least two Iraqw had been taken by lions as they staggered up the escarpment road.

For the Maasai lions, by night or by day, were a minor threat. And from what Lofty and I could see the subtleties of first-world food hygiene didn't trouble them either. One gaunt Maasai elder was enjoying his mid-day meal without troubling the local chefs. Standing by a butcher's kiosk little bigger than a long-drop lavatory, he was holding aloft a large, raw fillet of beef, half-blackened with dried blood and flies, with one hand, whilst tearing at its lower end with his teeth and much enjoyment. "Rather him than me..." muttered Lofty, he himself not known for being over-fastidious.

Vesey soon returned. He had left Chilufiya at the park hostel at the foot of the Rift wall, to sort out our rooms and prepare dinner. We were there within minutes, after driving through the park headquarters and up a short, steep track to the hostel itself. It was a low, broad-fronted and sparsely furnished building with wooden floors, as basic as Vesey had promised. A narrow balcony ran along its front, overlooking the ground-water forest that characterizes the northern end of the park, and the lake beyond. Vesey would be staying at the warden's house nearby, so having dropped us and shown us to our room, where simple beds and mosquito nets had been set up, he excused himself. "Chilufyia", he assured us before leaving, "will organize dinner. Don't expect Dover sole bonne femme! And he'll do breakfast in the morning. I'll come over about 9 and we'll go and take a look at the park. And meet Iain".

He had kindly left a few beers in a cool-box and armed with one each we went out to sit on the balcony after setting up two of the hostel's camp chairs there. From this perch on the precipitous wall of the Rift we looked down over the canopy of the trees below and across the northern sector of the lake. For some time we sat in silent satisfaction, watching a small variety of birds flit among the nearby branches and marvelling at the pink swirl of flamingoes along the nearer shore of the lake, happy just to be there without feeling compelled to possess everything by speaking its name. But with the early dusk, for the cliffs behind and above us soon blotted out the sun, the mosquitoes began to whine and we moved indoors, quite pointlessly as the ill-fitting door and screened louvre windows were far from insect-proof.

Chilufyia soon appeared to light our paraffin lamps. In Vesey's absence he seemed more relaxed, as most servants (or workers generally) usually are when their employers aren't around. Servants are also, of course, very quick to pigeon-hole strangers and perhaps the young Zambian, intuitively aware of our own lowly socio-economic status, felt more at ease with us than with most of Vesey's guests. And more able to take advantage, for after serving an unusually early dinner he disappeared into the night.

Vesey, we found out the next morning, had given Chilufyia permission to go into Mto wa Mbu "after dinner as long as you get back by 11 o'clock this evening – *Mzungu* time!" ("white man's time"). In Swahili time, which is 6 hours out of phase with ours, 11 pm would have been 5 a.m. the next day and even then Chilufyia would have missed the deadline, for he had apparently staggered in at 7 a.m. To be intercepted by a non-too-pleased Vesey and ordered to organise breakfast for the *Wageni* (guests) "*sasa hivi*" (right now) as we were already behind schedule. Chastened and with blood-shot eyes, Chilufyia had turned up at the hostel soon afterwards to crack open and fry a few eggs and to toast and butter a few rounds of bread, all of which Lofty and I could have done for ourselves an hour-and-a-half earlier. For excited at the day's prospects we had been up since daybreak, sitting out on the balcony, ravenously hungry but reluctant to embarrass Chilufyia by taking over his job.

Vesey, now driving one of the park's Land Rover pick-ups, drove up as Chilufyia was stacking our packed lunches and a huge flask of coffee into Vesey's old picnic chest. Soon afterwards, with Lofty and I standing in the Land Rover's open bed ("You'll get a better view from up there but watch out for overhanging branches") we set out for the park. Chilufyia waved us moodily on our way before, I imagine, sleeping off the previous evening's excesses. Minutes later we were at the park gate. The duty ranger saluted Vesey smartly and exchanged a few pleasantries before raising the counter-weighted log that served as a barrier representing, as it still does, an abrupt division between two very different Africas.

Passing beyond it we found ourselves immersed in the gloom of the "ground-water" forest, as if we had fallen asleep in the Rift and awakened in the Congo. A world of green silences and shadows penetrated only by occasional shafts of sunlight and the calls of certain monkeys or birds. Vesey, familiar with the forest's biological lore, and wanting as always to share it, stopped to show us a male blue monkey among the under-storey. And as a man in love will bring the object of his desire into every conversation, took the opportunity to name a few trees, pointing out what we had failed to notice, that unlike the trees in a true rain forest, these were bare of lichens and mosses, due to the drier air. Duly educated, where we had recently seen trees we now saw cape mahoganies and sycamore figs and crotons, and occasional swampy glades thick with *Phragmites* reeds and fringed with star-grass.

Soon afterwards he stopped again for the troop of olive baboons that then, as now, treated the forest as its fiefdom, fearing nothing but the occasional passing lion or resident leopard, and even them, I feel, without too much trepidation. For the male baboons in Manyara are many and powerful and not to be challenged with impunity. One old male approached the Land Rover and sat on its haunches a few metres away, fingering its long, thin penis. "Next time you pull yourself, pull yourself together!" laughed Lofty, repeating a lower deck cliché when the fingering stopped.

The baboon, unamused, regarded us with eyes that were literally "shifty", wavering from side to side like those of a would-be thief, which baboons, from an anthropomorphic point of view, undoubtedly are (the Manyara baboons will rip tents apart in their search for easy food). Of course baboons are no more to blame for their opportunistic plundering than lions are for killing cows or pet cats for murdering "innocent" birds, but because baboons are so much like ourselves their "crimes", like those of chimpanzees, somehow seem much worse. They are certainly not to be trifled with. As if to make this clear, the large male suddenly rushed, with bared canines, at a smaller male that was edging in, sending him and the troop into a screeching, squalling panic that simmered, just as quickly, into silence.

We soon emerged into a more open world, bountiful with sunlight, sending a sounder of warthogs trotting high-tailed into the adjacent scrub. Vesey, delayed by Chilufyia's overnight antics and with important work to do, was hurrying now along the main track, slowing only to negotiate the causeways across the narrow, boulder-strewn rivers, the Mkindu, the Mchanga and the Msasa. After crossing this last watercourse he slowed and shouted up; "This is *Acacia tortilis* woodland where the tree-climbing lions are sometimes seen – keep your eyes open!". The Manyara lions were, as they still are, famous for their tree-climbing habits, though lions climb trees in many other parks. Longing for my first sight of a wild lion I scanned every likely branch. We saw little, however, but pale grey doves and brightly coloured starlings and a small herd of impalas that performed, as we passed, a half-hearted ballet under a proscenium arch of thorns.

A few kilometeres further on we crossed the Chem-Chem and soon afterwards Vesey slowed again, to turn off along the northern bank of the Ndala. Another kilometre brought us to the park's Research Camp, a stone rondavel set among the gallery forest alongside the stream's rocky banks, close to a small waterfall. Vesey parked and we got down. The ground outside the rondavel was cluttered with elephant skulls. While Lofty and I were examining these, the young man responsible for collecting them, the "madcap" that Vesey had mentioned, came out to greet the ecologist affectionately before turning to us.

"Navy chaps, Iain...", explained Vesey, "on leave from the Gulf and looking for a bit of excitement. I thought you might show them your elephants".

Iain stared at us with the steady, reproving gaze that might have been expected, in the circumstances, of a scion of the Scottish nobility (the Dukedom of Hamilton) when confronted by two English naval ratings. "Hmm..." he murmured, reaching out to shake our hands. He was Ian Douglas Hamilton, now well-known as an authority on elephants. At the time he was in his early twenties, an unmarried, undergraduate zoology student. Already beginning to make a name for himself in East African wildlife circles, as much for his unconventional research methods as for the research itself. Even Vesey thought him "a bit reckless" though he put this down to Iain's youthful exuberance. And to his genes: "His father was a Spitfire pilot, what can you expect?"

Iain's "madcap" reputation was scarcely dispelled by reality. For despite his thick-rimmed glasses he reminded me of a younger (if more studious) "Tarzan of the Apes". He certainly had some Tarzanic attributes, a tanned, muscular body and shoulder-length, wavy blonde hair. Hair that had been brushed, if at all, by an abstract stroke of the hand some time earlier. But any casualness suggested by his nature or his dress was belied by the intelligent, observant eyes behind the glasses, and by Vesey's obvious regard for him.

Not that Vesey was uncritical. His opinion of Iain as " a bit of a mad-cap" soon seemed validated when the young student revealed that he was still recovering "after being kicked in the back by a rhino". Vesey had also hinted that Iain's unusual methods of studying elephants were perhaps unnecessarily risky and invasive, though he had done so with a fatherly and forgiving smile. Thus acknowledging, I imagined, that an unconventional and sometimes foolhardy young man, if his capabilities matched his adventurous high spirits, was preferable to a whole coach-load of cautious, paper-chasing Ph.D students. Despite their differences Vesey and Iain had much in common.

As soon as their conversational "catch up" was over Vesey stood and said "OK, Iain, I'll leave them with you – I'm off to check my plots. See if you can find them a lion or two and then introduce them to Boadicea". After Vesey had left Iain excused himself and went indoors, returning with a small tape recorder around his neck and carrying a large-bore rifle and a camera. "Let's go" he said, leading us off to his Land Rover pick-up, similar to Vesey's but even more battered and with an open-topped cab.

A Tanzanian ranger, wearing National Parks green and a crumpled bush hat, was standing by the vehicle. Iain introduced him as "Moja" ("One" – or "first-born") causing the Tanzanian to smile broadly and greet us with a double-barreled "*Jambo-Jambo!*". "You people will have to travel economy, I'm afraid" Iain continued, "Moja is my co-pilot". But it's more exciting in the back, eye-to-eye with the elephants". With that he heaved himself into the driving seat and Moja hauled himself up alongside him. Lofty and I climbed into the pick-up bed, where a measuring stick, like a giant ruler, lay along one side. "Don't tell me he's going to ask us to jump out and measure the bloody things!" muttered Lofty but he, like me, knew that another little adventure was looming and was eager to embrace it.

Iain had handed his camera to Moja and placed the rifle between himself and the driving seat door. He now checked the small tape-recorder and satisfied that all was well turned around to make sure that we were ready to go. "We'll be going off-road", he told us, "so hang on". And with that he started the engine and drove off, with Lofty and I standing upright, knees flexed as if on board our bouncy mine-sweeper in a choppy sea, and gripping the anti-roll bar just behind the cab. We headed back up the main track through the acacia woodland but soon turned off along a loop road.

A minute or so later Iain braked. "See the elephants over there, among the wild dates?" he called up, "It's Leonora and her family. Part of Boadicea's kinship group. I was hoping to find Boadicea herself – she's always good for a thrill. But never mind, hang on and we'll go and say hello". We had seen the elephants, eight or nine of them, including two very small calves, feeding calmly at the edge of the palm grove beyond a grassy clearing. I knew that cow elephants get particularly aggressive when their babies are threatened so as we turned off the track I braced myself mentally as well as physically. We bumped quickly over the grassland, heading directly for the pachyderms. "This," murmured Lofty, "is going to be interesting".

It was. Leonora, the matriarch and largest member of the group, wheeled as she heard our approach. Her family wheeled with her. Then we were among them. Iain stopped the Land Rover and switched off the engine as fifty tonnes or so of displeased elephants backed, wheeled, trumpeted, screamed, squealed and mock-charged, trampling emergent palms into a green mash in a display of violent outrage. They soon backed into a defensive arc, Leonora mock-charging us to within a few metres, while we, being "eye-to-eye" with her as Iain has predicted, stood exposed as the objects of her resentment. Iain was clicking away with his small camera. After a few more demonstrations, one by a tiny bull that charged from the colonnade of massive legs like a giant mouse, round ears outstretched and tendril-like trunk trumpeting defiance, the hullabaloo died down. To our amazement the elephants soon resumed feeding.

This is when Moja got down, on the blind side of the Land Rover, and asked for the measuring stick. With this in hand he edged around the vehicle and towards Leonora, until he was between her and Iain, who was leaning on the sill of his open window, camera ready. Leonora, becoming aware of Moja, went for him with a gurgling scream. Moja stood perfectly still, holding the measuring stick upright, one end against the ground. When the matriarch pulled up in a cloud of dust, standing tall, she was within an outstretched trunk of him. But after making her point she shook her head, ears flapping, and turned again, to work off her anger on an innocent bush that she proceeded to demolish.

This aroused the whole family into a further frenzy. But again the pandemonium subsided and one by one the group turned their attentions to the far more important matter of eating. "Displacement behaviour", Iain explained once the uproar had died down. "She was doing to the bush what she would have liked to do to us – if elephants weren't so civilized". "I don't know about displacement behaviour", whispered Lofty hoarsely (nodding towards the back of Iain's head) "it's *this* bugger's behaviour that worries *me*!" If the grandson of the 13th Earl of Hamilton heard the remark he didn't let on.

"This bugger's" behaviour, in fact, would soon result in a very popular book, *Among the Elephants*, an account of Iain's research in Manyara. And later in Iain being awarded the Order of the Golden Ark, one of conservation's highest honours, plus an O.B.E, C.B.E and much more. For the moment, however, "Lofty's" concerns had much to recommend them. Yet Moja had survived – he walked back smiling to return his stick to me, and himself to the cab – and Iain had got the photos he had hoped for.

The stick, of course, enabled Iain to assess the height of individual elephants. He would gradually refine these simple techniques and develop new ones, but his basic theory was that getting elephants to charge was the best way to photograph them for identity purposes. Head on, with both tusks visible and ears usually outspread, an individual elephant's distinguishing features were fully exposed. I doubt that he would defend such methods now but he was twenty-three at the time and like us, eager for adventure as well as enlightenment. More importantly, his methods worked.

Hours later, after a fruitless search for lions and for Iain's elephantine drama queen, Boadicea, we disembarked at the research camp. We thanked Iain for the morning's excitements whilst trying, as young men do, to appear unmoved by them. "But", Lofty couldn't help admitting, "I'm bloody glad you had that gun with you!" "This thing?" asked Iain, lifting the rifle. "It isn't loaded", and to prove it he slammed back the bolt to reveal an empty breech. "I don't even have any ammo. I take it along just to keep the parks people happy. If you carry a loaded gun, sooner or later some poor elephant is going to get shot and that's the last thing we want". "Not loaded?" growled Lofty in disbelief, "That's a bloody rum how'd you do, isn't it?".

Life in East Africa, I was to learn, is often "a rum how d'you do" but (for the relatively privileged like ourselves) rarely boring. Lofty and I were becoming addicted to its excitements and Vesey, aware of this, now took over where Iain had left off. Two hours or so after a simple alfresco lunch, leaving Iain to write up his notes, he drove us back through the acacia woodlands and towards the lake, to look for a male lion that he had seen that morning. "Let's hope he's still there", said Vesey. "Normally they move into the shade once the sun becomes strong but it's cloudy and cool today and cats have never embraced the Protestant work ethic. They don't move unless they have to so we might be lucky. One of my plots is very close to where he was, so we can combine business with pleasure". He made it sound as if the lion was incidental to his botanical obligations but I knew that he was going out again for our sakes. And perhaps because he had never lost the thrill, as I never have, of seeing lions in the wild.

Having braced myself for disappointment my heart suddenly leapt as Vesey called out "He's still there! On the old termite mound straight ahead". And there it was, my first lion in the wild. I was ecstatic. Since then I have seen more lions than rabbits, without ever losing that little rush of adrenalin that comes with each sighting. Yet that first experience in Manyara half a century ago was more nerve-racking than Iain's elephants had been. I was yet to learn that elephants, together with buffaloes and at times hippos, can be far more dangerous than the so-called "king of beasts".

Knowing this, and determined to send us back to our ship with tales to tell, Vesey drove close to the lion and switched off the Land Rover's engine. Lofty and I were again standing exposed in a Land Rover pick-up's open bed. From the moment the reassuring throb of the engine died to the moment it was restarted we kept as still and silent as reedbuck expecting to be flushed, trusting Vesey's experience but feeling the adrenalin prickle through our veins.

Lions have four basic ways of looking at you. One is what I call "the cocktail party look", as if they are looking over your shoulder for more exalted and interesting company. The second is directed at you but casually, as a king might register the presence of a palace electrician, come to replace a blown fuse. The third look transfixes you with sustained intensity, watchful of your every move. And the fourth, the "fight or flight" look, burns with unmistakable hostility. This particular lion had sat upright at our approach, apprehensive but controlled. Spellbound by its unwavering, amber eyes with their dot-like pupils, I did not notice, at first, the flies that crawled around them. When I did notice them the sharpness of their outlines startled me, emphasizing, as they did, just how close we were.

I felt several years older, not quite the same person, when eventually I heard the Land Rover engine start. But the cough and growl of the engine caused the lion to spring to its feet and Lofty and I to stiffen even further. When you are fully exposed, as we were, and within a few metres of a lion that is poised between fight and flight, time and one's heart really do seem to stop. Vesey, cautious now, backed off slowly and, just as slowly, turned. I became aware that I was still holding my camera in one hand, half-raised for pictures that I never took. As we moved away, as if in slow motion, Lofty and I, eyes still on the lion's, had to remind ourselves to breathe – as dolphins are said to have to do. Vesey must have been smiling to himself as he drove over to his nearby plot. Parking alongside, still within an easy stone's throw of the distrustful predator, he got out to examine his beloved grasses, as if he was a curator in Kew Gardens, watched by a tortoiseshell tom-cat.

To us it seemed quite fool-hardy. But Vesey knew his lions as well as his plants. Kneeling by the wire-mesh cage that protected a square yard or so of grassland, identifying and measuring the grasses and other emergent plant life and making brief notes, his kindly face was suffused with absent-minded absorption. For him the lion had almost ceased to exist. After some time he stood up, rubbing the circulation back into his ageing legs before walking the ten or so metres back to the Land Rover. His movements caused the lion to flatten itself menacingly against the ground, emitting a series of low growls, ears back and tail switching.

Later Vesey drove us through the park to the deserted Endobash area. Here the acacia woodland gives way to more nondescript, open country of low bush, scrub and grassland, half-enclosed by a curve in the Rift wall and bisected by the Endobash River. Country in need, it seemed, of a good curry combing. Characterised, Vesey explained when we stopped on the causeway that spanned the river, by shrubby wild caper and patches of paperbark acacia. The Endobash is a sand river in the dry season but there were traces of surface water downstream, where a few fat-bellied zebras grazed on the riverside sward, and a family of waterbuck, dark against the sand, stood watching us from mid-river.

Vesey checked a few of his plots on either side of the river before we headed back north, branching off once we were back among the *tortilis* to drive along a little-used secondary track. Soon afterwards, in attractive open thorn-bush country, the kind of terrain I would come to associate with lions, Vesey stopped, inviting us to get down. "I have a few more plots to check in this area", he explained. "Why don't you chaps walk ahead and I'll pick you up later? But keep to the track or I might miss you. And keep an eye open", he added, pointing the stem of his pipe at a host of unmistakable lion prints, some sharp and clear in the sand. "Probably passed through this morning", he said, "but they won't have gone far, they'll be lying in the shade somewhere up ahead". I felt sure, looking back, that Vesey had seen the prints before he had stopped, and had "invented" his plots, another big-hearted gesture to provide us with more adventure. Once we were out of sight he would, I imagine, have climbed back into the Land Rover, enjoying his pipe and the solitude.

Some way along the track the prints died out where the lions had padded off into the bush. But a few kilometres further on, just after Vesey had picked us up again, a rhino suddenly burst from the bush immediately ahead of the Land Rover, puffing and posturing. It came to a halt some thirty metres away, in a small clearing, agitated and bristling with menace. It soon trotted off, none too happy, but with our recent foot-safari in mind I found myself examining all the prominent trees in the vicinity. None were remotely climbable. That is how it is on foot safaris.

"Well", Vesey called up as we drove on, "If I'd turned up five minutes later you might have had a very interesting tale to tell when you got back to your ship…" "*If* we had got back", replied Lofty. But Vesey's comment had reminded us that our safari was coming to an end. Tomorrow, as we passed through Arusha, Vesey had promised to drop us off by the bus station for our journey back to Nairobi and our onward flight via Aden to Bahrein. Saddened at the thought we both lapsed into silence. Vesey, as if empathising, lapsed into silence also. He must have been tired after his day in the field but instead of driving back to the hostel he headed towards the lake and the natural hippo pool on the Simba River. To share one last evening of hopefully mutual pleasure.

It was an evening that I shall remember until death or dementia overtakes me. An evening capable of persuading atheists that God exists after all, if only to give them someone to thank. Vesey was no god but he was a very special man. He stood outside the Land Rover, pipe clenched between his teeth, as Lofty and I climbed up on to the bonnet and sat on the roof of the cab. We all looked out towards the lake, which was immaculate under a cloud-terraced sky of tropical early evening blue. Before the sun dropped behind the darkening Rift Wall it electroplated with copper a herd of impalas as they emerged from the bush, and picked out, on the broad, lawn-like margins of the lake, a congregation of buffaloes, some zebras, a single giraffe and beyond them, in the shallows, drawn-out curlicues of pink, like absent-minded flourishes in a Japanese brush painting, where the flamingoes were feeding.

CHAPTER V

Return to the "Troubled Continent"

In 1970 I left the Navy and signed on "the dole" at the local employment exchange. In order to draw my weekly hand-out I had to register with the "Men's Employment Section" to ensure that I was serious about looking for work. For some bizarre bureaucratic reason, considering that I had left the Navy as an Acting Leading Hand, I was registered as "professional". I was interviewed one Friday morning by a thin, bespectacled little man wearing a suit and tie, the shoulders of his jacket powdered with dandruff. After a few formalities he asked me what kind of job I was looking for and I found myself saying "Well, if I had the choice I'd be a writer".

If I had said "Trapeze artist" he could not have looked more flummoxed. "Writer?" he murmured to himself, scratching his head and setting in motion another mini-avalanche of dandruff. He had a large, official-looking book on his desk, a catalogue of different jobs and professions, which he now consulted, flicking slowly through it. "Writer", he repeated softly, after reaching the "W's", falling silent again as he read through whatever was on the page. "Mmm…" he murmured at last, closing the book (and the door to my ambitions), "I'm afraid you've had it. You need two "A" levels…" (he knew that I only had one). "Shakespeare didn't have two "A" levels", I reminded him, rather flippantly. He smiled a tight, weary, thank-God-it's-Friday smile. "You're not Shakespeare..." he said.

The next morning I read in the local paper that there was a vacancy for an "Employment Officer" – at the same Employment Exchange. I applied for it, got it and was soon working in the next department to the man with the dandruff, though in the more down-market "Manual Labourers" section, interviewing brick-layers and boiler-makers rather than misguided, aspiring writers. Life there was pleasant enough but hardly adventurous and eventually I went into teaching, starting my career in a small junior school on the outskirts of Liverpool. Teaching wasn't particularly adventurous either though it had its moments, not least when a python escaped from its box in my classroom. The python perhaps reminded me of Africa. Whatever the case my thoughts began to turn more and more frequently in that direction.

On my days off I would walk my Labrador in the fields and open spaces close to home, often lapsing into fantasies, conferring the romance of East Africa upon the rather less glamorous features of south-west Lancashire. The local colliery tip was my Kilimanjaro, the Sankey Valley my Manyara, the remnants of an ancient moss-land my Serengeti. I was still very much infatuated. Unilaterally, of course, for Africa is indifferent, but one-way love is still love...

When you are in love opportunities seem to arise out of nowhere. Or perhaps, if they don't, you just don't notice. Late in 1976 I saw an advert for a job at the International School of Tanganyika (I.S.T.), Dar es Salaam, and applied. The interview – and the interviewer – were quite eccentric, but it is enough here to say that I got the job. I was, after all, the only applicant. After leaving the Oldham school where the interview had taken place, I stepped into a stationery shop by the bus stop, to shelter from the rain. And out of politeness felt obliged to buy something.

I asked the elderly shop-keeper for a packet of felt-tipped pens, "something that won't dry up in the heat". He stared at me over his glasses. "Tha won't be seein' too much o' that around 'ere", he said, "Where are tha' off to – t'Sahara?".

"Not quite", I answered, "I'm going to Tanzania". He stopped for a second or two whilst sliding a plastic wallet of pens into a brown paper bag.

"One o' me nephews is out there", he said "'e loves Australia".

"You're thinking of *Tasmania*", I responded. "Tanzania is in Africa".

"Africa?" he murmured, scratching his balding head and staring out through the rain-beaded window, as if trying to remember which bus route Africa was on. He turned to scrutinize me through the thick lenses of his glasses. "*Africa*?" he repeated. After a dramatic silence and with discomfiting gravitas, he added "Troubled continent, that…"

He got that one right. But a month or so later, after telling my mother that I would be back in two years, I flew from a snow-covered England and emerged into the damp, drying-room heat of a Dar es Salaam night, the palm trees along one edge of the airfield dark and sharp against a rising, immaculate full moon. The city – and the country – would be my home for the next 34 years. I had been taken hostage. Even now, seven years after leaving, East Africa will not quite let me go; the laptop on which I type is still set to Tanzanian time.

Life in a big international school in Dar es Salaam was very different from that in my previous school on the edge of Liverpool but that is another story. The main reason for me being in Tanzania, apart from my job, was my passion for safari. But first I had to prepare for it. I was determined to be as independent as possible, which meant that I needed a car, a tool kit and a small tent. But I also wanted company – what I would come to call "safari partners".

I soon made friends with two of them, John and Barry. Both were about thirty, some six or seven years younger than me, and single, as I was. Both would contribute something memorable to our lives on safari though they could hardly have been more different. John was a little under six foot though he walked with a forward stoop, shoulders hunched and elbows out, as if push-starting a car (a very useful trait on safari). His interest in wildlife was marginal but of all my safari partners he was the most practical. One of those DIY geniuses who could put together an IKEA flat-pack wardrobe with nothing left over. On the downside his attitude towards money was cautious to the point of obsession, an inclination unredeemed by his narrow, permanently furrowed brow and neat black beard. But this was balanced by a high intelligence, a quick wit, a ready sense of humour and the practicality already mentioned.

Barry, whom in "laddish diminutive" British style we knew as "Baz", was in many ways John's antithesis. At six foot two he was rangy and loose-limbed but unlike John not the kind of man you would expect to find in a B & Q store, examining sheets of plexiglass or comparing epoxy resins. He could seem slow off the mark (I once joked that it would take a time-lapse camera to capture any movement, especially in the early mornings), though he ran rings around me, sometimes literally, on the squash court. He also had an astounding general knowledge, a profound interest in and familiarity with the world of birds and a willingness to undertake the kind of chores – collecting firewood, fetching water etc – that no one else wanted to do. Least of all when the firewood-rich zones are shared by elephants and buffaloes and the water inhabited by crocodiles that haven't eaten since the previous dry season.

John, Barry and I never travelled on safari as a threesome but I valued the company of whichever of them was with me. Strangely, though both could drive, neither wanted to. My other main safari partner, before I met my wife-to-be Anjum, was another colleague, Kevin, who joined the school in 1980, soon after John and Barry had left. Kevin couldn't drive at all at that time but he made up for this deficiency with a wonderful (if quirky) sense of humour and a sharp, entertaining wit. He was also a very good camp cook and soon became a dedicated (in later years outstanding) bird photographer. Tall and well-built, he had dark, curly hair, a neat little beard and the kind of good looks and blue eyes that had more than a few women weak-kneed with adoration. Qualities that fortunately for Delta-males like Barry and I were rendered redundant on safari, when the only females we usually encountered were either feathered or four-legged.

Unlike John, Barry and Kevin knew nothing about car maintenance or repairs; changing a tyre would have challenged them. Which raises serious questions about my choice of partners, though I was happy to be behind the wheel, especially in the bush. The long journeys from Dar to the more remote parks and reserves were always tiring and often stressful but (I convinced myself) good for the soul – a kind of martyrdom-for-beginners. And I took pride in always piloting my car back to base, if only "on a wing and a prayer".

CHAPTER VI

The Little Blue Renault

Finding a "safari-worthy" car that I could afford was a contradiction in terms. But a colleague lent me a book called *The Winds of Mara*, written by a young American who had hired a little Renault 4 in Nairobi and driven it down to the Maasai Mara Game Reserve. And more importantly driven it back again. A sketch in the book showed the tiny car confronted by a huge bull elephant, deep in the "Mara Triangle". I looked at that picture again and again. If he could do that, so could I. And second-hand Renault 4's were relatively cheap.

I began to take an interest in the model. Essentially the Renault 4 was a tin box on wheels (one at each corner, which might explain the "4", for the Renault was certainly not 4WD). Its gear box was situated towards the front of the engine compartment and operated by a kind of metal walking stick that projected – horizontally – into the car's interior via the dashboard, its curved handle being twisted, pushed or pulled one way or another by the driver to effect, if one was lucky, the appropriate change of gears. The engine (847 cc.) looked more like a sewing machine than something designed to power a motor vehicle; a Land Rover engine of the time was almost three times as powerful.

But what it lacked in horse-power it made up for with self-belief; it was a Shetland pony with the convictions of a

Clydesdale. Its body seemed inspired by a biscuit tin, secured to a chassis that sloped down towards the front, as if the vehicle was intended to double as a snow-plough in the wintry Haute Loire. But the tiny box-on-wheels had a heart as big as a bucket. In Columbia it was known as *amigo fiel* ("faithful friend") and in Spain *cuatro latas* ("four tins") but throughout East Africa, where the challenges were more extreme, it became known as the "Renault Roho", (*roho* meaning "heart" or "spirit" in Swahili).

Contrary to popular opinion, four-wheel-drive is not essential on safari, even (at least in the dry season) off-road, though when it *is* needed it is needed badly. In any case I couldn't afford to be choosy. Renault 4's were common in Dar in the late 1970s but finding the right one, which for me meant the cheapest, was another thing. After seeing one advertised in the local *Daily News* I asked a rather colourful colleague, Dylan, if he would help me check it out. "I'll come with you, mate", he had answered "– cost you a couple of beers in the *Palm Beach* afterwards. But if you buy it, don't blame me if the fuckin' thing conks out half-way to the Serengeti, O.K?"

Dylan was English but had spent a good many years in Africa, working his way from the Cape to Tanzania country by country, one step ahead, it seemed, of the local police. He was a linguistic schizophrenic in terms of his accent, which alternated between Cockney and a clipped, white South African variation. The former was normally adapted when he was drinking and relaxing with friends, the latter on more formal occasions. In his early thirties, he looked like a recently retired rugby league centre accustomed to a few punch-ups on the field and off. Except that unlike most retired rugby league centres he always dressed in a smart Kaunda suit (a safari-like style outfit made popular by Zambia's first President) and had gained a First in Classics from Bristol University. He was also said to be gay before the expression (and "coming out") became popular. And when homosexuality in Tanzania was legally subject to a life sentence with corporal punishment.

All this was enough to make Dylan stand out in most school staff-rooms but it was his bacchanalian lifestyle that elevated him to legendary status, the epicentre of his home range being the school's local, the *Palm Beach*. He once admitted that he drank half a crate of lager per day during the school week and a full crate (24 half-litre bottles) per day at weekends and during holidays. When I once asked him for advice should we ever get stuck or break down on safari (hoping to learn, for example, how to lever a car from black-cotton mud using a tree branch and a rock whilst being charged by a bull elephant) he said "Always make sure you've got a crate of fucking beer in the boot".

He knew more about beer than cars but I had no one better to turn to. So one Saturday morning he and I set off in his own dilapidated V.W. Beetle to the address given in the ad., conveniently close to the school. It turned out to be an apartment block, its balconies adorned with drying clothes, many brightly coloured. Dylan, a cheap Sportsman cigarette dangling from his lips in defiance of gravity, gave a disapproving grunt. "Asian area", he growled, "Don't expect any fucking bargains".

The thin, bespectacled young man who answered the door-bell soon afterwards was indeed a "Tanzanian Asian", an educated Ismaili bound for a new life in Toronto. He led us to his car. Dylan gave the nearest tyre one of those ritualistic kicks that certain male second-hand car-buyers, for some unfathomable reason, are unable to resist. This having revealed little other than that the tyre was hard and Dylan's flip-flop quite unsuited to the occasion, he switched his attention to something of far greater import when considering a vehicle for safari-worthiness. "Fuckin' awful colour!" he growled, as if the car was to blame for having been re-sprayed in a flat, institutional Brunswick blue. Then, after focusing upon two further serious defaults (a cracked number plate and the lack of a roof rack), he asked for the keys and ordered me to "'op in", before informing the car's owner that we were "going for a test drive".

The young man smiled helplessly and said "Sure...", very unsurely. Dylan, after a long drag on his cigarette, opened the driver's door and squeezed inside, "Oh fuck!" he remarked immediately, "I'd forgotten! It's got these weird gears!" The young Ismaili politely assured him that the gears were "not a problem once you get used to them" but Dylan was already yanking and pushing at the horizontal gear-stick while I ensconced myself in the front passenger seat, which I found (important on safari) surprisingly comfortable. Starting the engine, Dylan listened, head cocked, for a few seconds. "Sounds like a fuckin' *piki-piki* (small motor bike)", he muttered, before slamming his door shut and shouting, somewhat unoriginally, "Chocks away!".

The test drive had included "putting this packing crate through its paces" (we briefly topped 50 mph); a "hill start" on the neighbourhood's steepest incline, which would almost have required a spirit level to detect any slant (and without the aid of the handbrake, which never worked throughout my subsequent six-year ownership); and an "emergency stop" that, due to the inefficiency of the foot brakes, seemed to go on for fifty metres. As the car had rolled to a gradual halt Dylan had muttered "Jesus! I wouldn't like to drive down the Rift Wall in *this* fucking thing!". A comment charged, if only I had known, with dramatic irony.

The Rift Wall seemed to figure strongly in Dylan's catalogue of safari challenges. For after the unconvincing "hill start" without a hand-brake he had growled "Talking of the Rift Wall, if you come to a standstill going *up* it just turn the bugger round and reverse to the top. Leaving me to try, unsuccessfully, to envisage driving up to the Mbulu Plateau, via the steep, winding and rocky escarpment track, in reverse gear in a 2-wheel drive Renault. Something, I concluded, to anticipate with minimal enthusiasm.

Feeling that he had now earned his two beers for services rendered, Dylan drove us back to the yard where the young Ismaili man was anxiously waiting. "What do you think?" I ventured to ask, as we approached the block of flats. Dylan, removing what remained of his cigarette from his lips with fastidious care, burst into a phlegm-cracking laugh, spitting the resulting mucous into the road.

"What do I *think*? I'll tell you what I think, mate – I think it's a fuckin' *wreck*!" He laughed again. "But what do you expect on *your* salary? It depends how much this guy asks. He ought to pay you to take it off 'is 'ands". But don't involve me in any haggling, O.K? You pays your money an' you takes your choice, pal".

The Ismaili gentleman, relieved at seeing his car again, and in one piece, asked for 20,000 Tanzanian shillings, causing another, rather over-dramatised outburst of laughter from Dylan. Who, when he saw how pathetic I was at haggling, ignored his recent warning and soon knocked the young man down to 15,000. Today this would buy about eight bottles of locally brewed lager or, in the currency of the time, about 125 crates (Dylan's fiscal system being based on the bottle-of-beer unit). In return for my money, which represented three months' salary, I drove away a seven-year-old Renault 4 that I was to own for the next six years.

Throughout those years the Renault's handbrake, as I have said, never worked at all, the regular brakes negotiated with the road-wheels rather than imposing their will and the headlights were so dim that at night in the bush I sometimes had to ask my front-seat passenger to help out by shining a torch. He (before I met Anjum my safari partners were all male) was also responsible for braking when we lost momentum on steep uphill gradients. Two wooden blocks were kept for the purpose in the front passenger foot-well. In emergencies my partner would leap out and stick them behind the two inside wheels.

When restarting the car on such slopes the partner in question was obliged to push the Renault to help provide the necessary momentum. He would of course be left behind as the car gained speed, following me on foot to the next level stretch of the track, where I could safely stop and wait. If such a convenient stopping place was some distance up the slope, and if the track was in a national park, such as the climb to the rim of Ngurdoto Crater in Arusha National Park, where the adjacent forests were home to elephants, buffaloes, rhinos and leopards, my companion would not hang around admiring the view.

Yet for all its shortcomings the Renault had the big heart implicit in its Swahili nickname. It was to take me, and various safari partners, including my wife-to-be, Anjum, many thousands of kilometers across rural and wild tracts of Tanzania, to and through and around some of the greatest national parks on Earth. I have never been one of those men who drool over their cars and give them pet names; to me they were never more than devices designed to get me from A to B and back. Except for the little blue Renault. I came to adore it, if only in retrospect.

CHAPTER VII

The "Unspoiled Wilderness"

My first long safari in the Renault took place during the ensuing dry season, with Barry alongside me and four other colleagues travelling in convoy in a Land Rover. We were heading for Ruaha National Park, 620 km. from Dar in Tanzania's south-central region. Extended in recent years, Ruaha, even in 1977, covered 13,000 sq. km, more than four times bigger than my home county of Lancashire in England. Together with the Selous Game Reserve, which is one third as big as England itself, and several smaller sanctuaries, including Mikumi, it now forms part of Tanzania's "Southern Circuit".

These southern sanctuaries are quite different from their more famous northern counterparts, partly because, even now, they are less accessible; most modern tourists opt to fly in rather than travel by road. In the old days we had little choice. Ruaha was virtually undeveloped and although the Selous had three basic safari camps, passenger flights between it and Dar were very infrequent and beyond our budget. I understand, of course, why today's tourists choose to go by air. They have more money than we did but less time; and flying is more comfortable. Journeys by road, even though the roads are much-improved and though most tourists now travel in air-conditioned, reliable 4WDs with a local expert doing the driving, can still be tiresome and at times harrowing.

But therein lies the paradox. For safaris are not just about "game viewing", any more than Homer's Odyssey is about a pleasure cruise. Safaris are odysseys in themselves, kaleidoscopic journeys of discovery and adventure and intense personal involvement. In avoiding the discomforts and challenges of travelling by road, those opting to fly miss much of what life on safari is about. And the satisfaction, at times joy, that comes from overcoming adversities in order to reach a distant, eagerly-anticipated destination. Without being self-righteous (in later years, thanks to generous safari operators, Anjum and I sometimes travelled by light aircraft and thoroughly enjoyed the experience), I am pleased that my safari partners and I "earned our stripes" the hard way.

In 1977 Ruaha was still, in the words of the eminent ornithologist John Williams, East Africa's "park of the future". "It's greatest charm," he maintained, was that it was a "completely unspoiled wilderness". I agreed with him. Selfishly, I was glad that there was not one safari camp or lodge (there are now at least 15), glad that we had the huge "wilderness" more or less to ourselves and glad, in a masochistic kind of way, that Ruaha was many gruelling miles by road and dirt track from what passed, in Dar es Salaam, for civilisation.

Its "greatest charm" was also Ruaha's greatest challenge, not least if you attempted the journey in a 2WD Renault 4. It was essentially a two-day drive each way, with an overnight stop in Mikumi National Park, which the Tanzam Highway (the main road between Dar and Zambia) bisects, or in the little Southern Highland town of Iringa, 500 km. west of Dar. Any anxieties involved, and for me they were fairly constant, were offset by the adventures, the "champagne tingle" of adrenalin in the bloodstream. And by the excitements of the route itself.

Beyond Mikumi the road from Dar climbed through the Rubeho Mountains before dipping into the scenic (and then quite lonely) Ruaha Gorge, then climbed again on to the open, upland plateau. At Iringa a steep secondary road curved up to the ridge on which the town is situated. And from the town a dirt track, thick with sand in places, led down to Ruaha National Park's entrance gate (no more than a counter-balanced barrier across the track). After paying our dues we would cross the Ruaha by means of a hand-hauled "ferry", a raft kept afloat by empty oil drums and good fortune, and drive through the park towards Msembe, where the park headquarters were based. A short distance from the headquarters we would turn off on to a little-used track, no more than twin tyre-marks through the grass, that led to Campsite No. 2.

How such an idyllic glade, bordering the river, shaded by attractive winterthorns, figs and tamarinds and overlooked from the south by the 4,000 ft. bulk of Chariwindi, could be known by a mere number is beyond me. The bureaucratic minds involved were British rather than Tanzanian, for the practice of numbering rather than naming campsites began before the country's independence. But a rose by any other number smells just as sweet and whatever poetic imagination the British officials lacked they made up for in other ways. Many campsites, as with this one, were wonderfully well-located.

Campsite No. 2 was as appealing to animals as it was to us. Elephants, giraffes, impalas, waterbuck, warthogs, baboons, vervet monkeys, banded mongooses and sometimes buffaloes would wander through to drink from the river or feed on the winterthorn fruits. Greater kudu or wild dogs, among others, would occasionally appear on the opposite bank. Hippos and crocodiles occupied the river's deeper pools and monitor lizards, four foot long or more, patrolled the waterside sandbanks, hunting for the eggs of crocodiles or White-headed Plovers. We never saw lions or leopards there though they would have passed through from time to time. Certainly, after dusk and before the dawn, we would often hear lions calling.

We would pitch our tents at the edge of the low cliffs just to one side of the glade, facing the river and the bush beyond, thus providing us with an escape route (down the banking) should over-inquisitive elephants threaten our peace of mind. The elephants and other herbivores were drawn to the camp-site by the winterthorns (which I insist on calling *Acacia albida* despite the fact that a committee of botanists has declared all African acacias null and void). The tree's common name derives from the hoary appearance of its broad crown, with its lacy network of silvery branchlets and white thorns that in the southern winter are swept with a snow-storm of blossom.

None of which attracted the elephants. Their life is essentially one long meal and it was the acacia's fruits that they were after; they find them as irresistible as we find potato crisps. Even I loved the winterthorn fruits, though for different reasons. The fallen ones, as with newly-fallen horse-chestnuts in England, defy you not to pick them up and hoard them. Coiled into loose spirals like apple peelings they are delicately crinkled and pastel-shaded in peach and apricot as if they had been brushed with butter and baked. I sometimes wished that I, like the elephants, enjoyed their taste as well as their appearance but I stopped short of experimenting. They contain cyanide, for one thing. Elephants don't seem to mind but for me, possession was one thing, poisoning another.

I harvested the fallen fruits with the intention of passing them on to the elephants, a gesture not entirely altruistic. Between the low cliffs and the river a single *Acacia albida* grew from the sand-flats. In the dry season it attracted elephants, always bulls. Wanting to photograph them at close quarters, without risking life or limb, I devised what I called my "elephant trap". To the amusement of friends I would go down on to the sand-flats when it was safe to do so and collect the *albida* spirals in a plastic bowl. I would then strew a trail of them between the tree and the foot of the cliffs, below our tents, where I would leave a terminal pile of the fruits. Having set the trap my friends and I would wait alongside our tents, cameras ready.

It worked. Elephants would come to the tree, lock on to the trail of fruits and follow it, hoovering up the *albida* rings until they reached the terminal pile. By this stage we would be lying face down, immediately above the elephant in question, clicking away just out of reach of an outstretched trunk. The clicks would arouse the animal's suspicions, causing it to spread its ears and look photogenically threatening, which is exactly what we wanted. Iain Douglas Hamilton would have been proud of me.

This happy "win-win" situation ended when the elephants suddenly got bigger. Ruaha's elephants, when I first encountered them, were the biggest I had ever seen. A short time earlier, in the Ivory Rooms in Dar, I had seen a massive pair of tusks taken from a Ruaha elephant allegedly shot by a corrupt policeman. One weighed just over 91 kg, the other just under. The second heaviest tusks on record, they were the equivalent, in elephantine terms, of walking around with two heavyweight boxers hanging from your upper jaw. Surprisingly, in many visits to Ruaha, I never saw outstandingly big tusks though I certainly saw outstandingly big elephants.

On that first visit to the park, in addition to my "elephant trap", I decided to get further elephant close-ups but from directly above. At the time it seemed like an unconventional thing to do and like many people I sometimes confused "unconventional" with "creative". I also didn't realise that photographs of animals from above are usually disappointingly flat. So I put my next plan into action. By the edge of the campsite, where the low cliffs declined to the level of the riverside sands, stood a large fig tree. Elephants and other animals often passed under it, on their way to or from the river. All I had to do was to climb into the tree, establish myself in a fork that was, I hoped, beyond the reach of an elephant's trunk, and wait.

In the event the biggest threat lay elsewhere. As I checked my camera to make sure that the settings were right I was distracted by an ominous, increasingly loud hum. Created by an approaching swarm of African "killer bees". The African (more properly "Africanised") Honey Bee is a sub-species of its British counterpart. Its sting is no worse, but the African bee is much more aggressive and when aroused to anger releases an attack pheromone, causing its hive-mates to join in. Which is why Africanised bees often pursue and sting victims in great numbers, and why they are known as killers.

This is something of a non-story as the bees obviously didn't kill me. They went humming by like a great fighter plane fly-past in miniature. But as I settled thankfully back into my perch I saw Barry, normally the most phlegmatic of men, waving frantically and pointing upriver. "Elephant!" he called, in his excitedly understated way. As Barry rarely got animated about anything other than larks, pipits and the Six Nations rugby union series I assumed that the approaching animal was somehow out of the ordinary. As it soon proved. For the biggest elephant I had ever seen lumbered into view along the sand-flats, towards the isolated *Acacia albida*, where it stopped to eat the fallen fruits.

Just as we were coming to terms with its great size two larger elephants appeared. They were against the light and broadside on. Dark, silent and immense. They looked implausibly, long-leggedly tall, like computer graphics elephants disproportionally stretched by an amateur graphic designer. This and their stealth-like silence, combined with their shadowy silhouettes, gave them a forbidding aura, as if the exaggerated evening shadows of ordinary elephants had detached themselves, to wander with a vengeance through the wilds. As they greeted the first elephant, the elephant that we had just regarded with awe, with outstretched trunks, they made it look normal.

To watch wild animals go about their lives, especially from close quarters and when unaware of or unconcerned by your presence, is one of the great joys of safari. Our camping days provided many such opportunities. Sometimes, on the Ruaha site, I would sit in the shade of a tree, browsing through my field guides or preparing the evening meal while the elephants came and went, or a herd of impalas or waterbuck grazed nearby, or a troop of vervet monkeys watched from the winterthorns, conspiring to steal our precious bread. It wasn't always the larger mammals that held our attention, or the monkeys that raided our pantry. On one occasion we returned to the campsite for a late breakfast to find that a marauding party of banded mongooses, forty strong, had got there before us. And one evening, as we sat down to eat on a log by the fire, a striped sand snake slithered from a crevice in the log and melted into the night.

Sunrises were often splendid along this gentle curve of the Ruaha, emblazoning both sky and river from downstream. But the evenings had their own charms after the heat of the day, preceded, in the dry season, by a mysterious wind that would whip itself into a fury soon after sundown. Alarming in its suddenness and strength it sometimes blew down any tent that wasn't adequately pegged down. After an hour or two the wind would drop as dramatically as it had arisen, leaving behind a vacuum of sound and motion as if God had flipped a celestial switch. The silence would be broken by the shrieking calls of Thicknees, dying away in mournful, echoing cadences, like the cries of lost souls descending into the Underworld.

On that first trip to Ruaha we camped overnight in Mikumi. The night itself was uneventful but the morning brought a little excitement, especially for one of our party, Sam, a laid-back Science teacher from Indiana. The campsite, like all national park campsites at the time, was just a vaguely designated area of wild bush, known in this case as Campsite No. 1. If you were lucky a large patch of grass would have been slashed into submission by the rangers, using cutters shaped like hockey sticks and appropriately known as *sleshas*. If you were luckier still the rangers would have collected a pile of uncut branches, for use as firewood, and dumped them by the "fireplace" (a circle of old ashes with three or four rocks on which pots and pans could be balanced once the fire was going). The only semi-permanent structure on most campsites was a pit latrine or hole-in-the-ground lavatory, like a sentry box made of cement blocks, set some distance away from the camping area itself.

Early on the morning of our departure for Ruaha, when we were all packed and ready to leave, Sam had wandered off to the "long drop" lavatory. He was built for comfort rather than speed and walked with the slow, rolling gait usually ascribed to sailors fresh from sea. In Sam's case it seemed to have evolved in synchrony with his Indiana drawl. I had never known Sam to run, even when playing tennis. This was about to change. I happened to look up as he approached the lavatory through knee-high grass. Something beyond him, on the far side of the latrine, caught my eye. A male lion that I had come to know as "Red Mane". It and Sam were on a convergence course, concealed one from the other by the intervening lavatory.

I called out, causing Sam to half-turn. "There's a lion walking towards you!" I yelled.

"Suuure…" he drawled, without pausing.

"Sam!" shouted another American colleague, Bob, as we all watched anxiously, "He ain't *joking*!"

"I hear ya!" replied Sam, still walking. And then he saw the lion. It had veered slightly off course to round the lavatory. For a long moment Sam stood paralysed. Then he turned and bolted back towards us, legs pumping like pistons. Not ideal tactics in the circumstances, for like all cats lions are hard-wired to chase moving objects. This particular lion, however, was as shocked at seeing Sam as he was by it, and shot off towards the relative safety of the highway.

Sam, having reached us, collapsed on to a large fallen log by the ashes of our campfire, wheezing and panting. It was some time before he regained his breath. Slowly he shook his head from side to side, as if in disbelief of his deliverance. Looking up at me with his soulful eyes he said, in his drawn-out Indiana way, "Gray-am, Ah tell yuh… ah saw mah whole ly-aff pass befoh mah eyes! An' ah almost didn't need that damned outhouse…"

There were more adventures to come when we got to Ruaha. Apart from a family of Scandinavian expatriates who were camping further downriver, and of course the park rangers at the nearby headquarters, we had 13,000 sq. km. of wild Africa to ourselves. As there was also, at that time, a minimum of bureaucracy in Tanzania's southern parks and reserves, we enjoyed a sense of freedom denied to modern visitors. In the hope of taking advantage of this I decided, on our first morning, to introduce myself to the Chief Park Warden. To ask if my colleagues and I (with the exception of Martha and Dthim, who wanted to go fishing) could go out on foot instead of in our respective vehicles.

I was well aware that walking (and fishing) in the parks were officially forbidden to anyone other than TANAPA (Tanzanian National Park Authority) employees, but accompanied by Martha, a lovely, tall, slightly built young American, I drove to the headquarters to try our luck. We found the door to the Chief Park Warden's office open and the man himself alone behind his desk, bent over some paperwork. Calling out "*Hodi!*" (the Swahili alternative to knocking), I waited for the expected response, "*Karibu!*" (Welcome!). It didn't come immediately. Even when he did respond and we edged inside, the warden was still engrossed in his paperwork.

At last he looked up, though hardly invitingly. He bid us a polite "Good morning" in perfect English and asked what we wanted. He was good-looking and for someone in his position quite young, smartly dressed in his green TANAPA uniform. And unsmiling. Tanzanians, with the general exception of police, customs and immigration officials and bureaucrats in general, usually greet guests, especially *wageni* (strangers), with a natural warmth. This one was an exception; he might have been English.

Apologising for disturbing him I suggested that we might come back later when he wasn't so busy. "I'm always busy", he replied. After some seconds of silence he asked again what we wanted.

"Well", I began, "We are staying on Camp Site No. 2. This young lady would like to go fishing with a friend. And I wondered if my other friends and I could go walking. We thought…"

He was staring at Martha. "Fishing? Are you not aware, Madam, that fishing is not allowed in our national parks?"

"Well, I guess I thought it might not be allowed but my friend here (she glanced at me) suggested that we could at least ask…"

"Oh – I see. And is your friend here the Director of TANAPA?" Martha and I stood silent, like schoolchildren called to the Head's office for some behavioural lapse. The Warden glared at Martha, his eyes straying from her face to her figure. "You are very thin, Madam", he said.

"*Thin*? What's that got to do with it?" Martha was beginning to bristle.

"I'm suggesting, Madam, that you could be suffering from protein deficiency".

Martha, the most gentle of souls, was flabbergasted. "Protein deficiency? I don't *get* this!"

"Let me explain Madam", said the Warden calmly. "I am authorized to allow fishing in the park to counter protein deficiency. The wives of my wardens go fishing every day. Just downstream from your campsite, by that big fallen tree".

"We've seen them", said Martha, "but I don't understand what that has to do with me being thin?…"

"Madam", said the warden, "You are protein deficient. Take my word for it." Reaching behind his head, where a row of fishing lines hung from nails in the wall, he took two of them down and handed them to Martha,

"Go and talk to the women and *watotos* by the fallen tree. If you ask them they will give you some bait and show you where to fish. Don't worry about the crocodiles – they won't bother you. But keep an eye open for hippos. And elephants. And let's hope that your protein deficiency is soon reversed. As for you", he said, turning his attention to me, "Don't tell me that you didn't know that wandering around our national parks on foot is forbidden? But anti-poaching patrols are allowed. Be outside this office at 7 tomorrow morning with your friends. I will make sure that one of my rangers is here to meet you. He will take you out on patrol. But don't expect special treatment. My rangers are tough…"

This was an African warden not only with an excellent command of English but with an English reserve and a deadpan English sense of humour. And, like my old skipper David Haslam, and that outstanding ecologist Vesey Fitzgerald, a man with "the Nelson touch", that rare and refreshing ability to turn a blind eye to bureaucracy and officialdom. Sadly, I was never to see him again, except to thank him and say goodbye before we left Ruaha. What became of him I never found out, though he seemed a man of great promise, with uncommon leadership and man-management skills. The sort of man that TANAPA, soon to experience terrible challenges from organized poaching gangs and other major problems, badly needed.

Meanwhile, thanks to his generosity of spirit, we male members of the group set off early the next morning on our "patrol", leaving Martha and Dthim to address their protein deficiency at the riverside. The ranger who met us at the headquarters introduced himself as Nick Mringo, a studious-looking man of medium height and perhaps in his mid-thirties, friendly enough and quiet but as hard and fit-looking as a special forces veteran. As his boss had warned, we were not about to be spoilt.

We set off in Bob's Land Rover but after guiding us across an extensive salient of *commiphora/combretum* bushland, around which the Ruaha curved, Nick ordered us to park by the water-course. This marked the starting point of the "River Drive", a stretch of dirt track that follows the Ruaha to its confluence with the Mwagusi Sand River 10 km. to the north-east. And the starting point of our "patrol". Fortunately we didn't know then that we were expected to cover a total of 20 km. at a steady ranger's pace, for although we were all relatively young and active none of us were super-fit. And although the dry season is the coolest time of year in East Africa it can be searingly hot once the sun is up.

In a vehicle the " River Drive" is a leisurely and pleasant drive, with the Ruaha and its attendant woodland on one side and open bush and long-grass plains on the other. Elephants, buffaloes, lions, leopards, greater kudu (and, in the grasslands between the two rivers) Grants gazelles and cheetahs are sometimes encountered, while impalas, waterbuck, warthogs, yellow baboons and vervet monkeys are quite common among the riverside acacias, figs and tamarinds. Hippos and crocs live in the deeper reaches of the river and the waterside margins attract a wealth of birds, including the Spur-winged Goose, the decorative Crowned Crane and the unusual African Skimmer, which as its name implies skims low over the water, the tip of its extended lower mandible ploughing the surface in the hope of scooping up small fish.

On foot, as I have said earlier, you experience a different wild Africa. A much more threatening one. Yet the prevailing atmosphere, even when you are not accompanied by an armed ranger (a now obligatory safety measure in the national parks and reserves), is not one of menace but of freedom and independence and adventure. Underpinned, if one is wise, by a respectful caution. A caution sometimes justified as you almost walk into a pride of lions, a wandering bull elephant or something else to jolt you out of your complacency. And yet such moments are mere exclamation marks in a predominantly peaceful tract of living prose.

The outward leg of our trek along the river, though punctuated by pleasing distractions, was by African standards uneventful, though at one point we coincided with a large herd of buffaloes making its way down to the water. The buffaloes panicked and went thundering back up the slope, causing momentary alarm. But otherwise our anxieties were limited to the increasing heat and Nick's unrelenting pace. By the time we reached the confluence we were all bathed in sweat and dehydrated. Gratefully we rested under a large fig, gulping down the contents of our water bottles. Foolishly we had brought insufficient water and all we had in reserve (10 km. behind us in the Land Rover), were six bottles of Coca Cola, not the most thirst-quenching of drinks in the bush, least of all after they had lain in an oven on wheels for several hours.

When Nick, who had remained standing, eventually roused us to our feet to begin the return journey most of us responded as if we were being asked to re-cross the *Rub al Khali*. The explorer Wilfred Thesiger, well-acquainted with the Arabian "Empty Quarter", would have dismissed us, rightly enough, as "pansies". But suffering, like so much else, is relative and after a kilometre or so we came to a standstill. And soon a sit-still, in the shade of a trackside tamarind, for the walk was proving too much for some of us.

Except for Nick we were all thirsty, but otherwise I felt reasonably comfortable and asked Nick's permission to press on alone to the Land Rover and drive it back, with its precious if inappropriate cargo of Coke. Nick, perhaps reflecting the risk-taking attitude of his Chief Park Warden, agreed. My Canadian colleague Art insisted on coming with me and, with all our water gone, we set off on the 10 km. hike back. Before long Art branched off to walk along the broad, sandy margins of the river, where visibility was unencumbered by trees or bush. I continued along the track, and because of Art's detour was soon well ahead of him.

I was aware, despite the relatively placid outward trek, of the dangers of complacency. But as the heat increased I was more worried by the effects of dehydration, and kept up a good pace. At last, in the far distance, I saw our parked Land Rover. I would never have guessed, until then, that the thought of a lukewarm bottle of Coca Cola could arouse near-hallucinatory longings. Encouraged by the sight of the Land Rover and the scant relief that it promised I abandoned all caution and left the track to take a shorter course through the riverine bush.

My progress was soon barred by a *korongo*, a narrow seasonal watercourse that during the rains drained into the Ruaha but that was now dry. Such *korongos*, usually thickly wooded, choked with undergrowth and much favoured by leopards, sometimes harbour larger animals during the heat of the day. But to skirt around it would have involved a time-consuming detour. Clapping my hands and getting no response, other than startling a pair of Red-billed Hornbills, I eased my way down into the bed of the gully. The far bank was steep and covered in dense scrub and tall grass.

As I began to pick my way through the entanglement there was a heart-stopping clatter as some large animal broke free. Above me reared a huge beast, its size exaggerated by its superior position and a set of enormous, spiralled horns. A male Greater

Kudu. These antelopes, five feet high at the shoulder but much higher at the tips of the horns, are impressive enough when seen from a distance. Up close and rising from the scrub halfway up the opposite bank, this one seemed enormous and improbable, a diabolical monster from prehistoric times or Classical mythology. I stood immobilized, simultaneously chastised and thrilled as the kudu, despite its size, vanished within moments. As if, like the mythical creature it had seemed to be, it had never existed.

There was nothing mythological about the bull elephant that I saw as I emerged from the *korongo*. Like the kudu it had appeared from nowhere, as elephants often do. It was browsing close to the Land Rover, some 500 metres away. I was dismayed. Bull elephants can be frustratingly stubborn when you want them to move. But by now I was desperately thirsty and in no mood to wait. Stepping slowly and quietly in a wide loop I gained the far side of the Land Rover without attracting the elephant's attention. Quickly opening the driver's door I jumped in. Alarmed by the noise the elephant wheeled to face the Land Rover, working itself into a convincing little lather.

Ignoring these histrionics I grabbed a bottle of Coke from the *kikapu*, the woven grass basket, in the back of the vehicle. Prising off the cap with my pen-knife I drained the bottle of its hot, frothy, sickly-sweet contents in seconds. It was preferable, as Sam pointed out later, to "drinkin' rivah wardah or wardah from the Land Rover's radiatah or…" (lapsing into melodrama) "…mah own yoooor-ine".

The elephant had bustled off after its show of pique and Art now appeared. Together, as Art finished off one of the remaining Cokes, we raced back for the others, finding them where we had left them. They grabbed their Cokes and gulped them down (Nick politely refusing even a sip) and we all climbed into the Land Rover and drove back to the headquarters. After dropping Nick and thanking him we drove on to the campsite. Here, as we all guzzled pints of lukewarm water and rested our aching legs, Martha and Dthim showed us their morning's catch, a collection of small catfish.

"It was great! enthused Martha, "And the hippos were fan*tas*tic!"

"And the giraffes"' added Dthim. "Three of them came down to drink, right across from us! And we saw this family of elephants crossing the river, with two tiny babies hanging on to their mother's tails with their little trunks…"

"Then", said Martha, "these wild dogs chased a small kudu down the bank and into the river, and…"

"Ee-nough, ee-nough, ladies…", interrupted Sam wearily, "Next tiy-am, ah'm stayin' right *here*! We walked our butts off for my-als an' my-als in this goddam heat an' saw *nuthin'*!" Which was not exactly true, though none of us argued.

That evening was typical of so many that I spent on Ruaha's Campsite No. 2, except that in subsequent years I rarely went on safari with more than one or two companions. As Dthim cooked a catfish stew over an open fire I walked out to our "fridge", the river, where our bottles of lager were cooling in the shallows. Watched by a small, presumably teetotal crocodile, I retrieved the bottles. Soon afterwards, as the sun sank beyond the river in a great flare of colour we sat by the fire, Barry and I on my tin trunk, our companions on convenient logs, sipping our lagers and waiting for the sudden dry wind to come rushing in, shaking the branches and tents and whipping up spirals of straw in its short-lived fury. When the sun had gone and the wind had died and the dust and shreds of straw had settled we ate the stew and drank more lager and felt glad to be alive. And in Ruaha. Overhead a line of three bright planets, like the draw cord of a net, was about to loose a shoal of stars into the well-deck darkness of the night.

CHAPTER VIII

Night among the Maasai

The following December I embarked on another long safari in the Renault, this time with John. We were heading for the Serengeti, via Lake Manyara and Ngorongoro, hoping to climb Kilimanjaro on the way back. In a small, ageing 2WD car and at the time of the "short rains" this was ambitious, with breakdowns inevitable. The first occurred at Mombo at the foot of the Usambara Mountains when a thin trail of dark smoke began to issue from the engine compartment accompanied by a smell of burning.

Sooner or later everyone broke down in Mombo. It was that kind of place. Perhaps, in those days of pot-holed roads, old vehicles and shortages of spare parts, the nondescript little town, 340 km. from Dar and 378 km. from the northern safari hub of Arusha, was a critical "breakdown distance" from either. Certainly the rustic bar and little garden restaurant of the roadside "Mombo Hotel" always seemed patronised by delayed or benighted expatriates, exchanging stories over a few beers while their cars were being cobbled back together in some nearby workshop. Fortunately we were close enough to the town to limp in and find a "mango tree *fundi*" (a mechanic based under a roadside tree, where the overheads are limited to leaves) before whatever was smoking burst into flames.

The bearings of the Renault's generator had seized and while it was being repaired John and I sat just across the road at the edge of the pavement. After a while two Maasai *ilmurran* (men of the old warrior age-grade) walked down the road towards us. One, who could speak a little English, approached and introduced himself as Yakob. His companion, Gideon, was moodily keeping his distance. "He is frightened of you", said Yakob.

I found this flattering. Striking fear into the heart a Maasai "warrior", armed with a spear and a short-sword and whose recent ancestors had terrorised great swathes of East Africa, was strangely elevating. Yakob later revealed that Gideon had thought we were some kind of police. He and Yakob had recently killed a leopard with a shotgun and sold the pelt to a German expatriate, part of a sadly increasing trend at that time among the pastoralists, who traditionally had lived in harmony with wildlife. Which helped to explain Gideon's unease.

Yakob (the Swahili rendering of "Jacob") and Gideon had presumably been given their Biblical names at some mission school in the back of beyond. If so, like many Maasai youths, they must soon have run away and returned to their *enkang*, culturally unchanged except for their new Christian names and, in Yakob's case, a smattering of English. They were in their late twenties, approaching the end of their lives as carefree bachelors and senior *ilmurran*. For another two or three years, perhaps, they would wear their hair long, painstakingly fashioned into braids with sheep's fat and ochre, and live a life of relative abandon, pampered by proud mothers and pleasured by the Maasai girls, the *nditos*. Then, at the ceremony of *ng'esher*, reality would kick in. Their hair, until now their pride and joy and the subject of countless hours of attention, would be shaved to symbolise their passage from "warrior-hood" to the more sedate (though not necessarily sober) roles as junior elders.

Yakob, after explaining Gideon's anxieties, walked across the road to the Renault and looked, solemn-faced, into its open engine compartment. After some moments he rejoined us. "*Pole*" (Sorry), he said. "Your car is broken". But they will fix it, *hamna tabu*. And then where will you go?" When I told him that we still hoped to reach Arusha that evening he asked if we would give him a lift. "I want to go to my *enkang*, my home in the forest", he said, using the word "forest", as many rural Africans do, for what we know as "bush". "There is a place ten miles along the road where you can leave me. From there I will walk to my *enkang*." It was the name, as I knew, for a Maasai family settlement, the huts forming a circle around a central cattle enclosure, the whole surrounded by a circular thorn *boma* or brushwood fence. "Gideon", added Jakob, "will stay here in Mombo".

I agreed, on condition that the car was soon back in running condition. Otherwise we too would spend the night in Mombo. While we waited, Yakob sat with us and we conversed in a linguistic muesli of halting Swahili on our part and on his the little, sometimes quaint, English that he had picked up in mission school. The conversation, thanks to Yakob, centred upon cows. The traditional Maasai (as opposed to those who work in offices or banks or as computer technicians and so on) will talk about cows until the cows come home.

Their former reputation as fierce, wide-ranging warriors stemmed largely from their belief that all the cattle on Earth belonged to them, having been sent from Heaven by their god Engai via the aerial roots of a giant fig tree. As a result cattle raids became common as Maasai *moran* claimed their "divine rights", appropriating huge expanses of land as pasture, often with considerable bloodshed. Skirmishes over cattle still occur sporadically and as late as the year 2000 a Maasai *moran* that I was travelling with pointed out a Datoga pastoralist as we drove by with the comment "Datoga very bad", adding, after a brief pause, "When we meet them on the grasslands they mix their cattle with ours but when they go away they take many of our cattle with them."

"And what do you do?" I asked.

"We kill them", he replied.

Yakob, I imagine, would not have thought twice about despatching the odd Datoga herdsman but right now he was more concerned with interrogating John and I. The Maasai are by nature curious and direct but Yakob began in a more English way, the "Where-are-you-from-and-what-do-you-do?" approach to pinpointing social status.

"You from German?" he asked.

"No", I replied, "From England".

"Eeeeh! From England! From London?".

"No, not London. I come from the north of England. John comes from the Midlands – the middle of England. But we work now in Dar es Salaam. We are teachers. *Walimu*"

"Eeeeeh! *Walimu*! It is good."

Teachers, though very poorly paid, are more respected in Africa and the East than in Europe so we were off to a reasonable start. In traditional Maasailand, however, one's social standing is established by the number of cows one owns. It wasn't long before Yakob's questioning assumed an inevitable slant.

"How many cattle", he asked me, "do you have in Dar es Salaam?"

"Cattle? I don't have any" I admitted.

Yakob looked stunned, as if I had admitted to having no penis. His eyes, their "whites" discoloured yellow, stared in bewilderment,

It took him some seconds to gather his composure. And then:

"No cattle? But your *father* must have cattle, yes? In London?"

The thought of my father, a shift-worker in a south-west Lancashire glass factory, looking after cattle during his "48 off" was vaguely amusing, especially as two cows in our back yard would have been company, three a crowd. But in Maasailand, if cattle don't exist, it is necessary to invent them. And to many Maasai (as to many Londoners) the concept of an England beyond its capital is unworthy of serious debate. The simplest way to bridge the cultural gap, I decided, was via that much-maligned but extremely useful social skill, the art of telling a barefaced lie. This John and I now did, with a facility that ought to have been embarrassing but wasn't.

Our fathers, we remembered, did have cattle in London. "Eeeeeeeeeeeh!" Yakob responded, for the Maasai, like England's own taciturn pastoralists the Yorkshire hill farmers, tend to communicate in monosyllabic bleats and groans and grunts, a linguistic short-hand picked up, perhaps, from their livestock. These "Eeeeeeehs!", in Yorkshire or Maasailand, convey anything from "Bloody hell!" to a less-than-impressed "Mmm…", depending on context, length and emphasis.

I would never have thought, as a "war baby", that I would ever regard Joseph Goebbels as a role model, but his belief that "If you tell a lie big enough and keep repeating it, people will eventually come to believe it" now came to our rescue. It certainly worked on Yakob. It even began to work on me; it is disturbing just how quickly one begins to believe one's own prevarications. "It is good", Yakob said when I admitted to having cattle in London after all. But then came the expected follow-up: "How *many* cattle?".

Numbers, of cows or of wives (the number of the former often determining the number of the latter), are important to the Maasai. I had no idea how many cows the average pastoralist in his mid-thirties might possess but I guessed and said "Four hundred". Lying was becoming intoxicating. Yakob's yellowed eyes rolled and his lips soundlessly formed the words "four hundred" as his brain slowly converted them into Swahili. "*Mia nne?*" he eventually asked. "*Ndio*", I confirmed, "*Mia nne.* Four hundred." He emitted a long sigh, like a punctured beach lounger. "Eeeeeeeeeeeeeeeeeeeh! *Mia nne!*", before turning to John and asking him how many cattle he had in London. "The same", answered John, rather unoriginally, I thought. "Four hundred".

"Eeeeeeeeeeeeeeeeeeeeeeh! Sighed Yakob, "You are *rich*!"

We were basking in our our newly acquired affluence when we heard the Renault's engine splutter into life. Jumping up and going over, we were informed that the generator was now "*safi sana*" – in good health. One of the *fundis* banged down the car's bonnet in confirmation and after giving the car a little test run we paid our dues, thanked the two mechanics responsible and drove off. Darkness had fallen but we were soon cruising north on a deserted road, Yakob alongside me. John sat to one side in the back, keeping head and neck well clear of the business end of Yakob's spear.

After fifteen or twenty minutes Yakob ordered me to stop, alongside a large sisal plantation. This, he said, was where he would begin his walk home, through the bush. When he got out, however, he stood for some moments and then bent down, not to bid goodbye but to invite us to spend the night in his *enkang*. "It is dark", he explained, "and Arusha is *mbali sana* (far away)". Which was true. Besides, the opportunity of spending a night in a Maasai *enkang* was too good to miss and after a brief consultation we agreed. Yakob was pleased. He rejoined us in the Renault and carefully propped his spear back into position. "Now go this way", he told me, indicating the entrance to a narrow track that led off into the darkness, alongside the sisal fields.

Beyond the sisal the track disappeared into an expanse of tall, pale grass. "*Pita!*" ordered Yakob, "Go ahead!". Regretting our decision to accept his invitation I eased the Renault cautiously into the wall of grass. It shone white in the headlights and was almost as high as the car's roof, but it parted and folded back as we advanced and the ground itself felt firm and level. Trusting Yakob's judgement I motored slowly forward. The grassland eventually gave way to open bush, interlaced by a confusing tracery of cattle trails.

Yakob guided me with stabs of his finger and we slalomed slowly through the thorns. I was expecting a punctured tyre at any moment but none occurred and after what seemed a long time the headlamps of the Renault weakly illuminated a wall of thorn-brush ahead, four or five feet high. It was, I realised, the outer *boma* of Yakob's *enkang*. "My home" confirmed Yakob. Ordering me to stop he opened his door and eased himself out. Retrieving his spear he stood upright, adjusting his *shuka*. "Come", he commanded.

John got out and after switching off the Renault's engine I joined him. The night was warm and still, the air infused with the pungent smell of cow dung. We could hear the shouts and squeals of children from within the *enkang*. Between the spiky sillouhettes of the nearby trees I could see the Usambaras, beautifully outlined against the light of a rising but as yet invisible moon. "*Twende*" said Yakob, "Let us go". We followed him to the *boma*, where he removed a large branch, revealing a crude kind of stile. Stepping over this he turned to face us. "Are you afraid of Maasai?" he asked.

"No", I replied.

"Let us go then".

We followed him over the stile and, turning again, he replaced the branch he had removed.

Yakob led us through a dark gap between two huts and into the open space beyond. The light of the rising moon hardly penetrated the *enkang* and all we could see were the shadowy huts between which we had just passed. Yakob disappeared into one of them, returning with an elderly lady, short but straight-backed. Even in the semi-darkness she exuded a quiet, bright-eyed dignity. "My mother" said Yakob. She smiled and we shook her hand but after a few moments she returned to her hut. "She is old now", said Yakob, by way of explanation.

Two other figures detached themselves from the darkness. Yakob spoke to them in Maa, the Maasai language, before introducing them as his sister and brother-in-law. They too shook hands, welcoming us in Swahili. "*Karibuni, karibuni!* ("Welcome! Welcome!"). The man, middle-aged and with short, naturally curled hair rather than the long, elaborate tresses of the *ilmoran*, offered me the stool he had been sitting on, while his wife brought a similar stool from the adjacent hut, for John.

The wooden, three-legged stools, their upper surface slightly concave and polished with use, were comfortable. With Yakob, spear in hand, on one side and his brother-in-law on the other, John and I sat enthroned like Victorian explorers, a modern-day Burton and Speke without the outrageous brilliance of the former, the clinical stoicism of the latter or the nagging question of the Nile to distract us. A further figure, a senior *moran*, tall and slender as the Maasai *moran* stereotype, stepped out of the shadows, to be introduced as Joseph. He stood alongside Yakob, spear in hand, looking down at us. Yakob's sister returned. Now that our eyes had adjusted to the strengthening light we saw that her head was shaven, indicating that she was married. She wore an extravagantly beaded necklace, traditionally circular in form, beaded earrings and armbands and bracelets of polished copper. She had brought another stool, for Yakob.

Children, as children do, especially in Africa, appeared as if summoned by a conjurer, leaving off their running and jumping games when word reached them that there were two *Wazungu*, two white strangers, in the *enkang*. They materialised as shadows detaching themselves from the darkness, hesitant and alert and silent like bushbuck emerging from the forest gloom, wary of John and I but wary too of Yakob's authority. With a few assertive commands he soon had them seated on the ground in front of us, like an experienced teacher marshalling his young students into the "reading corner" for a talk by visiting V.I.P.'s. They stared at us as if we were creatures from another planet, which for them we almost were; Yakob told us later than some had never, until now, seen a white man.

A few women edged into view to stand behind the children, followed by a small number of elders, forming an amphitheatre of onlookers. John and I stood as Yakob introduced us, one by one, to the women, who out of embarrassment or more probably good nature laughed or giggled as we shook their hands. The elders, scorning such familiarities, kept their distance, their shaven heads, like those of the married women, shining in the slowly gathering moonlight. Yakob's sister had disappeared but soon returned, carrying a calabash the size of a fruit-bowl, which she handed to Yakob, who was sitting on my right. Yakob passed it to me. "Drink", he insisted.

The calabash was filled with milk, which, as I knew, is central to the Maasai diet. I also knew that Maasai men sometimes mix blood with their milk, though less often than is sometimes supposed. The blood is obtained by firing a specially adapted arrow into the jugular vein of a cow, after which the wound is plugged with clay and the cow released, none the worse for the blood donation. But it wasn't so much the thought of drinking blood that bothered me as knowing that the Maasai will happily drink milk that is badly curdled, from calabashes rinsed with cow's urine.

In the circumstances I had little choice and besides, I was extremely thirsty. The milk smelled fresh as I raised the bowl to my lips and I took a few exploratory sips, watched by many pairs of eyes. The milk was cool, with a slightly sharp but not unpleasant flavour of wood-smoke or ash. I took a few much longer draughts. I heard murmurs of amused approval from the children and the women. The elders maintained their dignified silence. Relieved and refreshed, I passed the calabash to John.

Yakob protested. "No!" he said sternly. "It is for you. Drink!" Retrieving the calabash I slowly drained it, gulp by gulp. Yakob took the empty bowl and handed it to his sister, who disappeared to refill it. On her return she handed it to Yakob. Yakob handed it to me. I handed it to John. "No!" ordered Yakob. "It is for *you*! You are Maasai now!" Already feeling bloated, I reluctantly gulped down what I could. I tried again to pass the calabash to John but again Yakob intervened, insisting that I finish the whole bowl. Somehow I did. I do not know how much milk I must have disposed of altogether, perhaps five pints. What I do know is that I have never drunk milk since, except with tea and coffee and with cereals.

Dreading another bowlful I braced myself to refuse, regardless of etiquette. But once it had been refilled a third time Yakob took it, rose from his stool and handed the calabash to John. The whole process was repeated. "Now", said Yakob after the trial by milk was finally over, "you are Maasai *morani*!". "Don't tell me…" muttered John in exaggerated despair, "He'll have us circumcised next. Or send us out on a bloody lion hunt! Or both!". This was a little melodramatic, I thought, but a lesser ordeal was beginning to emerge, reminding me of yet another East African explorer, the young and slightly wacky Scot, Joseph Thomson.

The first outsider to cross Maasailand, Thomson first encountered the pastoralists by Kilimanjaro in 1883. With a whimsical eccentricity unexpected, perhaps, in a Victorian Scot, this young man (only 25) entertained the *moran*, at that time dangerously unpredictable, by waggling his false tooth at them or (even more provocatively) by subjecting them to electrical shocks from his galvanometer. Whilst simultaneously, for greater effect, having one of his servants fire off a shotgun just outside his tent. Tactics hardly conducive, one might think, to securing good Caledonian-Maasai relations. Thomson got away with it but didn't escape the natural inquisitiveness of the Maasai or their disregard for personal privacies. Nor did we.

Thomson bemoaned "their annoying attentions, letting them touch me on the face, feel my hair, push up the sleeve of my coat and examine with intense curiosity my boots". John and I suffered much the same fate, though with more amusement than irritation. It started when the children closest to us began to touch our own boots, and trouser legs. It quickly developed into a game, the children naming each item of clothing or body part in Maa, John or I repeating the name in English.

One of the children was a pretty, fine-featured girl of around twelve, her slender body enclosed in a plain-coloured shift, tight enough to accentuate the developing curves of adolescence. Her shyness had gradually given way to a bolder curiosity, focused, it seemed, upon me. She spoke softly in Maa to Yakob and Yakob told me that she was asking my name. When I told her, she tried to repeat it. "Grar-ham" she said, pronouncing it as many Africans do. The other children chuckled and the girl smiled. I asked her own name but she looked puzzled. Yakob spoke to her again and smiling shyly again she said "Leah". "She is Leah", confirmed Yakob. "My sister. My young sister".

This inspired a "name game" and a lot of laughter as each child spoke his or her name and John and I did our best to repeat it. The children soon reverted, however, to the "body part" game, but as the visible parts of the human body are far from inexhaustible in number, things began to get a little discomfiting. Becoming bored with pointing at our various limbs, extremities and facial features, one or two of the children, including Leah, now came and touched them. One boy, fascinated by John's black beard, asked Yakob if we were human beings or animals. Things got worse when Yakob decided to join in. Motioning one of the boys to come closer he grabbed at the edge of his *shuka* and pulled it aside, exposing the boy's penis and naming it in Maa, causing the boy to writhe out of the way with an embarrassed laugh and much laughter among his friends.

Yakob then began to tease Leah and suddenly reached out, pulling down the top of her shift to reveal her bare breast, once again naming it in Maa. As she snatched up her dress Yakob reached down between her thighs, threatening to expose her to much greater discomfort. With a little cry of protest Leah forced her hands, and her shift, down between her legs to cover herself. Thankfully Yakob left off his teasing (as he would have seen it) but it was an interesting insight into traditional, male-dominated Maasai culture. And into the difference between cultures, for Yakob's behaviour, accepted as nothing more than playful in traditional Maasailand, would be viewed in modern western society as highly offensive.

It only hinted at more liberal sexual norms. The German anthropologist Ulrike von Mitzlaff, in her book *Maasai Women*, writes: "Twelve to sixteen year-old girls test out and practise the behaviour and rules of the game between the sexes with men who are adult…who have often had sexual experiences and are either already married or having affairs with married women". The white Kenyan author David Read, who spent his early years among the Maasai, goes a little further, expressing doubts about the existence of Maasai virgins over the age of ten. And in his autobiography *The Worlds of a Maasai Warrior* Tepilit Ole Saitoti talks of losing his own virginity at the age of nine to "a Maasai girl who was about three or four years older than me". Leah's age.

John had shifted uneasily in his seat at these latest developments though he was probably just as uneasy of the heightened excitement that Yakob's antics had aroused among the children. His classroom control back in Dar was notoriously strict for the progressive 1970s – his wing of I.S.T's elementary department was known to Barry and me as "Death Row" because it was so quiet. Whatever the cause, John had had enough. "This" he muttered into his much-abused beard, "is getting a bit out of hand".

The elders and the women must have thought so too, for they faded away into an *enkang* now dappled with moonlight and shadow. Soon, with the exception of Leah, the children followed, to resume, for a little while longer, their running and leaping around the outside of the *enkang's* central enclosure, where the cattle were penned. Yakob's older sister and brother-in-law stepped over to bid us a Swahili goodnight, "*Lala salama!*" and then took their leave. It was time to press our case with our host. "Yakob", I ventured, "We are tired and would like to sleep. It is late".

Yakob looked a little chastened, but not for long. Perhaps inspired by my reference to the lateness of the hour he now transferred his attention to John's watch. He had shown interest in the watch earlier, pointing at it and remarking that it was "good". Now his interest became less casual. "You give me watch?" he asked. John, reluctant to part with it, said that he needed it in school, but that Yakob could wear it for a while, and taking it off he passed it over. Yakob fastened it on his own wrist, among his beaded bangles, and with an innocent, childlike half-smile on his face, sat admiring it.

More worryingly, Leah had stood up and come to my side, slightly behind me. The Maasai are often fascinated by the hair of the *Wazungu* – the white people – and Leah was no exception. She began to touch my hair lightly and then to run her fingers through it. Coming to stand directly in front of me she then asked me shyly, in Maa and by mime, to touch her own hair. I reached up to oblige. Her hair was dry and coarse and probably rarely washed though soon, when she was married, it, and in fact all her body hair, would be shaved off.

Yakob was preoccupied with John's watch but Leah gained his attention for long enough to whisper something to him. He looked up at me and said "Leah likes you". The intercultural alarm bells were beginning to ring a little more insistently. "That's nice", I replied, adding, a little guardedly, "I like her, also". John groaned at this attempted gallantry but Yakob hadn't finished translating what Leah had whispered. "She wants to kiss you on the lips". "Oh God!" said John. Which is just what I was thinking. This was a cultural gap that I was not prepared to cross. Yakob, undeterred by our unease, told Leah, good-naturedly, to "Go kiss your husband". For a moment I braced myself uneasily but perhaps sensing my discomfort she backed off. "If you need a best man", said John unhelpfully, "Let me know". And with that he somehow managed to retrieve his watch from Yakob and remind him that we badly needed to sleep.

This time, to our relief, Yakob agreed. "You will sleep here," he said, indicating a nearby hut, "It is the home of my mother". He then spoke to Leah and Joseph, who disappeared into the hut. While they were gone he began to talk, yet again, about our cattle "in London". This time, however, the question and answer session was punctuated by remarks about John's watch. We were spared further questioning by Leah's return. She murmured something to Yakob and turning to us he said "Come! Let us sleep. The bed is ready".

The plural "us" and the singular "bed" concerned me but I was too weary to care. And there was, in any case, something of more immediate concern. Thanks to our earlier "ordeal by calabash" our bladders were swollen almost to the point of incontinence. In the excitements of the evening the need to relieve ourselves had somehow gone unnoticed until now. John put it into words. "I'm bursting", he complained, "for a pee".

Yakob, who had begun to lead us to his mother's hut, stopped and turned. Sensing our distress but only half-understanding John's remark, he posed a question that seemed to come straight from one of those little phrase books one sometimes encounters in the back streets of places such as Cairo or Aden. "Do you", he asked, "wish to deposit your dung?" Adding, presumably in case we thought he meant there and then "In the forest?" Depositing our dung was not, at the time, a priority, but emptying our bladders was, and to save time I said "Yes". Yakob murmured something to Leah and then, to us, said "Go with Leah. She will take you into the forest." And with that Leah led us back between the huts, through the gap in the *boma* and a little way into the bush. She stood at the upper end of a grassy slope in the moonlight while John and I walked to the shadows at its lower end and urinated as if peeing for an Olympic gold.

It seemed to go on forever but eventually we zipped ourselves up and emerged from the shadows, where Leah, at the top of the slope, was waiting. Yakob was also waiting, inside the *enkang*. "Let us sleep now", he said, leading us to his mother's hut, a traditional, loaf-shaped construction made of springy *leleshwa* branches plastered with cow dung, divided into two rooms. Yakob led us behind a screen of saplings that led to the low and narrow doorway, half-blocked by a cow, which like us was trying to get in. "There is a cow" warned Yakob, somewhat unnecessarily.

Pressing aside the warm barrel of the cow's flanks we stooped through the doorway into the narrow passageway that separated the hut's two rooms, and into almost total darkness. "Another cow!" warned Yakob and I squeezed through the gap between a small calf, presumably belonging to the cow outside, and the wall of the passageway. Having successfully negotiated this obstacle I was less successful in avoiding the next, almost falling headlong over two kid goats that had bleated out their presence as Yakob had passed through. John, behind me, was easing his way past the calf as, perhaps by way of protest, it defecated sloppily. He then stumbled, as I had done, over the two kids. "This", he said, "is going to be an interesting night".

Just beyond the kid goats the passageway opened on either side into the hut's two rooms. Yakob led us into the room to the right. A tiny fire, composed of small, slender twigs, was smouldering in the narrow space between a low, broad bed and a wall of the hut. In the fire's faint light I saw that the bed was covered with cow-hides, on which someone had earlier dumped our rucksacks and sleeping bags. The wall at the far side of the bed was hung, here and there, with small clusters of gourds. "This is how Maasai sleep" said Yakob.

But sleep was the last thing on Yakob's mind. After kneeling down and blowing a little life into the fire he invited John and I to sit on the bed. Fashioned, like the hut itself, from *leleshwa* saplings, it was firm but springy. Yakob stood by the fire, and soon, not without some consternation on my part, Leah joined us and sat on the earthen floor by my feet. To our dismay Yakob then started, yet again, to talk about our cattle "in London". John, glancing at his watch, said "Yakob, it's time for us to sleep". Yakob switched his attention to the watch and in resignation John took it off and handed it over. "You can keep it", he said. "But please let us sleep now".

Yakob was thrilled. Sitting next to John on the bed he put the watch back on to his wrist and admired it, before reaching out towards Leah to show it off to her in the faint firelight. "What time does it say?", he asked. "Half-past ten" said John. "Half-past ten", repeated Yakob, proudly. John showed him how to rewind the watch and how to set the time. Yakob sighed at each little demonstration to signify that he understood. For some time afterwards he sat staring at his acquisition, announcing, at intervals, the mantra "Half-past ten".

Finally he stood up. Looking again at his watch he said "Half past ten. It is time to sleep" and we murmured our agreement. He spoke briefly to Leah, who also stood up. Bidding us "*Lala salama*" he turned and left, followed by his sister. We listened as they made their way out, negotiating the kid goats and the calf, then, fully clothed except for our shoes, for the dry season night was already cool, we rolled out our sleeping bags and snuggled into them. And were soon asleep.

I awoke some time later to the sound of a woman's voice, singing softly, almost inaudibly. Looking up I saw a shadowy figure standing in the dying light of the fire. A girlish figure. Her face, in the near-darkness, was defined only by the highlights on the cheekbones and in the eyes. It was Leah. For a few moments she looked down at us, before kneeling by the fire. The singing stopped as she breathed new life into the fire with soft, rhythmic exhalations. With each breath the intensifying light outlined her fine features and upper body in a copper-coloured glow, like the profile of a young, Nilotic princess impressed upon some ancient coin. After a while she leaned back, as if admiring the result of her efforts. Then standing, she resumed her song, looked down at us again for another few moments, then melted into the darkness. I heard her edging through the passageway, then Yakob's voice from outside and Leah's soft reply, before falling back to sleep.

After a while I was awakened again. The room was once more in near-darkness but someone had just sat down on the foot of the bed and was squirming around on the lower end of my sleeping bag. John had also woken up. "What now?" he murmured. He was answered by a plaintive bleat as the second kid goat jumped on to the bed with a thump, to settle down across our feet with its companion. "Don't kick them off", I protested as John sat up to shoo them away, "They're Maasai hot water bottles!". And indeed the weight and warmth of the two kids was comforting, for the night was growing increasingly cold. "As long", said John, lying back again, "as that bloody calf doesn't decide to join them…"

It wasn't the calf, however, that caused the next disruption but Yakob. After smacking the kid goats from the bed he ordered us to "Come!". John and I moaned our displeasure. "Come *where*, Yakob?" I asked, irritated at this third disturbance . "Outside", he replied, "We must talk" "Talk?" grumbled John, "at this hour of the night? Not about bloody *cows*, I hope!" But Yakob insisted and with further rebellious mutterings we levered ourselves wearily out of bed and pulled on our boots. Quite annoyed now we followed Yakob out of the room, nudging aside the kids and squeezing past the calf.

We emerged to find the *enkang* transformed by the full moon, now high overhead. Yakob was standing with Joseph, their long-bladed spears silver-plated by the moonlight. It was the moon, not cows, which Yakob wanted to talk about. He pointed at it with his spear. "This moon" he said, "Is it true that Americans have walked upon it?"

"Yes, Yakob, it is true".

"Eeeeeeeeeeeeeeeeeeeeeh!" He stared at the moon for some seconds before turning to Joseph to translate. "Eeeeeeeeeeeeeeeh!" sighed Joseph and "Eeeeeeeeeeeeeh" repeated Yakob, "They have walked upon this moon!".

He stared at the moon in wonder, screwing up his eyes as if to scrutinise the lunar surface for footprints. "Eeeeeh! How is this possible? How did they get there? Did they walk?"

"No! They went by rocket", I responded, adding, on seeing Yakob's puzzlement, "a special kind of plane". He was familiar with planes, which often cross Maasailand.

"Eeeeeeeeeeeeeeeeeeeeeeeh!" He sighed, staring at the moon yet again. "That is a *long* safari!" Then, in Maa, he relayed my words to Joseph. "Eeeeeeeeeeeeeeeeeeeh!" breathed Joseph.

Having dragged us from our beds, Yakob was loath to let us return. He had something other than the moon on his mind and the conversation now turned, not to cows, but to that other passion of the Maasai *moran*, the *nditos*, the young women. Or more accurately one particular *ndito*. His sister Leah. Addressing me he asked, as he had asked a few hours earlier, "Do you like Leah?"

"Oh no!" murmured John, "Here we go again!" as I tried, in vain, to change the subject.

"Leah likes you," said Yakob, undeterred. Not getting a response he added, "She will be your wife". And, after another pause, "She will go with you. To Dar es Salaam"

"Now you've done it!" muttered John, as if I had spent the evening seducing the girl.

"My wife?" I protested, "But Yakob, Leah is only twelve – and I'm thirty-six!"

"It is nothing. Many Maasai *wazee* (old men) marry very young girls. You are strong. And your father has many cattle. In London".

"This is what you get," insisted John, "for inventing all those bloody *cows*!"

"Yakob", I insisted, I can't marry Leah! She's just a child"

"She is becoming a woman".

This was irrefutable. And Yakob was not just referring to Leah's physical development but to a more symbolic one. Soon she would endure the agonising ritual of *emuratare*, female genital mutilation, after which she would be married off, almost certainly to a much older man; a forty or fifty year age difference is not exceptional among the traditional Maasai. In desperation I played the cultural card: "But in my country, in London, Yakob, men cannot marry girls until the girls are sixteen. *Kumi na sita*". Yakob thought about this before murmuring, quietly and as if to himself "Your ways are not like ours…".

"That's true, Yakob, but can we not talk about this in the morning? We are very tired now and need to sleep..."

Thankfully he let us go. Not that I could get back to sleep. The idea of marrying a 12-year-old Maasai girl was not easily disregarded. And to make matters worse, the mosquitoes that we had hardly noticed until now were whining insistently in our ears like tiny dentists' drills. We were glad, in the end, to hear the clank of cattle bells, the occasional lowing of cows and the sound of women's voices from outside, signalling the break of day. Quickly we got out of bed, pulled on our boots and anoraks and went outside. The moon was still quite high and clear above the bush to the west but in the growing light of dawn we saw the cattle huddled at the heart of the *enkang*. Women and girls moved among the cows, or knelt by their flanks, carrying out the morning milking.

Yakob appeared and greeted us, still holding his spear. I feared that he might rekindle the debate over Leah but Yakob only insisted on showing off the family cows. Cattle, figuratively at the centre of life in the *enkang*, are also at its literal centre, discouraged from straying by a circular inner *boma* of low thorns. Yakob led us among the animals as the women and older girls continued their milking, using long, slender gourds as receptacles. We soon encountered Leah. She was still wearing her simple shift, her pretty face pressed against the flank of the white cow that she was milking. She was half-kneeling, her bare feet caked in cow dung, a girl at peace with herself and her role in the continuum of traditional Maasai life. She contrived to greet us, as we passed, with a smile that was shy and coquettish at the same time.

Soon afterwards I helped Yakob, Joseph and a third senior *moran* to rope and hold down a cow so that it could be vaccinated, watched by a small, unsmiling group of elders. The cow bucked and kicked like a rodeo bull and we had to dodge around to avoid being hoofed in the shins. Or worse. The elders looked on in critical silence. Finally the animal was subdued, vaccinated and set free, bucking and plunging its way back into the herd. "Now", said Yakob, smiling, "you are Maasai!". The elders, their faces as impassive as those of driving test examiners, remained unconvinced.

Then with John, who had sensibly stood well clear of the lively cow, I witnessed the morning exodus of the cattle from the *enkang*. It has, like so many other aspects of Maasai life, a timeless, ritualistic air about it, like some minor religious observance, unimportant in itself but vital to the rhythm and continuity of the church's, or the *enkang's*, daily life, and therefore to its self-esteem. The cattle disappeared into the bush, escorted by herds-boys, to the evocative, discordant clunk of the larger cowbells and the pleasant tinkle of the smaller ones.

After watching them go Yakob led John and I back to his mother's hut. The old lady was busy preparing breakfast for us on a small open fire in her own room. She invited John and I to sit on her bed and soon presented us with roasted cobs of maize and tin mugs full of tea, strong and sweet enough, as my own mother would have said, "to stand a spoon in". We had hoped to leave for Arusha immediately afterwards but immediacy, in Africa, is a foreign concept and goodbyes, like hellos, are not to be hurried. Guests are more important than time and are expected to understand that. To dash off just "to reach Arusha before dark" makes little sense to most Africans and none to the pastoral Maasai.

In any case I had made the mistake of seeing a young boy with a torn and badly infected ear, black with blood and flies, and had volunteered to help. Fetching our rudimentary first aid kit from the Renault I cleaned the infected ear with Dettol and plastered it with TCP ointment, watched by half the *enkang*. Apart from these items our medical kit boasted only sticking plasters, anti-malarial tablets, aspirins and a plaster of paris bandage that after about 20 years had petrified into a kind of small prayer-wheel. But the possession of a first aid kit in rural Africa, no matter how inadequate its contents, invests its owner with almost Messianic powers.

Having performed one minor miracle (the antiseptic cream had at least kept the flies at bay) I was now called upon to perform a second that would have challenged Jesus of Nazareth. Yakob asked me to treat an old lady who was, he said, "very sick". And without waiting for an answer he led us towards her hut at the far side of the *enkang*. He entered before me, turning briefly at the doorway to motion me to follow. As my eyes adjusted to the darkness inside several Maasai women, themselves mostly elderly, moved respectfully back from the bed, around which they had been standing.

The sick woman was covered by a blanket, her head exposed and supported by a pillow. She looked very old, her face withered and hollow-cheeked, her eyes closed. I knew at once that she was dying. She could expect no "white man's magic" from me. But Yakob, and the watching women, and the crowd that had followed us over and was now waiting silently outside, had their own expectations.

And so I took a wad of cotton wool from the first aid kit, dabbed it with Dettol and leaning over the old woman, gently rubbed her forehead. Her eyes opened slightly, gleaming with the unnatural brightness that signals the final flaring of vitality. The watching women stirred and sighed. The old lady's eyes closed again but she seemed more relaxed and after I had soothed her forehead for a few more minutes appeared to fall asleep. I took some anti-malarial tablets and aspirins from the box and feeling as fraudulent as a snake oil salesman instructed Yakob to give the woman two of each every day until they were gone. The tablets, I felt sure, would outlast the patient. And soon after that, without ceremony or sentimentality, her corpse would be carried into the bush for the hyenas and other scavengers to dispose of, for the traditional Maasai only bury their distinguished elders and *laibons*, as their wise men or prophets are known.

With my mountebank's work over and the all-important cattle safely out to pasture, Yakob's thoughts were free to return to Leah, whom he now sent for. She came running with a girlish awkwardness, looking almost unrecognisable. She had changed into a blue, two-piece tunic and was wearing earrings and a simple necklace, her upper and lower arms encircled with shining copper bangles. A broad, beaded leather girdle, symbolic of her uncircumcised state, encircled her slim waist. Yakob smiled. "She has dressed for you", he said. "For her husband". I was speechless. John began to hum, *sotto voce* (and, I thought, somewhat peevishly) a few bars of Mendelssohn's *Wedding March*.

Yakob, serious now, was talking to Leah in Maa. She answered just as seriously. It went on for some time, when Yakob paused before addressing me.

"Leah likes you. She is happy to be your wife. She is happy to live with you in Dar es Salaam. She is happy to go with you to London. But the ways of the *Wazungu* are not the ways of the Maasai. She knows this. Now she only asks for one thing…"

"A signed photograph of her fiancée?" suggested John, flippantly.

"Not photograph", said Yakob, dismissively. "She wants to ride in your car. Leah has never been in a car".

Yakob insisted on me bringing the Renault inside the *enkang*, he and Joseph widening the gap in the outer boma so that this could be accomplished. I drove the car through, and between the two nearest huts, and parked just beyond. It was soon surrounded by children, peering through each window. Yakob ordered them to stand back and called Leah forward. "Sit with your husband!" he commanded. Leah, overcome by the novelty of it all but with her friends shouting out instructions and encouragement and giggling with excitement, slipped shyly into the front passenger seat alongside me.

Yakob, like an over-zealous football referee supervising a free kick, ordered the unruly mob of children to move back. And further back still. Had he possessed a whistle he would have blown it and dished out a few yellow cards. Satisfied at last, he got my attention, flung out an arm to point out my way and shouted "*Nenda!*" ("Go!"). Slowly, to a cacophony of yells and shrieks and laughs from the watching crowd, for many adults had now joined the children, I drove the car forward and guided it in a wide circle around the *enkang*, between the huts and the inner *boma*.

Leah was thrilled. We drove three times around the enclosure. Each time we passed them the children erupted in a high-pitched outburst of sound and Leah smiled proudly. As I brought the car to a stop after the third circuit the children cheered and Leah, like a Maasai Cinderella escorted back from the ball by a rather charmless Prince Charming, alighted from her low-key "coach" with the kind of calcium-enhanced smile normally seen only in toothpaste ads.

We had hardly stepped out of the car when a new wave of excitement gripped the children. "*Morani! Morani!*" they were calling, all looking towards the gap in the boma. Yakob looked up. "Come!" he commanded, "It is the *morani*! They have come to see you!" And through the gap, in single file, came six junior *moran*, armed with spears, their lithe bodies rubbed with sheeps' fat and ochre and glistening red-brown. "They have come to meet you!" said Yakob, "Come! Come!" The youths marched towards us and out into the open, then stopped. None spoke but as if choreographed they lined up side by side to face us, spears erect, like a guard of honour.

Yakob addressed them and then turned to me. "Are you frightened of the *morani*?" he asked. I answered "No". "Come then", he said, and led John and I towards them. They were all staring at me, surprisingly shyly, and not knowing what else to do or say I shook hands with each one in turn. In doing so I noticed that I, at 5 feet 11 inches, was taller than all of them except one. And he was comprehensibly cross-eyed. So much for stereotypes. Not that any of this detracted from their overall presence, which was imposing.

One man, in addition to his spear, was carrying a length of rubber tubing. This, said Yakob, was "for making music". The *morani* had come to entertain as well as impress. There would be a dance that evening in the *enkang*, at which John and I, according to Yakob, would be the guests of honour. Could we stay one more night? Reluctantly we declined, but I asked Yakob if I might photograph the *moran* before leaving. They refused and loped off, to be admired by the women and children at the centre of the enclosure.

We also prepared to leave, shaking hands with Joseph and Leah, and with Yakob's older sister, brother-in-law and mother, who had all come out to say goodbye. Yakob himself was to accompany us as far as the main road. And so we drove off, Yakob alongside me, John in the back. On hearing the Renault's engine start up the *enkang* children came racing over, followed more sedately by a few more adults. John and I waved at them all as we pulled away and they all waved back.

Before driving between the huts and through the gap in the *boma* I turned to wave one last time. At the forefront of the group, among the waving arms and excited faces, I saw Leah, her own face set in a touchingly wistful smile. I was never to see her again. Many times since, however, I have thought of her, and of our fascinating night in the *enkang*. Life can be harsh and uncompromising in Maasailand, especially for women, but the women that I have encountered out on the Steppe and in the Rift have mostly welcomed or acknowledged me with a ready smile and I like to think that Leah would do likewise. And that she is happy and married to a man with many cattle and who treats her well, and blessed with children. I wonder also if she sometimes remembers me, and her drive around the *enkang*, so long ago…

As we threaded our way back through the bush Yakob asked if we were going to the "Siringet" – the Serengeti – after reaching Arusha, and I said that we were.

"There are many lions there", he responded gravely. It was a warning, not a commendation. "That's why we are going", I assured him. He was not to be put off. "Lions are dangerous", he insisted. "You *Wazungu* do not know lions. We Maasai live with them, here in this forest. You do not know them".

This wasn't completely true though when it came to living dangerously I was happy to concede that the Maasai were in a different class. After all, not so many decades earlier, a group of *moran*, armed only with spears and buffalo hide shields, would encircle a lion and kill it to prove their manhood. As they occasionally still do, though without the shields. "Lions are very dangerous", he repeated. "So you must have *dawa* (medicine). From the *laibon*. He will give you *dawa* to keep you safe from these lions. He lives in the forest near to Samé, I will take you there".

The opportunity of meeting a Maasai *laibon*, a much-revered tribal prophet-cum-medicine man, was tempting but John and I were anxious to press on and I told Yakob that unfortunately we didn't have time to spare. To most Africans "having no time" is unthinkable, and in a last effort to change our minds Yakob played that ace in the Maasai pack – cattle. "Your father has many cattle in London", he reminded us. "One day those cattle will be yours. The *Laibon* will give you *dawa*. Stop your cattle becoming sick. Stop lions attacking them". I assured him that our cattle in London were in good health and under little immediate threat from lions, but John, money-minded and curious, asked how much the *laibon* would charge for his services. "You must speak to him", answered Yakob. Maybe a cow. Maybe two goats. I don't know". When John replied that we had no cattle in Tanzania, Yakob, not to be thwarted by practicalities, murmured "He will take money instead".

We were now at the main road but Yakob, before getting out, made one last effort to change our minds. "The *laibon* can give you other medicine. Powder. It will make all women like you. They will come to you". "Now", said John, "you are talking". And indeed the thought, to two lonely bachelors, of becoming instantly irresistible to the world's most attractive women, seemed well worth the odd cow or a few thousand shillings in lieu. We contemplated the thought in a long, imaginative silence.

Experience had conditioned us, however, to the fact that we didn't figure highly in the eyes of the world's women, and that a handful of powder was hardly likely to improve things. Yakob seemed baffled that for the sake of a few shillings and a short detour, two youngish men would opt for loneliness over a lifetime of endless, rampant sexuality. But he accepted it and, after shaking hands and bidding goodbye, he picked up his spear and levered himself out. As we drove up the road I looked in the rear-view mirror and saw him, already reduced to a small figure, standing watching us go, his spear raised in a lingering farewell. And then, like Leah, he was gone.

CHAPTER IX

"The Milk Run"

We drove on, through sisal estates and then dry, unpopulated expanses of greyish thornbush and reddish soils, where we saw a man hunting with bow and arrow. And then back into more cultivated areas of occasional villages and roadside *shambas*. The Usambaras a little way to the east petered out, to be replaced almost immediately by the South Paré and then, at Samé where the Maasai *laibon* lived, by the North Paré.

A little way beyond Samé, at the crest of a long, upward slope, we found ourselves looking over a broad valley. Beyond it rose Kilimanjaro, its main peak Kibo breaching from its blue-grey base like Melville's great white whale from the deep, causing us to gasp in awe. And me to stop the car. From no other vantage point does Kilimanjaro seem so preposterously high, so sublime. And yet so paradoxically empyrian – of the sky rather than the land. Like the ghost of a mountain rather than a mountain.

It is the highest free-standing mountain on Earth and the intervening valley exaggerated that height. For a few minutes we stared in wonder at the vision that stretched across the Renault's windscreen like the beginning of a Cinema Scope film, as if half-expecting to see it over-written by opening credits and with stirring theme music in the background. But true greatness, in mountains as in men, proclaims itself, requiring no stirring words, no fanfare of trumpets. And as if confirming its self-assurance, Kilimanjaro vanished as we watched.

We drove on through Moshi to Arusha, where we stopped off for a "Big British" brunch at the tiny "Jambo Snacks" café, which was to become a great favourite. It was run by a taciturn, doleful English expatriate who would sit behind the counter listening to the BBC News on his radio as the Empire and all sense of order, political, social and moral, collapsed around him. It always seemed to be the top of the hour in "Jambo Snacks", with *Lillibullero*, the theme tune of the BBC's Overseas News Service, blaring out from the owner's little portable.

This "corner of a foreign field" was indeed 'forever England". From his chair behind the counter the owner would gaze forlornly at the opposite wall a few metres away, under which we customers sat at the three or four simple tables. The wall was covered, end to end, by an enormous photographic print of Tarn Howes and the Langdale Pikes, in full colour. And so we would sit, to all intents and purposes picnicking in the English Lake District, to be served with huge plates of bacon, eggs, sausage, buttered toast and great mugs of tea by becomingly shy Waarusha or Wameru waitresses. To male travellers their presence, incongruous as it was in this reconstruction of rural northern England, was a delightful distraction after (or before) the rigors of safari. On that first visit John, after eliciting a smile but nothing further from the prettiest of the girls, was moved to murmur, as he chewed reflectively on his toast, "We should have gone to see that *laibon*".

After brunch John and I drove on through Arusha, then little more than a frontier town beneath *Ol Doinyo Narok*, "the Back Mountan", Mount Meru, and across the Ardai Plains to Makuyuni, where the land slips gently down into the Rift. "Gently" only in terms of the declivity itself for in all other respects the passage across the Rift to Mto wa Mbu in those days was hellish, as I had discovered years earlier in Vesey's Land Rover. But Hell, in this case at least, was closer to Heaven than we had been led to believe at Sunday school. For within a minute's drive of the western end of that infernal road lay a heavenly national park, Lake Manyara.

John and I had decided to camp in Manyara rather than stay overnight in Arusha. After picking up a few fresh vegetables and eggs in Mto wa Mbu we were soon pitching our small tents in the lovely glade close to the park's little gate-house. A beguiling yet strangely sombre place, screened from the sun by a natural fan-vaulting of foliage, the overhanging branches of broad-leaved crotons, Cape mahoganies, wild mangoes and sycamore figs. These splendid trees stand around the edges of the glade like great gothic columns, part of the park's ground-water forest, so called because it is mainly nourished by water filtering down the Rift wall through the porous volcanic rock.

Dusk descends quickly in Manyara as the sun dips beneath the western wall of the Rift, and even more quickly in the confines of the ground-water forest. In the gathering gloom, as we prepared our evening meal, a large bull elephant glided past, silent and slightly sinister in that elephantine way when they are travelling purposefully, as if on some secret mission. It ignored us completely but in the middle of the night, awakened by a mysterious trembling sensation, I assumed that the elephant had returned and, accidentally or purposefully, had tugged at or brushed against the tent's guy ropes.

I lay still, in that state of excited helplessness familiar to anyone who has camped in the bush when a potentially dangerous animal is just outside. Elephants can move as if on tip-toe; I have seen one stepping between the guy-ropes of my tent without disturbing them. But they announce their presence through frequent stomach rumbles, the results of a flatulent and inefficient digestive system, or by the tearing up of grass. Everything now, however, was as silent as night in an African forest ever is. It was some time before I went back to sleep. The next morning, when John asked if I too had been awakened by "the earth tremor", I remembered that we were camping in a geologically volatile area, itself created by immense volcanic forces.

For me Manyara was full of memories. Vesey, a decade after Lofty and I had first met him, had been dead for four years. And Iain Douglas-Hamilton had left Manyara, though many of the 50 or 60 elephants that John and I saw there would have been familiar to him. And in 1977 it was still possible to encounter a rhino in Manyara; earlier that year Barry and I had seen seven there within 24 hours. And the lake was still fringed with a pink froth of flamingos, as it had been on the last evening that Lofty and I had enjoyed with Vesey. Safaris are as much about people, and remembrances of people, as about animals and birds. As time passed, especially during our last few years in Tanzania, the bush became populated by ghosts.

Soon after leaving Manyara John and I, sharing an Ngorongoro Conservation Area Land Rover with a Japanese girl, saw four more rhinos in Ngorongoro Crater. And two lions, and a whole host of other creatures. It was my first experience of this celebrated natural arena, the realisation of yet another dream. I still find it astonishing that the caldera of an extinct volcano, ringed by steep cliffs and quilted grassy slopes, a place that in most other countries would be celebrated for its scenery alone, is also one of the greatest wildlife sanctuaries on Earth. And the former home, at various times, of people as disparate and fascinating as the Datoga, the Maasai, the hunter-gathering Dorobo and a handful of colourful colonial eccentrics.

On leaving Ngorongoro we drove around the southern crater rim to where the track curves down to the short-grass plains, skirting the magnificent Malanja Depression with its background triad of expired volcanoes, Oldeani, Satiman and

Lemagarut. It is a voluptuous landscape of smoothly plastered folds and curves, the green slopes grazed by zebras, eland and wildebeeste as well as Maasai cattle and made more glorious at times by swathes of golden daisies. Here and there on the lower slopes and floor of the depression the close-cropped grasslands are darkened by the well-trodden, circular enclosures of the Maasai *enkangs* and often a *moran* or elder will be seen striding out across their hallowed pastures, *shukas* a translucent, poinsettia red against the green.

It was to become a much-loved panorama but on that first descent my eyes were drawn to the point where the track rounded the south-west shoulder of Ngorongoro. From that location I knew that I would look out upon a prospect familiar only through photographs or films, but one that had haunted my imagination for years; the celebrated Serengeti plains (much of them within the Ngorongoro Conservation area). The Maasai, who still roam the plains on the Ngorongoro side of the Serengeti border, once inhabited the Serengeti itself. They knew it – or rather the region's southern grasslands – as the *Siringet* ("the Plains Without End"). As the bend around the Malanja straightened I saw, beyond the intervening savannah, these exquisite grasslands stretching out before me, as if indeed without end, sunlit and tawny and brindled with cloud-shadow, under the smooth and shapely heights of Lemagarut.

My excitement was soon dampened, for as we approached the Serengeti boundary we experienced a mishap. We had just negotiated a narrow causeway across the bed of a rocky ravine, choked with thorn-bush. The sides of the ravine were far from steep but the Renault, engine racing, had stalled as I tried to drive out. "Clutch-slip" said John, as he jumped out to stick our two wooden "brake blocks" behind the nearside wheels to stop the car rolling back. With this emergency "hand brake" in place I switched off the engine and got out.

"Try adjusting the clutch," John suggested, but a quick examination revealed that the adjusting rod had been bent out of shape, presumably on the rough, rocky stretch leading down from the Crater Highlands. John, pragmatic as ever, set about making tea on our camping stove as I began to remove the distorted rod. Our colleague Dylan would have shuddered at the idea of having tea when we had a full crate of beer (his safari cure-all) in the boot, but in my opinion tea is best in emergencies, alcohol once the emergency is over. Unless, of course, one is about to go "over the top" on the Somme or be hung, drawn and quartered at Tyburn, when a timely tot of rum or pint of ale would no doubt be better appreciated.

The only hammer we had was buried under all our camping equipment so having removed the adjusting rod I looked around for a suitable stone with which to beat it straight again. I soon found one that fitted snugly in my hand and using a flatter stone as an anvil hammered the rod back into shape and re-fitted it. I was then able to adjust the clutch to give it sufficient grip, allowing me to drive out of the gully to the level stretch of track just beyond.

John followed, camping stove in one hand, kettle in the other and we were soon standing by the car enjoying our tea. It was only then, as I looked back into the ravine, that the irony of our situation struck me. For I realised that we had broken down in Oldupai Gorge, Tanzania's so-called "Cradle of Mankind", made famous by the Leakey family and their anthropological discoveries. One such discovery had been the skull of *Homo habilis* ("Handy Man"), believed to be the first of our ancestors to use tools. As I had crouched by the track out of that same gorge, using two stones as tools, two million years of evolution had telescoped into twenty minutes.

By the time we got moving again it was too late to try to drive on to Seronera, our intended destination. We headed instead for Lake Ndutu Lodge on the Ngorongoro/Serengeti boundary, then the only lodge between Ngorongoro and Seronera. After breakfast the next morning we resumed our journey, along the narrow grassy track that formed the northern edge of the "Ndutu Triangle", that delightful slice of short-grass plain that lies beneath Naabi Hill, the signpost-in-the-sky overlooking the Serengeti's southern gateway. There were gazelles everywhere, the restive, tail-flicking "Tommies" and the larger, more sedate Grant's, scattered like seeds by some celestial hand.

Beyond Naabi the short-grass phases into an intermediate zone. It was here that we saw the spectacular Serengeti migration for the first time. File after file of wildebeeste and zebras streaming southwards, mostly at walking pace, some, on seeing the Renault, breaking into a loping canter, all wondrously clean in the afternoon sun.

The migration, like much of life itself, is all about eating, drinking and procreating. The herbivores involved are said to consume about 4,000 tons of grass every day and, in the same period, recycle 420 tons of it as dung (don't ever say that the researchers at the Serengeti Institute don't earn their keep). As grass depends upon the seasonal rains so too do the various movements of the migration. And as the rains can be unpredictable the annual progress of the migration, generally conforming to a clockwise, cyclic pattern, can also be eccentric. At its most impressive, when the great menagerie leaves the southern plains for pastures new, the migration is truly awe-inspiring. It usually takes place in late April or early May, when the short-grass plains run dry and the recently-born wildebeeste calves run strong.

What John and I were experiencing on that first visit was more piecemeal and less dramatic, though impressive enough to shock us into silence. We saw no lions but here and there spotted hyenas lay in the trackside ditches or holes that they had scraped out or appropriated. Their fat, mud-caked bellies would soon be fatter still, for less than two months later, in February, as many as 8,000 wildebeeste calves, helpless as shucked oysters, might be born in a single day.

Seronera itself, apart from the old lodge, imaginatively built among the great granite boulders of a *kopje*, was disappointing, a scattered sprawl of functional concrete huts and outbuildings disfiguring the acacia woodlands. Suburbia-in-the-bush. But among the acacias we saw our first topi antelopes, their dark rufous coats gleaming like tarnished copper, casually polished, in contrast to the gun-metal grey on their upper quarters, their bodies raked from fore to aft to give them acceleration "out of the blocks". And, again for the first time, we saw Violet-backed Starlings, their colours shimmering from metallic, violet-blue to purplish crimson with the changing light. We also saw, a few days later, our first cheetah, lying languidly against an old termite mound among the Maasai Kopjes, as unconcernedly eye-catching as a leggy super-model relaxing between photo-shoots.

I can hardly believe, looking back, that when I first went to live in Tanzania in 1977, thrilled at the prospects of safaris-to-come, the Serengeti wasn't at the top of my "must see" list. Out of some kind of inverted snobbery, I didn't want to go to a place where everyone else wanted to go. I wanted to be different, to go to places that were not so well known. Not that there was anything wrong with that but to ignore the Serengeti was like going to Agra without seeing the Taj Mahal. Fortunately that first visit with John knocked all that nonsense out of me and looking back, I feel nothing but gratitude for the opportunities we had, in those early days, to see a place as sensational as the Serengeti in such never-to-be-repeated circumstances.

For apart from the fact that there were then only two lodges within a park the size of Northern Ireland, Tanzania's President

Julius Nyerere had recently closed the border with Kenya due to a political dispute. As most tourists in those days entered the Serengeti via Kenya his decision reduced tourism to a trickle. On that first trip in the late 1970s John and I shared the park, perhaps the best-known national park in the world, with fewer than 50 other visitors. In the week or so that we were there we encountered, outside Seronera itself, only three or four other vehicles, including a National Parks Landrover. We actually saw more lions (16) than cars, without venturing far from our campsite.

The campsite itself, at the base of a *kopje* or granite outcrop, was interesting enough. It was one of nine, just beyond Seronera, all of them, as far as I could see, unoccupied. Like all other national park campsites it was nothing more than a designated expanse of bush with a heap of firewood, a water standpipe and the inevitable long-drop lavatory. Except that this particular lavatory was relatively upmarket. It had a box seat (a luxury when camping on safari) and, even more excitingly, a double "stable" door. Allowing the incumbent to sit in reasonable comfort and privacy behind the closed lower section whilst looking out through the open upper one. Thus affording some remarkably intimate views of the Serengeti migration as the wildebeeste and zebras pounded past.

When the time came for us to strike camp it was, as always on safari, with a sense of desolation. I never got used to seeing my recent life, with all its excitements and adventures and enjoyments, reduced to a tiny rectangle of etiolated grass where my tent had stood – beneath the cumulous-clouded skies by day, the Milky Way and southern constellations by night, and among the creatures, great and small, that had wandered by. Always, as I drove away from a campsite, I would cast a last glance back, at the pale oblongs of grass and the nearby ashes of our fires. And wonder, disconsolately, if I would ever return.

This morbid sentimentality soon passed. And as John and I left Seronera we began to look forward, not back. To reaching Arusha in one piece and off-setting the more Spartan aspects of life on safari by celebrating with a big British breakfast at "Jambo Snacks" and a shower and proper bed at the Arusha YMCA. But as always on safari there were some underlying anxieties also, for the corrugations, outcrops of rock, thick sand and potholes encountered on the outward journey would be no less threatening on the way back. And at the time of the *mvuli*, the "short rains", the weather could turn spiteful.

Of all these challenges it was the corrugations that I most detested. Such tracks seem made of rock-hard corduroy, each transverse ridge two or three inches high in places. The main Serengeti track was one of the worst, especially on bends, where perhaps, because of the camber, they were more exposed to the sometimes persistent Serengeti winds. Such corrugations, as I have said before, can shake a car to its chassis – and beyond. As John and I were about to find out.

After leaving Seronera and passing its outlying air-strip I heard what I thought was another vehicle closing up behind. In my rear view mirror I could see nothing but our thick, billowing trail of dust. The Renault's windows, normally kept open as the car was not air-conditioned, were far from air tight even when closed, and if the vehicle behind overtook us we would be blinded and choked by its own dust cloud. I asked John if he could wriggle into the rear seat and somehow signal to the driver behind to slow down until I could wave him on without being enveloped in a sandstorm. John obliged but reported that he couldn't "see a bloody thing!".

The rumbles and growls from behind grew louder. Fearful of slowing down myself because of the pall of dust that would overtake and overwhelm us, I decided to pull off the road on to the adjacent plain to windward and let the impatient fool behind go belting past. Before I could do so, however, we were overtaken not by another vehicle but by events. John had stuck his head out of the rear window again, desperate to signal our annoyance to the driver behind, only to find that there was no driver there. "It isn't another car!" he yelled, above the grinding and the squealing, "The fucking *wheel* is falling off!"

Almost as he shouted the Renault lurched violently to one side with a drawn out, screeching crash. It took all my strength to keep it on the track, all efforts to brake proving futile. And unnecessary, for the rear offside stub axle, relieved of its wheel, was ploughing through the gravel and dust and slowing down the car more effectively than its brake-pads had ever done. As we came to a stop, with the car at a ludicrous angle and John and I thrown against our respective offside doors, we were engulfed in choking clouds of dust and an unreal silence. For a few seconds the dust poured in through the window that John had opened in acrid, suffocating clouds. When the air cleared I saw, through my own window, the detached wheel rolling across the plains, watched, with a mixture of curiosity and alarm, by a wildebeest bull. The wildebeest jinked away in panic before stopping and looking back, stupefied, as the wheel finally spun to a standstill.

With some difficulty we extricated ourselves. It quickly became obvious that a temporary repair job was out of the question and that we would have to go back to Seronera on foot to seek help. And so, after recovering the wheel and the various bits and pieces that had once been part of the braking system, we dumped them in the lop-sided Renault and set off. By chance, we soon heard the welcome sound of a car engine and saw, to our relief, a National Parks Land Rover, crowded with rangers, travelling at some speed towards Seronera on a nearby secondary track.

We waved like marooned sailors waving at a passing ship. They waved back but the Land Rover drove by without even slowing down and soon disappeared. "They must have thought we were researchers", I concluded charitably. "*Researchers*?" growled John. "Plastered in dust and walking through the Serengeti by ourselves, without a gun and in this baking heat? What the fuck do they think we're researching, death rates among suicidally-inclined white Caucasians in the African bush?"

We soon lapsed into silence, too concerned with the possible presence of large, aggressively-inclined mammals to think about much else. The country was quite open, the grass shorn to ankle-height by the passing migration. Any lions in the area would have seen us coming from miles away and hopefully loped off. Buffaloes, however, are more stubborn, and much more apparent. Just as the kopje on which the Seronera Lodge is built came into sight we saw a breeding herd of them, a little way ahead.

Normally such a herd, no matter how big, will charge off at the sight of humans approaching on foot, though we didn't know this at the time. In any case this particular herd was split into two, forcing us either to make a wide detour or to take a direct route between the two sections. We were too tired and dehydrated to care. The buffaloes, for their part, were in no mood to budge. They had stopped grazing to glower at us with eyes made all the more menacing by myopia. I felt like a matador, bereft of sword or cape or matadorial courage, sharing a rather large *plaza de toros* with John and about 150 fighting bulls. Most of them were in fact cows or calves but this did little to cheer us as we strode between the two groups, hoping that one would not try to rejoin the other.

Shuffling around to face us as we passed, both groups began to edge towards us, as buffaloes will, but only to see us safely off the premises. We were soon breathing normally again and within half-an-hour were sitting in the lounge of the Seronera

Lodge enjoying a couple of cold lagers before walking across to the garage compound at the Park headquarters. We were expecting to have to stay the night at the lodge but African motor mechanics (they get lots of practice) can sometimes fix a crippled car surprisingly quickly. The Seronera *fundis*, who must have dealt with most vehicular catastrophes known to Man, were wonderful. By late afternoon we were heading back out of Seronera and across the plains to Naabi Hill and Ngorongoro.

As we approached the Simba Kopjes, an archipelago of granite outcrops halfway between Seronera and Naabi, I saw what seemed to be a cluster of large, exotic blossoms, dark and round, springing from a low shelf of rock alongside the track. The "Mickey Mouse" ears of the first African wild dogs I had ever seen. Overcome with excitement I drove too quickly towards them. The dogs backed off but soon resettled, the boldest of them coming right up to the car to stare at us. The eyes of wild dogs, set in the black patches that extend from their muzzles, seem more sunken and beady than they actually are, giving them a disconcerting, dispassionate appearance that, like their former reputation for gratuitous ferocity, is undeserved. Their method of killing is certainly violent but they do what they have evolved to do efficiently, with neither compassion nor cruelty. They are themselves.

They are also visually attractive, their coats patterned with patches and whorls of black and tan and white, justifying the popular epithet "painted wolves". And amongst themselves mutually supportive and far less aggressive than their hunting and killing methods might suggest. To my knowledge they have never attacked a human being in the wild, though one was said to have bitten off the finger of a Tanzanian guide on Kilimanjaro. I was not aware of all this at the time but out of curiosity, when the nearest individuals had moved back a little to lie alongside the track, I got out of the Renault and took a few steps towards them. They jumped to their feet and one gave a brief bark of alarm, but they didn't retreat far and certainly didn't show any aggression. Feeling foolish and intrusive I returned to the car, got inside and quietly closed the door. The dogs again settled down.

Before long, however, they began to grow restless. I knew, from articles and books, that this was part of their pre-hunting ritual, in which the pack works itself into a high state of arousal. Down below us a large stream of wildebeeste and zebras was trailing through the shallow valley parallel to the track. The dogs, aware of them, began to show an interest. One began to walk down the slope towards the passing herbivores and the others followed, openly and unhurriedly. John and I got out of the car to watch. As the dogs reached the valley floor they stopped in line abreast, all eyes on the wildebeest and zebras. These also stopped, looking apprehensively at the dogs before breaking into a stuttering trot. The dogs began to move towards them at an easy lope. The wildebeest and zebras accelerated. The dogs followed suit. Through binoculars and at a distance it seemed unreal, too slow and silent and contrived for a drama that would end in death.

It was almost ceremonial, like some macabre, pre-sacrificial ritual, and just as inevitable. The dogs had selected their victim, a wildebeest yearling calf. Picking up speed they separated it from its mother as expertly as sheepdogs isolating a lamb. The calf, confused, came to a standstill and the leading dog seized it by the nose. The other dogs closed up fast, thrusting their muzzles between and around the calf's hind legs, to attack the groin.

Wild dogs are equipped with cutting teeth as hard and sharp as pinking shears and the strongest bite, relative to body mass, of any living carnivore. Their victims do not "go gentle" into their "goodnight" but they go relatively quickly. Not quickly enough for the wretched calf. Or for me. For minutes that must have seemed endless to the calf itself, it stood upright as it was disembowelled. The dog that had been holding it by the nose had joined its pack-mates at the groin. From a distance, through binoculars, the calf's pathetic, disproportionally large head, stilled by shock, seemed strangely oblivious to what was happening behind. Just as strangely the calf's killers seemed as innocent as mongrels in an L.S. Lowry painting. Which made the horror so much worse. The wildebeest's head sank lower as the animal, as if made of melting wax, was reduced to a sitting position, and then to little more than a smear of DNA upon the grass.

John and I, chastened, returned to the car. The death of the young wildebeest had aroused conflicting emotions. Violent death, so common in the East African bush (though not so commonly observed) is something that few of us witness. Our hunter-gatherer ancestors would not have spared a moment's thought for their own victims' pain or suffering; on the contrary they would have celebrated. But ten thousand years or so of evolution have changed us. The meat we eat comes from supermarkets, not abattoirs. And an animal in pain or distress, in most of us, evokes compassion. But we felt excited as well as subdued, and thankful for the morning's minor disaster. For had the wheel not fallen off the car we would have missed an enthralling act of natural theatre, and our first encounter with one of the most endangered, most fascinating and much misunderstood species on Earth.

"That", said John quietly as we drove off, "will happen to you one day." Fortunately he was no Nicodemus and over 40 years later, now thousands of miles from the nearest wild dog, I still haven't been ripped apart. "If the dogs don't get you", John added by way of elaboration, "the lions will". It was a reference to my habit, at that time, of getting out of the car and walking towards lions (or in this case wild dogs), to test their reactions.

My insistence that these idiotic exploits were in fact quite safe, and conducted with the advancement of scientific knowledge in mind, were rightly dismissed as "Bollocks".

We made it safely back to Ngorongoro, with the assistance of a Maasai elder who helped to push us up a fairly steep, rocky section of the track after we had stalled, and stayed overnight at Forest Hostel (now Rhino Lodge), a simple, downmarket place, set back from the crater rim. The next morning we headed off for Moshi. But as we descended the rocky track that dog-legged down the declivitous western wall of the Rift we saw the headlights of a procession of approaching vehicles. "Oh no", muttered John as the vehicles drove up at speed, trailing long clouds of dust, "it's the President or some other V.I.P! Pull over and stop!" This was (and is) the standard protocol throughout much of Africa and the developing world, where high-ranking politicians, fearful of would-be assassins, do not like to linger. Their well-armed body-guards, military and para-military and police escorts are not known for their forbearance – a few months earlier, in Dar, an expatriate had been shot in the back and killed for innocently driving through a road block.

It was the first time I had encountered such a procession and half-hypnotised by the headlights, the nearest of which were now flashing furiously, I was slow to react. Not that a quicker reaction would have made any difference to the Renault; its braking system, always poor, had not been improved by the wheel falling off in the Serengeti. "Oh my God!" groaned John as the vehicles raced up the rocky incline towards us, "It *is* the fucking President! STOP!" Too late. The cavalcade, headed by police motor-cyclists and jeeps full of Tanzanian troops in full camouflage gear, raced past in a spray of gravel and a smoke-screen of dust.

Through the dust I saw a blur of faces, contorted with rage, and a succession of waving arms and AK 47s commanding us to stop. We sailed on helplessly, past the irate police and military, past the cars filled with security men and minor V.I.Ps, and past the Presidential car with its official badge and flag. As we careered by I caught a momentary impression of the President's familiar face but it was the face of his guest, peering from the offside window, that had more impact. It was bearded and topped by an army-style field cap. "Oh God no!", groaned John, "It's Fidel fucking Castro!"

By then we were slowing down but once we had passed the presidential car I saw little point in stopping and every reason to keep going, which we did, grateful for the thickening clouds of dust but still threatened by an irate, weapon-waving succession of uniformed escorts in open jeeps, Land Rovers or astride huge motor cycles. I half-expected to be riddled with bullets or at least pursued and beaten up by a posse of police on motor-bikes but we soon skidded around one of the track's hairpin bends, shielded from the cavalcade by intervening walls of rock. The dust of its passing had drifted and thinned with the breeze and below us I could see the village of Mto wa Mbu at the foot of the escarpment.

I had given up on the brakes by now and we jolted down the lower, more gentle slopes, still expecting to be overtaken by police motor-cyclists or a jeep full of commandoes, headlights flashing in my rear-view mirror. "You idiot!" growled John when we eventually slowed down and rolled into Mto wa Mbu, "Those bastards could have *killed* us! Why didn't you *stop*?"

"We don't have any brakes", I reminded him. "Let's go and grab a beer".

CHAPTER X

Mountain of God

The following dry season another safari partner, Barry, and I set off on a very different kind of adventure. We were attempting to climb the active volcano *Ol Doinyo Lengai*, "Mountain of God" to the Maasai, in what was then a quite remote section of the Rift Valley, just south of Lake Natron. There is a little tourist camp at the foot of Lengai now but in those days there was nothing but isolated Maasai *enkangs* and *manyattas*. And the area's Maasai *ilmurran*, the young men of the old "warrior" grades, were not always well-disposed towards strangers.

Some time earlier, inspired by a chapter in Peter Matthiessen's beautifully written book *The Tree Where Man was Born*, I had foolishly attempted to reach Lengai in my Renault 4, accompanied by my colleague John. In the event we got little further than Monduli on the Rift's eastern edge, as the Renault steering rack had given way half-way down the Rift wall, which by Monduli is quite dramatic. A gang of Maasai *ilmurran*, on their way into town, had lifted the little car bodily, turned it around and helped push it back to the top of the escarpment. With darkness approaching we had decided to camp outside Monduli for the night and drive to Arusha the next morning, but were soon put under "tent arrest" by the Tanzanian army, which controls much of the area. Eventually, after accepting that we were not planning to mortar bomb their Monduli barracks, and with the help of a half-bottle of whisky that I often carried for such emergencies, they had let us go. When (due to the loose steering rack) we steered a zig-zag course through the night to Arusha.

Still determined to climb Lengai, I had planned a second attempt. By that time John had left the school but our friend Barry had agreed, with much reluctance, to come with me. "Baz", as I have implied earlier, was as different from John as one could imagine. His biorhythms seemed synchronized with the Earth's rotation. On crawling from his tent at dawn his metabolism appeared to have congealed overnight. But as the sun rose he would become more enlivened, reaching a climax in the evening when, aided by a few beers, he could be surprisingly animated. His intelligence and prodigious general knowledge, not least with regard to ornithology, was never in question. And of all my safari partners he was the most tractable, always willing to do, within reason, whatever I asked him to do. Not that I usually needed to ask; he was bright and sensitive enough to find a role for himself and quietly get on with it. While I faffed around hammering in tent pegs and lighting fires in an effort to look indispensible.

The idea of driving into the Rift to Lengai, however, let alone trying to climb a 10,000 foot, steeply conical and active volcano, was way beyond his comfort zone. In the end he agreed, almost certainly because the Lengai area, at that time rarely visited by anyone other than the Maasai, was ideal lark, pipit and cisticola country. This, to a birding addict who loved the "L.B.Js" or "little brown jobs" that the rest of us refuse to acknowledge, must have tipped the balance. Along with the fact that I had arranged to hire another colleague's Land Rover rather than go in the accident-prone Renault.

His concerns were justified. The Maasai in the Rift are no longer widely feared but at the time the *ilmurrani* could be restless and sometimes aggressive. Two tourists camping on the rim of Ngorongoro Crater had allegedly been murdered by disaffected Maasai and soon after our safari to Lengai two young Danes were murdered while camping not too far from the mountain. We had been advised to take a local guide with us "to be on the safe side", and been given the name and address of such a man. "He is Arusha, not Masaai", we were told, but he speaks the Maasai language. He is based in Monduli but knows the Lengai area well".

On arriving in Monduli we drove to the address we had been given. To our amazement we found ourselves outside a most un-African terraced cottage, built of red brick, with a little front garden bright with flowers and roses round the door. It was as if we had taken a wrong turn and ended up in the Cotswolds rather than the administrative heart of southern Maasailand. I had switched off the Land Rover engine but Barry and I had remained inside, staring at the house in a state of reverse culture shock.

Nothing in Africa goes unnoticed for long and within two minutes a small, wiry-looking man, middle-aged and dressed in casual western clothes, as if he had just finished watering his geraniums, emerged from the doorway. In those days, when Monduli was rarely visited by outsiders, it must have been quite surprising to find two white men parked outside your gate. But the little man, after scrutinizing us briefly from his doorway, strode briskly over to greet us and shake hands through the Land Rover's open window, as if he had been expecting us. His face, except for the curly grey hair that surmounted it, was that of a pastoralist elder, lined and weather-beaten, with eyes narrowed by looking into many suns and over great distances, his teeth like fine white porcelain.

He exuded and inspired confidence, spoke good English and confirmed that he also spoke Maa, the Maasai tongue, and that, as we had been assured, he knew the Lengai area well. He was just what we needed. But, he told us, he had other commitments. Greatly disappointed I asked if he could recommend anyone else. "No problem", he responded, "my daughter will come with you". Barry and I exchanged uneasy glances. A little offended, he chastised us. "Tanzanian women are not like your women", he inisted. "They are tough". And ordering us to "Wait" he strode back up the garden path and disappeared indoors.

Since a favourite aunt had taken me to see "Goldilocks and the Three Bears" at the local theatre when I was about five, and I had fallen for Goldilocks (I was seriously short-sighted) I have been susceptible to occasional but dangerously romantic fantasies. I watched the open doorway with sanguine curiosity. Arusha girls, like their Maasai cousins, can be distractingly good-looking and I was hopeful of seeing some slender and beguiling young maiden emerge, Africa's equivalent of Longfellow's Minnehaha.

The day-dream was short-lived. The spritely little man reappeared. Behind him came his daughter, filling the doorway as she passed through. "Good God", murmured Barry. My own first thought, after the initial surprise, was to wonder how so small and slim a man could have produced so gigantic a daughter. "At least", was all I could say, as father and daughter walked down the garden path towards us, "We should be safe enough with this one…"

On reaching the Land Rover she stood alongside her father, dwarfing him as he introduced her. Her face was as expressive as an Easter Island statue, and chiseled, it seemed to me, from the same solidified volcanic ash. "She doesn't speak much English", explained her father, but she speaks Swahili. And Maasai". At his prompting she shook hands with each of us, with the enthusiasm of a teenager dragged from a much-awaited sleep-over with friends to look after two visiting and boring uncles.

"What do you think?" I asked Barry as tactfully as I could. Barry stared into his foot-well, mumbling something to the effect that if she was capable of putting the fear of God into him she was probably, by extension, capable of instilling similar forebodings in anyone else. This was something of a *non sequitur*, it seemed to me, as a group of young and murderous *ilmurran* armed with spears, hacking swords and knobkerries might be rather less inclined towards mortal fear than Barry was. But this was no time for philosophical speculation, as the girl's father now indicated.

"Do not worry", he said, "You will be safe with her". Barry was fumbling to light a soothing cigarette.

"Does she know the area?", I asked, desperate for an opt-out clause.

"She was born in Monduli".

"But the Rift Valley? And Lengai?"

"She knows. She knows Lengai. But do not expect her to climb the mountain. Only you *Wazungu* do these strange things. But she will take you to Lengai. And wait for you. And" (after a significant pause) "bring you back to Monduli..." He didn't add "dead or alive".

I cannot remember the girl's name, and somehow it didn't seem to matter, for throughout the trip she maintained a radio silence that the *Bismark* on its final break for freedom would have envied. She communicated only when addressed, and even then in monosyllables. She became known to us only as "The Brooding Presence". By the time we were grinding down the precipitous Rift wall the atmosphere inside the Land Rover was as tense and silent as that during a driving test.

The tension eased after reaching the Rift floor for the recently engineered dirt track looked in pretty good shape and the scenery was distracting. The wind and the hooves of countless Maasai cattle had raised the red-brown dust into a faint mist, softening the edges of the landscape so that the trees and distant hills and Maasai homesteads looked as if they have been drawn with coloured chalks and deliberately smudged by a creative finger. We passed group after group of Maasai, mostly women with donkeys hung with gourds, brown and earthenware red and golden and polished with use, the shaven-headed women waving and smiling as we passed. Sometimes we weaved through long streams of cattle and at one point the "Brooding Presence" ordered me to stop while she spoke to a Maasai elder, at the head of such a herd. It was gratifying to hear her speak, though Maasai conversations, as John and I had found a few years earlier, are as full of eeeeeeeeeeeehs as the conversations of Yorkshire hill farmers are full of aaaaaaaaaaaaahs, and to an outsider as unfathomable.

"Don't tell me she's lost already", muttered Barry, more from mischief than alarm, though he was less chirpy a little later when a great volcano emerged from the mist, directly ahead. "Lengai?", I asked "The Presence", knowing that it wasn't. "Lengai", she confirmed, without hesitation. "Lengai?" queried Barry, addressing me rather than our guide, "We are *miles* from Lengai, surely?".

"We are indeed", I answered.

"I knew I shouldn't have come", he mumbled.

Below us, to our left, a small lake glimmered through the red-brown fog and a quick glimpse at my open map told me that it was Lake Magadi and that the volcano ahead was Kitmubeine. "*Bwawa Magadi*", I informed "The Presence", nodding towards the lake.

"*Magadi*", she replied.

"*Mlima pale ni Kitumbeine*" I continued in my inadequate Swahili, "The mountain there", I said, pointing at it, " is Kitumbeine".

"Kitumbeine" agreed The Presence, who had, a few seconds earlier, identified it as Lengai.

We passed Kitumbeine in silence. After a while another volcano materialised from the haze, this time rising from the Rift's western wall. "Lengai?", I asked.

"*Ndio, Lengai,*". But another glance at the map told me that it was Kerimasi, at the extreme north-eastern corner of the Ngorongoro Conservation Area. At least "The Presence" was getting close. Like a contestant in a pub quiz answering "Shakespeare" or "Manchester United" to every question on literature or football respectively, she would, sooner or later, get it right.

She didn't get the chance. A third volcano, Gelai, appeared in the distance, barely visible in the haze, but before she could turn it into Lengai the real thing stepped out from behind Kerimasi and shouted "Boo!" It was the archetypal volcano that any child would recognize, a grey-brown, steep-sided cone, fissured with shadowy ravines and bare of vegetation. "Lengai", I said, unnecessarily. Barry stared at it balefully, without needing to speak. The "Brooding Presence", peeved at not having been consulted, settled sulkily back into her rear seat.

As we neared the mountain I scoured its southern slopes. Peter Matthiessen, in *The Tree Where Man was Born*, had written that he was one of a group of four, including my old benefactor Vesey Fitzgerald and an experienced mountaineer, when he attempted the climb in 1967, from the south. They had been forced to turn back. Brian Hawkes, the mountaineer, had later said that the route "was a job for a four man team with ropes and ice-axes". Why, having read this, I now chose to take the same route I shall never know. I had a good map of the mountain and it was obvious from this that a northern approach would be more appropriate, as it was to prove years later, when a camp was established on the nearby shores of Lake Natron. Whatever the case, our "guide" was of no help. Once we had parked, a little way off the track, she stretched out on the back seat and fell fast asleep.

For a while Barry and I stood in the Land Rover's shade, looking up at the abrupt southern flanks of the mountain, which was topped by clouds, as if the crater was belching out white smoke. I identified what seemed to be the best of several unpromising routes, though from this angle the southern slopes were little more than a silhouetted outline. Somewhere in their middle section, however, one of the ridges, about two-thirds of the way up its steep profile, seemed to level off. This encouraged me, quite without reason as everything higher than the short, near-horizontal stretch was obscured by cloud. "If we can get as far as that level bit", I told Barry, "we should be O.K."

Wondering, no doubt, if the part of my brain that promotes intelligent decision-making had melted in the heat, "Baz" remained silent. He raised his binoculars – I assumed to examine the visible heights of the mountain before offering his own opinion. But on lowering them after a minute or so, and with an air of mysticism that the Delphic Oracle might have envied, he merely murmured "White Pelicans...". Sometimes, when he was deep into one of his bird-induced trances, I felt that a cryptologist was needed to decipher his pronouncements. All I could manage was "What?"

"White pelicans. A flock of them. Flying way above the summit. Heading north, towards Natron..."

With that I realized that any decision regarding our route to the top rested with me. And it needed to be made quickly. The ridge that I had identified as being the least of several evils was further away than I had planned to go. Driving across to it, even in a Land Rover, was too risky in this unknown country, covered as it was by knee-high grass and spiked with stabby little thorns. I was anxious to bivouac on the lower slopes of the mountain before nightfall, to give ourselves a good start the next morning before the sun became unpleasant. There was no time to waste.

We took out my two-man tent, our sleeping bags and a small amount of "hard rations", long-established safari staples, cans of corned beef, glucose biscuits and squares of *kashata* (peanut brittle). We then filled a good many water bottles, salvaged from the school's lost property store, stuffed some into our rucksacks and hung others around our necks. Rousing the "Brooding Presence" I informed her that we were leaving and hoped to be back the following afternoon. She nodded, uninterested. Barry and I then set off into the searing sun, loaded like two British infantrymen going "over the top" at the Somme and perhaps with as much chance of success. I was armed with a Maasai *simi* or slashing sword, not to keep lions or disaffected Maasai warriors at bay but to act as an ice-axe during the climb. The surface of the volcano, as I knew from Matthiessen's book, was composed of hard-packed, treacherously friable ash.

The vegetation around Lengai at that time, except for emergent thorns and some stunted acacias along the drainage line between Lengai and Kerimasi, consisted mainly of spike dropseed grass, *Sporobolus spicatus*, as vicious as its specific name. Barry described it later as "carnivorous". The grass's awns and splinters worked their way into our jeans and socks, lacerating our legs and feet. And the dehydrating heat was relentless. We sought relief, if only from the grasses, by walking along a "river" of black ash that seemed to lead towards the chosen ridge. The flat bed of the "river" was solid and smooth but scorching hot, even through the soles of my trainers. Eventually we had to take once again to the spiteful grassland. The hike was taking much longer, and much more out of us, than I had foreseen. By the time we were opposite the ridge the sun was beginning to dissolve in the dust-haze beyond the Rift's western wall. Every minute counted now.

Directly opposite the ridge and leading towards it we came across old tyre tracks, hardened like concrete and possibly made several years earlier by the Matthiessen party. Despite the fact that Matthiessen and his companions had failed to climb Lengai the tyre tracks, inexplicably, reassured me. Just to know that other human beings, apart from wandering Maasai, had passed through that desolately awesome land lifted my spirits. They did little for Barry's. He was all but done in. Dropping his rucksack he declared that he was going no further.

Alarmed, because I wanted as good a start as possible the next morning, I urged him to make one last effort before night fell, but, dispirited and dehydrated, he declined. Reluctantly I left him with the tent, saying that I would press on to the foot of the mountain and sleep in the open there overnight. I asked him to join me as early as possible the next morning, when hopefully he would be feeling refreshed and more optimistic. I then set off for the ridge, feeling lonely and tired, with my rucksack, sleeping bag and Maasai *simi*.

Distances can be deceptive anywhere but in the immensity of wild Africa such deceptions are commonplace, and the slog through the drop-seed grass took longer than I had hoped. Eventually, however, I reached the edge of the grass line, in those days no higher than the foot of the mountain. The exposed ridge, with its carapace of compacted ash, was gentle enough here, where it fanned broadly into the grasslands, but above me it rose precipitously. Its pale grey crest narrowed dramatically towards the summit, upper extremes still hidden in cloud. From this angle the relatively level little stretch two-thirds of the way up, that had looked encouraging from a distance and in profile, was invisible.

Turning, I saw my little blue tent already standing amid the russet grasslands between Lengai and Kerimasi. Through my binoculars I saw Barry adjusting the guys. Even at a distance he looked weary and woe-begone. Soon he disappeared inside the tent. Twilight seemed to creep up from the shallow valley, turning muted shades into monotones. Spurred on by the approach of nightfall I quickly found a reasonably broad, flat ledge of hard ash and laid out my sleeping bag.

While there was still a little light I conducted a brief exploration of the vicinity. I was close to the edge of a narrow gully, about eight feet deep and with near-vertical sides. I decided to leave a few bottles of water there in case of emergencies on our way down the next day. After secreting the bottles in a suitable niche in one wall of the gully, in case there were hyenas or other animals around, I hauled myself out, quickly built a little cairn of stones to mark the spot then settled down to eat a little food and quench my thirst. As darkness fell I could see the tent dimly illuminated by Barry's torch. The torch soon went out and I too retired to my sleeping bag. I badly needed to sleep well before tomorrow's climb, but my mind was too active. Being alone on the slopes of a sacred mountain, a remote and active volcano in the middle of Maasailand was stimulating. And slightly disconcerting.

I lay on my back, thankful for the sleeping bag, despite its lightness, for the ground was hard and the temperature falling noticeably. With the onset of the night the band of sky that I could see, above the valley between Lengai and Kerimasi, was transformed into a glittering superabundance of stars, stupendous even for wild Africa. Strangely, I felt that I was looking down, not up. Floating, as if in a state of levitation, far above some still and silent sea that twinkled and glittered and shimmered with phosphorescence. It was a little frightening, as if I might suddenly fall and go on falling forever. Disturbed by this sensation yet fascinated by the beauty above (or below!) me I lay mesmerized, until phasing into a fitful sleep.

I was awakened some time later by stinging grains of ash driven against my cheeks by a fierce wind that must have arisen in moments. It was like being sand-blasted. I withdrew my head into my sleeping bag but the wind and the ash were relentless and I decided to climb down into the gully, armed with my torch. I had tossed my *simi* and sleeping bag into the narrow cleft in advance. The gully was claustrophobic but calm. Finding a small, reasonably level patch in which to sleep I again wriggled into my sleeping bag. Earlier, by the ash river, I had seen the white, calcified droppings of a spotted hyena, and now I wondered, morbidly, if the animals ever explored the mountain's lower slopes and gullies.

The thought of being discovered by even one hyena in this narrow defile wasn't conducive to sleep but in the end, too tired to care and with the *simi* close at hand, I succumbed. After a while the wind must have stopped as abruptly as it had started, as if I had dreamed it. The sudden silence must have awakened me. Looking up I saw the stars, reduced now to a diaphanous, scintillating scarf by the narrowness of the crevasse. Encouraged by the stillness I climbed back on to the open slopes, where, longing for daybreak, I lay down once more.

Eventually the light was strong enough for me to see the tent. There was no sign of movement or torchlight. I rolled up my sleeping bag and climbing back into the gully stashed it into the crevice with my emergency water supply. Hauling myself out again I waited for the light to strengthen further before shouting Barry's name, again and again, towards the tent. There was no response, and I wondered, in that immensity where distance can be so deceptive, if my voice had failed to carry. Some time later Barry emerged, and comforted, I saw him dismantling the tent. I shouted again and waved and he waved and shouted something back, pointing across the bitter grasslands that we had crossed the evening before. He had, I realized, seen enough of Lengai and was heading back.

I felt like the last man on the planet, watching the second-last disappear into eternity. But Africa has little time for introspection and self-pity and I knew I must move on. As if to assert myself I turned my back on Barry and my face towards the mountain, head bent back to survey my intended route. It was no more encouraging in the cold light of morning than it had been the evening before. The white clouds that only yesterday had clustered around the peak were now ominously dark but waiting for things to improve was not an option. After a breakfast of glucose biscuits and water I slipped my rucksack over my shoulders, and with the *simi* in my hand and my binoculars around my neck, began the ascent.

It quickly became clear that I was on the wrong ridge, and I was forced to climb in and out of two almost sheer-sided and fairly deep gullies, using the *simi*, as intended, as an ice-axe. There was no danger but I was wasting precious time and energy. More worryingly, despite the early morning coolness, I was already dehydrating in the dry air. At last I gained the ridge that I had chosen as my intended ascent route. I feel sure, in retrospect, that it was the same route that the Matthiessen party had taken. It was broad at the base and initially I made pleasing progress, though the ridge began to steepen and narrow. After a while I stopped to drink. I looked down into the valley, encouraged by the altitude I had gained.

From this vantage point the straw-coloured grasslands below had lost their hard-edged vindictiveness but even through binoculars there was no sign of Barry or life of any kind other than the dessicated vegetation. Kerimasi looked much closer than I knew it to be, and more like a gentle Lakeland fell than a spent volcano in the African Rift. I felt even more like the last man on Earth. And a harsh, uncompromising Earth at that. But an imposing one, worthy of a land overlooked by the Maasai God, for beyond Kerimasi to westward the Rift wall curved away to the north, pale brown with darker furrows but sharp and clear in the morning sun, as if it had just been created and, in a strangely exhilarating way, utterly forlorn. To behold this barren yet beguiling beauty was reason enough to have come.

I resumed the climb. The gullies on either side had deepened now into ravines and were pressing in on me. I could not see far into them, nor was I tempted to try. But now and again, when I used the *simi* to steady myself on the crest-line, the compacted ash flaked away and clods went sliding down to one side or the other, causing me to stiffen and listen as they rolled and tumbled into the abyss. In the otherwise ear-singing silence it seemed to take an age for the sounds to end. Not caring to dwell upon this I moved on, more cautiously now, stooping to lower my centre of gravity and holding the *simi* like a long-bladed dagger, ready to stab down into the hard ash should it suddenly crumble beneath my foot.

The ridge narrowed to the breadth of a Clydesdale's back. More nervous now I sat down, legs astride the hump of the crest, edging forward and upwards, trying to avoid looking down. Not that looking up brought greater comfort, for the clouds that obscured the summit, in places damson black, were stealing towards me in a sinister, rolling boil, their ragged fringes writhing like tentacles. This seething mass of vapour had assumed a purposeful, malignant unity, bringing to mind the poisonous black cloud that Pliny the Younger saw rolling down Vesuvius 2,000 years ago, which vulcanologists know as a pyroclastic flow.

It was no such thing, of course. But it was unnerving. With it had come a stiff wind, suddenly, like the wind that had awoken me in the night. And something else. Startled by a loud caw, harsh enough to be heard above the wind, I looked up to see a conspiracy of White-naped Ravens. The collective noun could hardly have been more apt. There were six of them, battling into the squall and finally alighting on the ridge ahead of me, where it levelled off. They clung to its narrow crest, just below the cloud, wings hunched to maintain a hesitant equilibrium. Now and again one or other would be blown back into the void like a black umbrella wrecked by a gust of wind, only to recompose itself and fight its way back. Fellow creatures in that forbidding world should have been comforting but they were far from that. Why were they here, where no life, no form of sustenance, existed? It was a mystery. Until I realized that the place was not quite lifeless. I was there. The ravens were there because of me. Watching, waiting, hoping…

I had no intention of moving until the cloud lifted. Unless it came closer. To have been enveloped in that dark and forceful malignancy, on that exposed ridge, would have been frightening. Meanwhile I still hoped that if the cloud lifted and the wind dropped I could inch my way on to the more encouraging section of the ridge, where the ravens now were, to give myself some respite. And that the route to the crater rim, so far screened from view by the clouds, would somehow be less daunting. I sat motionless, legs gripping the flanks of the ridge as tightly as a Cossack horseman and with more reason, my upper body bent forward to lessen the buffeting of the wind. But my attention kept returning to the ravens, which were suddenly unsettled, as I was, by a more forceful gust that swept them into the air. And that rolled back the trailing edges of the cloud.

The cloud and the ravens soon re-established themselves but in those moments of revelation I saw that the ridge, beyond the short, more horizontal section, reared up again, steep and slender as the neck of a giraffe. My attempt to climb Lengai was over. Even with mountaineering experience and equipment it would probably have been impossible, because of the treacherous ash of which it was composed. My disappointment was outweighed by my relief. There was no shame now in turning back. The regret was in choosing this route in the first place, knowing that Matthiessen's party, with its accomplished mountaineer, had failed.

Turning around at this point was too precarious, so for some time I inched myself backwards until the ridge broadened enough for me to squirm around safely. The ravens followed, fluttering sporadically into the wind before re-alighting. As I had twisted around, turning my back on them, one of them cawed, as if resentful of my bid to escape. I levered myself forward, relieved to be losing height, however slowly, and to feel the ridge widening beneath me. When it became too wide for comfort I stood, hunched like an ape to keep my centre of gravity low, my *simi* ready to anchor me should I stumble.

The ravens, thwarted, peeled away but I was now faced with a new problem, less menacing but no less discomfiting. I must have stubbed a toe badly at some point, its effects unnoticed due to other distractions. It was now quite painful, causing me to limp. Sitting down again I took off my trainer. My sock was soaked with blood around the toes, and I decided to do without shoes altogether, stuffing them into my rucksack. The water bottles inside the rucksack reminded me that I had also become badly dehydrated, and I drained a complete bottle in a series of long gulps. On tucking the empty bottle back into the rucksack I noticed that my water supply was almost exhausted. But I had my emergency cache in the gully below and now that I was in stockinged feet, with the ridge widening minute by minute, I was losing height more quickly.

Another challenge now arose. The wind that had arisen so unexpectedly higher up the mountain had dropped just as abruptly but as the temperatures in the valley below increased a succession of dust devils began to form, twisting and weaving their way across the grasslands in whorls of flying dust and straw. All of them, presumably due to some obscure law of physics, headed for Lengai, and all raced up one or other of its ridges.

It seemed pre-planned and co-ordinated, as if they were out to get me. Apparently increasing in speed as they approached, they whirled past in a frightening rush of noise, hoovering a column of ash into the air as they came. Sooner or later, I felt sure, one was bound to coincide with me and I wondered, with some trepidation, what might happen if it did. There was little I could do except sit down, dig the *simi* deep into the crust of ash and hang on as each whirlwind attracted to my particular ridge broke free from the grassland and surged towards me. There was something uncanny about the way they sought out the ridges and kept to them, as if with computer-controlled precision.

Fortunately most of those that came my way were not the most intimidating, just adolescent versions of the real thing, whooshing towards me but burning out their bravado long before they reached. By the time I had gained the safety of the mountain's fan-slopes the dust-devils had almost died down. And soon I saw the little cairn of stones that I had built to mark the previous night's bivouac. On reaching it I lowered myself into the gully to retrieve my sleeping bag and water bottles. To my dismay I found that two of the bottles had leaked. One was completely empty, the other only one third full. The remaining two bottles were quite small.

These, once I had quenched my thirst with the water I still had in my rucksack, were all that I now had to see me back to the Land Rover. I wasted no time in getting off the mountain but once back among the razor-wire grasslands I was forced to stop and put my trainers back on. The soles of my socks were by now threadbare and my toe, back inside the crippling shoe, more painful than ever. I limped slowly through the grass towards the ash river.

By the time I reached it I was half-crippled. Sitting down on the low bank I ripped off my trainers again and packed them away. I stepped gingerly on to the smooth black ash and not so gingerly off again, for I could have fried an egg on its surface. Even so it was preferable to the grass and to wearing the trainers. Bracing myself for some mild torture I set off along the ash river, looking for shadows to use as rare stepping stones of relief. I hopped from one foot to the other, feeling like one of those Shovel-snouted Lizards in the Namib Desert that survive by lifting two diagonally opposite legs off the sand, pair by pair.

When I did find a more reasonable patch of shade, thrown by an extra tall clump of riverside grass, I stood in it gratefully. At other times, when the pain became intense, I sat on the bank, holding both feet off the ground. At one point, when standing up after such a rest, I was startled by a sudden noise and movement from across the ash river. It was only a golden jackal breaking from the grass on the far bank, fearful of my presence, yet reminding me that I was back in big game country, where lions often roam.

Lions did not worry me in this relatively open country but something else soon did. Shortly after seeing the jackal I made for an old termite mound and climbed it, as cheetahs often do, to scan the grasslands. Ahead, through my binoculars, I saw the Land Rover, much further away than I had hoped, and devoid of any sign of movement. Where was Barry? And the "Brooding Presence"? And then, beyond the Land Rover, along the convex crest of a long, low hill in the distance, blurred and wavering in the heat-haze, I saw about fifteen Maasai *ilmurran*. In line abreast. And armed with spears, held upright.

I was alarmed. They were spaced out like advancing infantrymen, seemingly heading for the Land Rover. Or perhaps away from it? At that distance and in the heat haze, the latter exaggerated by the binoculars, it was hard to tell. Had they, with their exceptional eyesight, seen me? If not, why were they motionless? I watched for some minutes without seeing a hint of movement other than that caused by the rippling waves of heat. I looked again at the Land Rover. Still no sign of life. Had Barry and our guide been attacked? Robbed? Murdered? The thoughts were absurd but real. What was I to do? Keep a low profile until they had gone? Or get back to the Landrover as quickly as I could?

Even as these thoughts passed through my mind I saw movement closer at hand. Two Maasai *ilmurran* were heading my way, spears angled back over their shoulders, from the direction of the Land Rover. They had been screened from view by an intervening dip in the land. My first instinct was to hide but they had already seen me. I then remembered reading that enemies of the Maasai, when facing defeat and probable death at the warriors' hands, would grab a tuft of grass, much revered in traditional Maasai culture, and hold it out as a token of surrender and peace. Ridiculously, I plucked some grass, gripping it conspicuously in my right hand as I continued my walk along the ash river, as unconcernedly as I could. I might as well have held out a stick of candy floss.

The *ilmurran* approached in the characteristic, loose-limbed Maasai way, their *shukas*, bright red in the sun, blown against their lean bodies by the breeze. They strode past, some fifty metres away, as if I didn't exist, bare-legged and in sandaled feet through the grasslands that had caused Barry and I, in our jeans and stout shoes, such discomfort. I saluted them with a raised arm, still clutching the ludicrous tuft of grass. Half-raising their free arms in token acknowledgement they passed on, without breaking stride. Here, in this remote and near-deserted land, at the foot of the Mountain of God, a lone white man in stockinged feet, with a tuft of grass in one outstretched hand and a Maasai slashing sword in the other, had appeared out of nowhere, as if from the very bowels of the volcano. To be hailed with the most cursory of gestures, as a Londoner might wave to a minor acquaintance across Peckham High Street.

I was too relieved to be affronted, and hurried on. From the next rise in the grassland I scanned ahead again through the binoculars. The Land Rover was much nearer now, but still no sign of life. The line of *ilmurran* and their spears was nearer also, still as statues and obviously watching me. Except that they were not Maasai warriors with spears but fringe-eared oryx with long straight horns. To anyone unused to African distances, the illusory effects of African heat and the often unlikely nature of African possibilities all this might seem exaggerated. It wasn't. My eyesight, with glasses, is good and with binoculars as good as anyone else's, and my fears had been genuine. I felt utterly foolish but happy to have been proved so. As I watched, delighted now, the oryx wheeled, one by one, then stopped, looking back over their shoulders to watch again. And then, like discredited myths, they vanished into the shimmering haze.

As I drew close to the Land Rover I called out. For a moment there was no response. Then a familiar figure slumped into view, stretching and muttering itself back into consciousness. It wasn't quite "Stanley meets Livingstone in Ujiji" but Barry and I were deeply thankful to see each other. In our stiff English way we demonstrated it by being undemonstrative.

"Where is our trusty guide?" I asked. Barry nodded towards the Land Rover.

"Sleeping. She's been sleeping since I got back. After eating most of the bloody food and drinking most of the water".

"Let's get out of here" was all I could think of saying. It was enough. We shared some water and peanut brittle and biscuits and I woke up the "Brooding Presence". As sullen as ever, she showed not the slightest interest in my return or my adventures on the mountain. I didn't care. After quickly cleaning my injured foot and applying ointment I put on clean socks and my trainers. And we left, without looking back.

In our eagerness to go I forgot my *simi*. Some wandering Maasai would have found it, and I like to think it is still being used, down in that dramatic country beneath the Mountain of

God. Meanwhile we drove back as quickly as the conditions allowed, stopping only to observe a host of marabou storks, huddled like undertakers around the corpse of a golden jackal, in the middle of the track. Soon after dark that evening, after paying off the undeserving "Brooding Presence" outside her home, we were heading towards the gate of our favourite Tanzanian park, Tarangire. "I have never", murmured Barry, "been so glad to see this place".

CHAPTER XI

Campsite No.1

Before flying to Dar es Salaam to join the International School of Tanganyika in January 1977 I had packed a tin trunk with a small, eclectic assortment of possessions and had it shipped out. Half of those possessions were books. These, like the objects stored in the tombs of the pharaohs, were to sustain me in the afterlife, or at least my life in voluntary exile. Among them was a copy of John Williams' *National Parks of East Africa* that I had recently bought from the "Philip Son & Nephew" bookshop close to the famous Cavern Club in Liverpool. After buying the book I had gone into the café next door, once frequented by the Beatles, to flip through it over a coffee. One national park listed in the "Tanzania" section excited me more than the rest, as according to Williams it was "an easy three and a half hour's drive" from Dar es Salaam, where I was to be based.

It was called Mikumi. So enthralled that I almost forgot to drink my coffee I read that "Game animals and birds" were "abundant" there and included the 'Big Five', though how all these creatures could fit into such a small and simple sanctuary was a mystery. For the map accompanying the text looked as if it had been sketched on the back of a bus ticket. Its symbols depicted three groups of trees (fifteen trees in all), three groups of hills (eight hills in all), three minor rivers (two of which didn't seem to flow anywhere) and a waterhole. The main Tanzania-Zambia highway cut through it from north-east to south-west and a railway line passed from south to north within its western boundary.

On the evidence of the map Mikumi could almost have been a municipal park in my home town and yet my future was to become so intertwined with it that my partner-to-be, Anjum, would come to call it my "second wife". It would certainly become intimately familiar. As it is still, if only in my mind. The outline of its hills, the disposition of its plains and woodlands, the settings of its waterholes and alignment of its watercourses, its various tracks and circuits, all as clear today as they were so long ago. Such mundane memories, not just the more dramatic, are a measure of what a place – or a person – has meant to you.

The map did little justice to the park. Even then it was 450 sq. miles in area. Superimposed on a map of England that would encompass most of present-day Greater Manchester. But Mikumi is now twice as big as Greater London. It has always been understated. And underrated. But not by me. I found it impressive, though the "easy three hour drive" that John Williams promised (an average speed of 52 m.p.h, 2 m.p.h. higher than the maximum Tanzanian speed limit) was optimistic even then. Now it can take an hour just to grind through the Dar suburbs and at least four more to reach the park's main gate.

In the early days my safari partners and I would almost always camp in our individual, two-man tents on Campsite No. 1. Every Tanzanian national park had a Campsite No. 1 but to us this title was always reserved for that in Mikumi. Partly because it was so familiar but mostly because it was so different. Not in itself, for in that respect it was unremarkable, like most others. It was no more than a natural area of open bush with the usual pit latrine on its periphery and a circular spread of ashes and a few rocks that served as a fireplace at its centre. And its location seemed deceptively reassuring for anyone anxious about camping in wild Africa, as it was only two to three hundred metres equidistant from the main highway (then relatively little used), the park's main gate and, close to the gate, the so-called "Tented Camp" (now Mikumi Wildlife Camp). Yet despite these man-made intrusions it was, for us, the most exciting campsite in Tanzania.

Few tourists visited Mikumi in those days and the locals that did, mostly from the various Asian communities, would stay at the reasonably priced state lodge in the nearby hills or at the Tented Camp, as did most expats. A few expats, however, chose to camp as we did, sometimes for economic reasons, more often because they wanted something a little more daring than a room at the lodge or the Tented Camp. Many would have thought that Campsite No. 1, thanks to the nearby highway, main gate and the Tented Camp, would have provided the excitement of sleeping "in the bush" without much fear of being disturbed by potentially dangerous animals. They could hardly have been more wrong.

A bull buffalo was actually resident in the campsite vicinity for some time. It kept itself to itself, grazing the longer grasses just beyond the area that had been slashed short by the rangers. It never bothered us but whilst enjoying a beer at the Tented Camp one afternoon I heard the crack of a rifle and on looking in the direction of the sound saw a pick-up full of rangers on the campsite. I drove over to find the buffalo lying dead. It had, I was told, "become dangerous."

A more common threat was posed by elephants, always bulls. They had become habituated to human presence by roaming more or less constantly between the lodge, the Tented Camp, Campsite No. 1 and the park headquarters, raiding the rubbish dumps for scraps of fruits and vegetables or (on the campsite) sniffing around vehicles and tents for evidence of fruits and vegetables left inside by unwary campers. There were about five or six elephants involved in this regular patrol, always travelling alone.

The park rangers had given all of them names but I knew them collectively as "the lodge elephants". I actually named one of them myself. Two or three young American biologists, wanting to know if Mikumi's elephants commuted back and forth between the park and the Selous Game Reserve fifty kilometres to the south, immobilised and collared an elephant and trailed around after it day after day in a little Suzuki jeep fitted with the usual tracking equipment. Unfortunately it was one of the lodge elephants, and over the next few months, whenever we were in Mikumi, we would sometimes see the poor biologists driving between the lodge, the Tented Camp, Campsite No. 1 and the park headquarters, following their elephant on its little circuits and looking a little nonplussed. I named the elephant "Fido" because of its huge "dog" collar. And the researchers "Dumbos". Had they only asked the park rangers or the staff at the lodge or Tented Camp about the elephant before darting it they would have saved themselves a huge amount of time and embarrassment.

Not every lodge elephant was as docile as Fido and not all had such homely-sounding names. One bull, with impressive tusks, was known as "Osama" after the notorious head of the Al Quaeda terrorist organisation. It gained its nickname after charging a ranger's wife at the park headquarters and attempting to kill her. She survived and was rushed to hospital, badly but not fatally injured. Soon afterwards, however, Osama pushed a tusk through the head of a six-year-old girl. He was, like his namesake, tracked down and shot.

The park's tourism officer, after telling me this tragic tale, went on to explain that the children at the headquarters would often "play with Osama and hang from his tusks". I was astonished, knowing just how dangerous wild elephants can be, that park officials had allegedly allowed this to happen. Most of us love elephants but living with them can be a different matter. Fortunately, by the time Osama appeared on the scene in the early 2000s, I had given up camping as my wife Anjum, by then my constant safari partner, had become too nervous of elephants to sleep among them in the bush.

Her nervousness was unsurprising. In the late 1970s and throughout the 1980s, when we often camped in Mikumi, elephant "incidents" were frequent and sometimes frightening. On one occasion we were with two Californian friends, Bob and Karen. On the first evening they went to bed under the raised roof of their V.W. Camper while Anjum and I retired to our little tent some 10 or so metres away. Bob was a generous host who enjoyed his sundowners (and sometimes his sun-uppers) and thanks to him I had gone off to sleep in a blissful mental fug. In this state of abstraction I had left my brand new camera in a *kikapu* (woven grass basket) on the front seat of Bob's Camper.

Bob, deliberately or otherwise, had left the window of the VW cab open. During the night, disturbed by strange noises, he had slipped out of bed to investigate. As he lowered one bare leg through the hatch above the cab he was shocked to find it being caressed by what transpired to be the tip of an elephant's trunk. Much to Karen's bewilderment and concern he quickly recoiled back into the sleeping space in shock. The *kikapu* in which I had left my camera also contained fresh fruit, and the elephant was helping himself.

Anjum and I always slept lightly when camping and we too had been awakened. Zipping open the tent I poked my head out to see the elephant, in bright moonlight, dragging a pineapple from the *kikapu*. I also saw my new camera lying on the ground by the animal's feet. As an adult African elephant bull weighs between 4 and 7 tonnes the future of my camera was circumscribed by doubt. Grabbing one of my safari boots and with Anjum imploring me "not to be stupid" I crawled outside, stood up and flung the boot as hard as I could at the intruder. It caught the elephant full on the flank with a loud "thwack!" To my amazement, for I was half-expecting the animal to turn and charge, it squealed as if shot and went charging off into the night. The camera was unharmed.

On another occasion, when camping alone, I was awoken in the middle of the night by something thumping against my head through the fabric of the tent. I soon realised that it was an elephant's trunk, tearing up the grass just behind the tent. Unable to sleep (and after shifting my pillow and head out of range) I lay listening, somewhat resentfully, to the tugging of grass and the usual rumbles and gurgles and rectal sighs that confirm the inefficiency of the elephantine digestive system.

Eventually things went quiet. Anxious to reassure myself that the elephant had wandered off I squirmed out of my sleeping bag, knelt down by the front of the tent and tried to unzip it. To my irritation the zip stuck a few inches above the ground but I managed to force my head under the gap and poke it outside. As my head was now trapped cheek down against the ground I could see nothing ahead of me, despite the bright moonlight. With some difficulty I turned my head to the left. There was no sign of the elephant. Twisting my head to face to the right I saw nothing to worry about there either.

I was about to yank my head back inside the tent when I saw the lower end of an elephant's trunk curling around the corner towards me, followed by the animal's forequarters. In my panic my head became stuck, and reluctant to alarm the beast I froze. It edged closer, the tip of its trunk sniffing towards my face, its great head and tusks directly above me. Elephants are big enough at the best of times, but when one's head is alongside their toenails – and trapped – they look very big indeed.

Some months later, accompanied by my brother-in-law-to-be and his cousin, I had driven from the campsite to the Tented Camp's "Buffalo Bar", where we were welcomed by the Tanzanian manager, Theodore. He was a good-natured, hospitable man but on this occasion suffering from malaria. After a while he excused himself to try to sleep off his fever in his nearby wooden hut. Malaria can inspire weird, discomfiting hallucinations but those that soon affected Theodore were particularly unsettling. He awoke to find his hut pitching wildly like a small ship in a gale. Meanwhile, from the bar, we watched in fascination as a bull elephant, for reasons best-known to itself, had lumbered over to Theodore's hut (raised above the ground by bricks at each corner), hooked its tusks beneath it like a fork-lift truck and started levering the whole cabin up and down.

Elephants were not the only members of the "Big Five" to disturb the dreams of people on Campsite No. 1, as an acquaintance of ours, Peter, would agree. Until he landed a job as a road engineer in Tanzania he had hardly travelled beyond his native London or seen anything in nature more threatening than a cow. His first African safari was to Mikumi, where my old safari partner Kevin had arranged to introduce him to the joys of camping in the bush. Anjum and I, then unmarried, had agreed to join them but had set out hours ahead. Kevin and Peter, in a borrowed Land Rover, were to meet us later that afternoon.

Anjum's younger brother Zia, only thirteen at the time, was with us, acting as a kind of unwitting chaperone (Anjum's father being unusually liberal for a Pakistani). Zia had been with us before and had acquired a justifiable nervousness with regard to elephants. On arriving at Campsite No. 1, where a few troubling memories came seeping back, his anxieties overcame him. In the end we decided to sleep at the much-neglected hostel at the park headquarters, about two kilometres away. Before driving there I left my two-man tent, still rolled up in its bag, on the campsite in case Kevin or Peter wanted to use it, with a note explaining where we had gone and that we would see them on the campsite around dawn the next day.

Kevin and Peter saw the tent later and read my note. Peter had his own tent but Kevin, knowing how eventful life on Campsite No.1 could be, opted to sleep in the Land Rover. Which must have done little for Peter's already depleted self-confidence. Kevin reassured him: "Nothing to worry about, *really* Peter, we've camped here many times..." Unconvinced, Peter set up his tent. It was a one-man affair of the type popular with mountaineers, resembling, with sinister dramatic irony, a nylon coffin. When he and Kevin eventually retired for the night the young Londoner must have lain awake for hours, assailed by misgivings.

He finally fell asleep but was awakened, in the middle of the night, by low but alarming noises just outside. The tent itself was trembling – and so, soon afterwards, was Peter. For having squirmed around into a kneeling position he had squinted through the tiny ventilation panel in the front of the tent to see the silhouette of a lioness's head, two or three feet away. She was tugging at one of the guy ropes.

Kevin, curled up in the Land Rover, had also awakened. Sitting up and peering through the windscreen he saw four lionesses, spectral in the moonlight, alongside Peter's tent. Three were full grown, the one tugging on the guy rope a sub-adult.

He watched, hypnotised. He couldn't start the Land Rover as Peter had the keys. He thought about sounding the horn but felt that this might panic the lions and make a bad situation worse. So he sat helpless as Peter, fearing for his life, called out "Kevin! Kevin!". The lions leapt up but soon resettled. After what must have seemed like hours the adult lionesses, in their languid leonine way, began to stir. One by one they stood up, stretched and padded off into the night. The last to leave, after one last playful twang on the guy-rope, was the adolescent female.

Peter cried out again, imploring Kevin to tell him what was going on. Not wishing to raise Peter's hopes, Kevin merely called out "Wait!", "The lions are leaving!". After a while, with the lionesses no longer visible, he opened the Land Rover door. Clad only in his underpants, he jumped down calling "Peter! You can come out now!" Upon which two full-grown male lions, that had been sleeping in the shadows behind the tent (lions lying on their sides can keep an astonishingly low profile) leapt up with startled little grunts. Kevin leapt back into the Land Rover like an Olympic high jumper and slammed the door. Peter was reduced to suppressed sobs.

The sight of Kevin in his underpants (not a vision calculated to calm the troubled human mind) was also too much for the lions. They bolted after the females. When Anjum, Zia and I arrived at the campsite the next morning we found Kevin (now thankfully fully dressed) making coffee on the embers of the open fire. Peter was sitting on a log nearby, shivering uncontrollably, and not merely from the cold morning air. When he had regained enough composure to speak he muttered, with feeling. "I will *never* go camping again! *Never*! Not even on Brighton beach." Which, on reflection, might have been far more dangerous.

A few months later a young married couple had a similar experience, except that in their case the lions pulled down their tent on top of them. The couple had clung to each other in what they must have thought was a final embrace, not daring to move until 10 the next morning when the sun was searing and when any lion with any sense would be sleeping in the shade.

I never had serious problems with lions whilst camping though once Anjum and I were roused from our slumber by a mating pair. They were growling and rumbling their sweet nothings about eighty metres away, and getting closer with each (very frequent) amorous encounter. When mating, lions can be aggressive and unpredictable so before the pair became too close for comfort we crept out and ensconced ourselves in the front seats of the nearby Renault. Sleep proved impossible, however, not because of the lions but because a field mouse had somehow got into the car, rustling and scraping and scurrying around until daylight rescued us – and it.

Having someone alongside you on safari, to share your anxieties as well as the happier moments, makes a great difference. When you are alone the anxieties can tend to dominate. Certainly, when camping alone on Mikumi's Campsite No. 1, I was more mindful of the pessimistic possibilities. The mornings and afternoons usually passed pleasantly enough and there was an added sense of adventure and a satisfying self-sufficiency in being alone that appealed to me. But as night closed in and I sat by my campfire, eating my evening meal and enjoying a bottle of lager, I missed the company of a safari partner. Once the meal was over I would retire to my tent and snuggle into my sleeping bag, reading by the light of a torch but always alert to what might be happening outside.

Sleep, when it came, would be light and often fitful. Disturbances might include the screams of a crowned plover, alarmed by some nocturnal intruder, the "whoop-whooo-up!" of a passing hyena, the call of lions or the unwelcome sounds of an elephant just outside the tent. I rarely felt threatened but on my early safaris, in case of emergencies, I would take a long-bladed Maasai spear, bought as a souvenir, and keep it alongside me during the night. It was almost certainly illegal and practically useless against big game, but if I was to be eaten alive or trampled to death I was determined to go down fighting.

On the first night of one solo trip, exhausted at the end of a long school term and the drive from Dar, I had broken with normal practice by going to bed without washing up after dinner – a great mistake. In the early hours I was awakened by a harsh, aggressive snuffling noise and the rattle of metal objects as some creature licked clean my unwashed tin plate and cooking utensils. Leaning forward in my sleeping bag and kneeling by the front of the tent I slowly pulled up the zip (restored to efficiency after the incident with the elephant) and looked out. The moon was almost full but as the cooking utensils were out of view I could see nothing unusual.

Filled with curiosity and hoping that the intruder would return to the plate and pan I knelt in anticipation, pondering the possibilities. I assumed that the creature was a hyena, though possibly a civet, genet or even a lion or leopard. Any one of these would have been exciting to see – if rather disturbing in the case of the larger ones. Eventually, thinking that the animal had gone, I cautiously squeezed my way out, armed with the spear.

I slowly stood upright in the moonlight. Naked except for a pair of British Home Stores string underpants (unfashionable even then) and a pair of National Health glasses, and brandishing a six-foot Maasai spear, I hesitate to think how improbable and unprepossessing a figure I must have presented. At the time it was the least of my worries. After edging further from the tent, I caught sight of the mystery beast. More troublingly, it caught sight of me. Had I walked into a Bible study class in some rural English vicarage, armed and near-naked as I was, the eyes of the elderly ladies of the parish could hardly have expressed more alarm than those that now transfixed me. But it was the animal's distinctive pelt that caught my attention. Its upper-parts shone silver-white in the moonlight, contrasting starkly with the black of its lower body. The unmistakable warning colouration of the Honey Badger.

My first reaction was one of excitement. It was the first honey badger I had seen. My second, following immediately, was less enthusiastic, triggered by the sudden recollection of a paragraph in one of my field guides. Describing the Honey Badger as "a courageous and bold animal, that does not know the meaning of fear, capable of charging an intruder and attacking big game (up to a Buffalo), biting the groin and genital organs, the animal then bleeding to death". A more modern internet blog confirms these morbid idiosyncrasies, adding that the Honey Badger is listed in the Guinness Book of Records as "the World's Most Fearless Creature" and ending by saying, rather curiously, "You just have to *love* that type of ferocity." The italics are mine.

I can only assume that whoever wrote the blog had never been alone, on foot and clothed only in his underpants within a few metres of a wild honey badger. If he had he would have known that love for the badger's ferocity does not, at such times, figure highly in one's emotional responses. Furthermore, being armed like an incompetent, unhorsed Bengal Lancer did little to help. Ironically I felt more entranced than endangered and the badger, instead of hurling itself upon me and unravelling my string underpants in one sudden, emasculatory lunge, merely peered at me with its deep-set, widely-spaced little eyes. Before wandering unhurriedly away, beautifully silver and sable in the moonlight.

On my next visit to Mikumi I found a honey-badger, perhaps the same one, dead on the main road, close to Campsite No. 1. It had been killed, as many creatures are in Mikumi, by a passing vehicle, its fearsome fangs bared in one final snarl of defiance. Those terrible jaws, seen at close quarters, inspired a brief series of awful imaginings. In which I and some of my most vulnerable body parts figured prominently.

Honey badgers, incidentally, are not just partial to honey and genital organs. Many years after my encounter in Mikumi an Australian friend, manageress of Stanley's Kopje Camp in the north of the park, told me that the local honey badgers had recently carried out several nocturnal raids on the camp bar, situated at the top of the camp's rocky outcrop. They were after the wine, breaking dozens of bottles and slurping up the contents. Curiously they only touched the red. After hearing this story I was always particularly anxious, when staying at Stanley's and making my way back from the bar to my tent in the dark, to avoid the four-legged binge drinkers. If they are capable of castrating a full-grown buffalo when sober, God knows what they might get up to when pixilated on Pinot Noir.

Despite the honey badger, the "lodge elephants", the lions and whatever else, the overriding tenor of Campsite No.1 was one of tranquility, as with the African bush in general. When I think back now, years after I last camped there, it is this serenity that predominates. The drowsy, dry season afternoons when the south-east monsoon, still cool after curving up from the southern ocean, swept across the coastal plain and over the Ulugurus, stirring up sudden flurries among the red-oat grasslands below the Vuma Hills and setting the chaff spinning across the intervening bush and the campsite in whirling dervishes of dust. Or during the rains, when everything was lush and green and lustrous and humming with life. When isolated flowers, elegant witchweed and wild ginger and tiny, sky blue *Commelina*, would spring up almost overnight.

There was a beauty in the grasses themselves and even in inanimate things, such as the blackwood logs that were provided there (and in no other park) for firewood. Blackwood (commonly if erroneously known as "African ebony") is carved, by Makonde craftsmen, into a range of sculptures, the best of which are genuine works of art, like three-dimensional abstracts by Picasso. To burn it on a fire seemed like desecration

Yet there was beauty too in its destruction. For the dark, dense wood, muscular and finely corded, burned with a near-smokeless, orange-red intensity, the logs retaining their form even as they turned to ash, with tiny tongues of blue flame flickering erratically among the remnants of the wood's reticulations. To sit by such a fire in the cool of the evening, with the sky above a bright embroidery of stars and the Southern Cross sloping down above the Lumange Hills, like a kite in a lessening breeze, was deeply, atavistically satisfying.

For we who loved the bush and Mikumi, spending a few days on Campsite No. 1 was a joy and a privilege. Which is why, when my Lower School Principal revealed that he and his girl friend were getting married and planning to spend their honeymoon on the campsite, I was delighted for them. The Principal in question, Ken, was an American in his thirties. His good-natured girlfriend Sue, also American, taught one of the Elementary classes. Knowing my passion for safari and my familiarity with Mikumi they had invited me to dinner to discuss (I thought) their intentions.

After a few celebratory drinks and the inevitable safari stories the talk turned to the anticipated "honeymoon weekend". "We're aimin' on goin' a week from Friday", said Ken, "You free then?"

"Free?" I asked, a little taken aback and hoping perhaps that he was looking for someone to look after his pet Dalmatian in their absence.

"What Ken is getting at", interrupted Sue, "is that we'd like you to join us. If you're free, that is…"

"*Join* you?"

"Yeah", answered Ken, in his southern American drawl. "Join us. You know, come *with* us…"

"On your *honeymoon*?"

"Yeah – that a problem?"

"Well…" I responded, once I had recovered some composure, "I suppose it could be. I mean most honeymooners want a little privacy, I would have thought…"

"*Gra*ham!" retorted Sue with not-so-mock irritation, "We're not asking you to share a *tent*! We're just asking you to share – well – a short *vacation*! You in your tent, we in ours! Now do you want to come or not?" Americans might be odd but they are direct in their oddness.

And so we found ourselves, a few days later, climbing out of Ken's Peugot Estate on "Campsite No. 1". As I began to erect my tiny tent I noticed that Ken and Sue were in a clinch, showing little interest in erecting anything. At least, anything to do with camping...

"Excuse me", I interrupted boorishly, "but hadn't you two better get your tent up before dark?" They broke off slowly and reluctantly, as I imagine mating earthworms might untwine when disturbed by a sudden beam of light.

"Ken's decided", breathed the still disentangling Sue, "that we are going to stay in the lodge..."

"In the *lodge*? But – er – what about *me*? Have you ever camped on this campsite? It's bad enough when you have a car outside your tent but without one..."

"Oh, *Gra*ham", cooed Sue in her honeymoon voice. "and *we* thought you were a roughy-toughy old Africa hand! Didn't we, Kenny Darling?"

"Kenny Darling" murmured his agreement and soon afterwards he and his new bride drove off into the gathering dusk, waving cheerfully, with Ken yelling "Have a good night! See you at daybreak!"

Sleeping alone and unarmed on the campsite didn't worry me. It could be a little too exciting for comfort and I rarely slept deeply, but excitement and semi-sleepless nights are what *real* safaris are all about. Or so I would have argued at the time. What did bother me is that I wouldn't have a nearby vehicle into which I could hopefully leap if need be. I would feel a little like one of those buffaloes tethered to a stake as tiger bait during the Indian Raj.

In fact the night passed uneventfully. I slept fitfully, as always on the first night of a camping safari, and long before dawn was ready and waiting. I was still waiting three hours later, when Ken and Sue finally drove up, contentedly bleary-eyed.

"Hi!" called Ken, "Sorry we're a bit late!"

"A *bit*? Only three bloody *hours*! Which daybreak were you talking about, the one over Manhattan?"

"Now now, Graham", smiled Sue, "We *are* on honeymoon, *aren't* we, Kenny Baby?

"Sure *are!*" murmured "Kenny Baby", knowingly. "You'll understand one day, Graham. Anyway, ready to go?"

"Ready to go? What do you think I've been doing since 5.30 am – shelling peas?"

"Shelling peas? Boy, you guys have some neat expressions!" said Sue. "Better get this guy outa here, Ken, you know how these Brits are when they have a bug in their bonnet!"

"*Bee!*" I growled, squeezing into the back of the Peugot.

As we set off into the park the car interior crackled with emotional static. "Kenny Darling", one hand on the wheel, his other arm around Sue, somehow managed to keep the Peugot from drifting off the high-cambered track, with Sue half-enfolding him like a microwaved tortilla wrap. After about half-an-hour we came across a cow elephant, browsing placidly among the riverine woodland, a small calf by her side. Ken switched off the engine but not Sue, who by now was half-lying across his lap. She sat up at Ken's insistence and on seeing the baby elephant began to gush with maternal affection. Ken, responding to Sue's murmured endearments as if they were still directed at him rather than the infant pachyderm, leaned over to nuzzle her ear and beseige it with softly whispered inanities.

As I squirmed in the back seat Sue transferred her affectionate attentions to Ken and began to nibble, like a peckish rabbit at a "Little Gem" lettuce, at one of his own ears. I watched in dismay, pleading silently for relief as her lips worked their inevitable alchemy. When relief came, however, it was via a greater threat. For the cow elephant, without any of the usual screams or preamble, suddenly lurched towards us, in that rare, controlled fury, silent but for the trampling or cracking of vegetation, that characterises a genuine charge. Mock attacks by elephants are common, however convincing. In all my safaris I have only experienced two that were not. This was one and I knew it immediately. I yelled a warning.

To give him credit Ken responded, proving that sex doesn't always take precedence over mortal danger. Fortunately the Peugot's engine started first time and we accelerated away in a high-pitched, low gear splatter of flying dirt and screeching tyres, moments before the elephant could convert the Peugot into an abstract metal sculpture. I watched, not without fascination, as she pursued us in that deceptively ground-covering jog that angry or frightened elephants adopt. I soon lost sight of her as we rounded a bend in the dense woodland. Ken drove on for some distance before stopping again, wiping his brow. "Phew!" he gasped, "Exciting, huh?"

Sue, proud of her man, draped herself around his broad shoulders. Within seconds, had I closed my eyes, I might have imagined that I was trapped inside a dovecot. The billing and cooing soon became unbearable.

"Hey!" I complained, "do you think you two could wait until we're a bit further away from this dysfunctional elephant before committing a public nuisance?"

"Oh come *on*, Graham", sighed Sue, "She was *way* back! And in any case – Oh My God!!! She's HERE!"

She was indeed. Looking back I saw her tearing through the bush to one side of the track with a great splintering of branches. By coincidence or design she had cut the corner and was still lumbering, despite the distance we had travelled.

Even honey-mooners recognize reality when it grabs them by the throat. Ken untangled himself from Sue and grabbed the steering wheel. Luckily the engine was still running. But so was the elephant. Again I looked through the rear window to see the enraged animal bearing down on us as we pulled away with another screech of tyres and gravel and shot down the track. This time we didn't stop until we reached Chamgore Water-hole, some miles to the north. I, at least, had learned an important lesson. Go on honeymoon if you must but make damn sure it's your own. But if you *do* agree to go on someone else's, don't say yes to anything wilder than the Taj Mahal by moonlight.

CHAPTER XII

More Mikumi Memories

Elephants figured in many of our adventures in Mikumi, including one of those rare safari days when everything falls into place as if pre-planned. The day began, as do so many in the East African bush, like the first day of Genesis, when you half expect Cat Stevens to start strumming into "Morning has broken, like the first morning". Full of promise and anticipation and with the light of the rising sun as hard and sharp and clear as light in the vacuum of outer space.

I was with Anjum in the Renault, and a Pakistani friend of hers, Nafeesa. Because of Nafeesa, who was on safari for the first time, we were staying at the old state lodge in the hills rather than camping. But we were up at dawn and soon afterwards down on the edge of the flood-plain, heading for the Hippo Pool. Nafeesa, not knowing what to expect, was quietly enjoying seeing impalas, zebras, giraffes and elephants in the wild, murmuring respectfully as I suffocated her under an avalanche of received wisdom.

"One zebra might look like another but actually their stripe patterns are all different – like our fingerprints..."

"Mmm...interesting..."

"The elephants in Mikumi are mainly grazers..."

"Oh..."

And so on.

We spent some time at the Hippo Pool, where Nafeesa learned that hippos don't usually stay underwater for more than a few minutes and that they eat grass, not water plants or fish. She nodded and murmured like a good Muslim girl and like a good safari guide I then drove around looking for lions. We found none and by this time Nafeesa, wilting under the information overload, was almost certainly dreaming of breakfast. As Anjum and I were. We set off back to the lodge. "Some days are like this", I told her, mistaking her silence for disappointment, "It's not a thrill a minute like you see on TV…"

"Right" murmured Nafeesa.

Anjum chipped in by saying that nothing is guaranteed in the bush but that we would be going out again that afternoon and "might see lions then. You never know". "That's good…" said Nafeesa, dreaming, almost certainly, of scrambled eggs and buttered toast and coffee. Just then we turned a bend and in the distance I saw a large, dark object on the track. Anjum saw it with sharper eyes. "Lions!" she announced in one of her excited stage whispers. "One of them is standing on something – it looks like an *elephant*!". She was right. A dead elephant, lying on its side. There were nine lions, one standing on the elephant's flanks, one inside its stomach cavity, its muzzle and much else dark and wet with blood. The other seven lay alongside, sated and swollen-bellied. We stayed for some time, watching and taking photographs.

Later, over breakfast, I told Nafeesa, just in case she didn't appreciate the fact, that finding nine lions on or inside a dead elephant is not something one sees everyday. Nafeesa, chewing contentedly on her toast, nodded her appreciation. That afternoon, at about 4 pm, we set out for our usual evening game drive. "Let's take a look down the Ikoya Circuit", I said, adding, half-jokingly and for Nafeesa's benefit, "and find you a leopard". We soon turned off the Tanzam Highway that bisects

Mikumi and on to the Ikoya circuit, opposite the park's main gate. Nafeesa, not knowing how infrequently leopards are seen, had taken my remark seriously. So, in a very different way, had Anjum. "Always say *insh'Allah!*" she snapped. "You should *never* take things for granted. Now we'll *never* see a leopard!"

Two minutes later, with the Tanzam Highway still visible in my rear view mirror, I saw a beautifully patterned Persian carpet, the size of a prayer mat, sliding across the track a little way ahead. I braked. As anyone seeing a Persian carpet crossing a track in an African game sanctuary would. Fortunately for my sanity the carpet metamorphosised into a cryptically coloured python. But too broad for a python, and too flat, like a python squashed by a road roller. And then the python, like one of those lenticular pictures that change with the angle of light, resolved itself into a leopard. But like the python, a flattened one. Not a leopard but the pelt of a leopard, like a hunter's trophy, only the head projecting above the surface of the track. This apparently mangled thing was pulling itself forward by the claws of its outstretched forepaws, the hind-legs also fully extended, the tail trailing behind along the ground.

For the only time in my life I experienced what it must be like to be high on psychedelic drugs. Everything was surreal, beyond comprehension. I watched in disbelief as an apparition that had hallucinated from a Persian carpet into a python and now into the pelt of a leopard hauled itself across the track. The kaleidoscope of bizarre images that had passed though my mind had formed and reformed in moments but to my brain each separate image was "real", the result of astonishing optical illusions – and the almost inconceivable ability of cats to switch (as it sometimes seems) from three dimensions into two. Anjum, more concerned with hard facts than fantasy, had merely gasped "Leopard!" as if announcing the onset of a heart attack. "I don't *believe* it! You *said* we would see one!"

"And I didn't even say "*insh'Allah*"..." I murmured.

Nafeesa leaned forward speechlessly. Not, I think, with wonder but because, being new to the bush, she assumed that seeing a pride of lions on and in and around a dead elephant and a leopard that looked like a Persian carpet (and in the same day) was par for the course. Why else would people pay so much to go on safari? But not wishing to seem ungrateful, she emitted some suitably approving noises. By now the leopard was focused sharply in my binoculars and I saw that it was perfectly normal and healthy, and that it was hunting. I had once seen a lioness, when stalking zebras on the open plain, flatten herself into something resembling a (rather large) ciabatta bun, but this was even more astounding.

The leopard was full-grown, yet only its head, held back, and its thick, trailing tail, suggested that it was, in fact, quite normal. As it reached the edge of the track, with a lingering, purposeful look along its nose at the family of warthogs that was feeding at the top of the roadside bank, it poured itself into the intervening ditch, as indeed a python (or a magical Persian carpet) might have done, and disappeared. Leaving me, to use a modern slang (but perfectly apt) expression, gob-smacked.

It soon reappeared, as a proper, recognizable leopard, further along the ditch, stalking up the far bank. Stopping at the top, head held back, it scanned the fire-blackened scrub and grassland beyond. I could almost see it thinking. There was no cover between it and the warthogs, a mother and four small piglets, all of which were grubbing around in the carbonized grass. "If I were the leopard", I thought, "I would go back into the ditch, come this way a little and then go back up the bank right there, so that I reached the top right by that clump of leaves". There are few things more satisfying, on safari, than being able to predict what a hunting predator will do next, and for once my bush-craft was equal to the challenge. The leopard turned in one fluid movement, as if remote-controlled by my thoughts, and slipped back into the ditch.

We watched and waited. Anjum suddenly whispered "It's here, right below us!" I looked and saw two beautiful eyes, green as glacial melt-water in the late afternoon light. They were fixed on Anjum. Then suddenly the leopard was gone again. Reappearing further up the ditch, it crept cautiously up the far bank and peered over the top once more, immediately behind the clump of green leaves. It stiffened, watching the movements of the piglets before locking its concentration on the nearest. But beyond the cluster of leaves there was nothing but burnt grass, and the piglet was some seven or eight metres from the leopard, just far enough to make the leopard hesitate. Then a slight shift of the breeze must have carried its scent to the warthog sow, which had been kneeling on her forelegs in typical warthog fashion to nuzzle for edible roots or tubers. She jerked to her feet and stood motionless.

There is a tide in the affairs of leopards as well as men. The problem, for both, is in knowing when that tide is at the flood. For this leopard it was on the ebb. The four piglets had frozen now into tiny facsimiles of their mother. She, watchful but without panic, was edging further away, tail aloft like a regimental standard shredded by enemy fire. The piglets followed in single file, as warthog piglets do (all, incidentally, with their own place in the line). The leopard watched, knowing that the opportunity had passed. And then, as if snapping out of a day-dream, it turned to glare at us, as if we were to blame. Before vanishing for the final time.

Anjum and I were thrilled. Nafeesa (I could see her face in the rear view mirror) smiled a vague smile, perhaps thinking that our excitement was exaggerated, to enhance her own pleasure. As we drove off again I said, jokingly, "Now for the wild dogs". "Don't be silly!" Anjum complained, "that's being *really* greedy!" Nafeesa gave a kind of self-deprecating gurgle and settled back in half-hearted anticipation of the wild dogs, as if we were touring a safari park in the UK.

About thirty minutes later we came across the dogs. Seven of them, right by the track. "I don't believe this" Anjum had gasped yet again as her sharp eyes had first picked out the dogs' huge, give-away ears. At least the dogs *looked* like dogs, not Persian rugs or flattened pythons. We parked alongside, within a few metres. They stared at us with their small, deep-set eyes. Just to impress upon Nafeesa, yet again, that she was having a most unusual day I said "They might not look all that exciting, but they are!" "I'm sure" she murmured, half-smiling towards the dogs as people smile at someone else's children, when told they can "read proper books now" or have been chosen to play the rear half of the donkey in their school's nativity play.

The dogs (though they are not true dogs) were a group that we called "the Magnificent Seven". Over a period of about three years we had often bumped into them in Mikumi. Then, as wild dogs often do, they disappeared and we never saw them again. While they were there they were fascinating. On one occasion, when we encountered them walking towards us on a woodland track, I stopped and reversed the Renault to observe them in motion. They broke into an easy lope, keeping just behind us, and for a few moments, as the track was straight at that point, I saw them as a hunted impala or other prey species would have seen them in its peripheral vision just before they closed in on it.

It was a sight to reflect upon, for having a pack of African wild dogs on one's tail rarely ends well. Except from the dogs' point of view. They are far more efficient hunters than lions, and unlike the big cats, possessed of great stamina. And, as I pointed out earlier, the strongest bite, relative to body mass, of any living carnivore. As I watched them loping after the reversing car I was glad not to be an impala or wildebeest calf. For as my eyes switched between my rear view mirror and the dogs I caught glimpses of those fearful shearing teeth and that effortless, tireless running style.

Like all wild animals (with the possible exception of certain higher primates), the "painted wolves", as the dogs are sometimes known, are incapable of cruelty. For cruelty has to be intended. The dogs only do what they have evolved to do in order to stay alive and to keep their pups alive. Widely regarded until quite recently as four-legged terrorists they can, in fact, teach us more than we might care to admit, for they have a remarkably collaborative social system, in which co-operation is paramount and confrontation rare. As perhaps one might expect of a social system headed by a dominant (alpha) female. Mutually submissive behaviour, and even begging (or "petitioning" as I prefer to call it) for food, which is regurgitated, is the norm.

Nevertheless they do strike terror into the hearts of certain other creatures. Anjum and I once came across the "Magnificent Seven" close to the old baobab that dominates Mikumi's Camspite No. 2. It was just after the onset of the short rains and the dogs were lying in and around a few small pools that had formed at the fringe of the *mbuga*, as seasonally swampy grasslands are known in Tanzania. Some three hundred metres away a large herd of impala was browsing by the still dry tributary of the Mkata River. Close to the impalas were two elephants, three buffalo bulls and several giraffes.

The impala herd's harem master, confident of his dominance, left the females to themselves and strayed unknowingly towards the dogs. Which, ignorant of the fact that the bush's equivalent of a "meals on wheels" delivery van was approaching, dozed on. The impala almost literally walked into them. One dog leapt to its feet, alerting the others, which also jumped up. The impala fled in panic, adopting, as certain antelopes or gazelles sometimes do, a "stotting" or "pronking" manner, bouncing stiff-leggedly up and down as if on a pogo stick. It always seems to me to be a very strange mode of behaviour as it must surely be slower than an all-out leaping sprint. Presumably it is just as bewildering to pursuing predators. It certainly acts as a very effective alarm system to other potential prey species in the neighbourhood.

Whatever the case the dogs didn't close with it and the impala pogo-sticked back to its herd, infecting them with panic. As the impalas bounded off the infection spread to the giraffes, the buffaloes and (more ludicrously) the two elephants, which all joined the absconding circus, charging across the dried-up *korongo* (seasonal watercourse) and the black-cotton *mbuga* beyond. En route a bushbuck, a reedbuck and a spotted hyena attached themselves to the charging melee and the whole menagerie, still pursued by the seven relatively small dogs, disappeared over the park airstrip in a cloud of dust and desperation.

Lions (now much-endangered throughout their ranges) were commonly encountered in Mikumi. We came across them almost every day, even without the professional guides, the VHF radio systems and the mobile phones that now ensure that a lion (or other big cat) soon attracts a cluster of vehicles. I always made a point of leaving the campsite (in Mikumi or elsewhere), at daybreak. Partly to be ahead of other visitors, who would sometimes, out of over-eagerness or ignorance, ruin a hunt or a photo-opportunity by impetuous behaviour, partly because the big cats tend to be more active and interesting in the early morning.

From time to time we would see lions hunting. To observe them in this role is to witness an extraordinary transformation, as if idle giant Labradors had been morphed into single-minded killing machines within minutes. When hunting, lions seem like a different species. As do human observers, for we often forget that we too are predators, and the thrill of the hunt can transform us as well as lions. It is almost impossible, when watching such hunts, not to "join in". Whether we identify with the lions or sympathise with their intended prey we find ourselves assessing the possible strategies and outcomes, breathless with nervous tension.

Lionesses, unhampered by manes, can flatten themselves into apparent bonelessness in the scantiest cover, their massive, muscular power as intensely concentrated as a crossbow ratcheted to its limits. Where more cover is available, experienced lions will use it with great shrewdness. Once close to prey – and they often get remarkably close before charging – the tension can cause an observer's heart to thud almost audibly. Few sights or situations in life are genuinely "breathtaking" but the final moments of a lion hunt seem to confound the fact that breathing is involuntary.

Hunting behaviour is learned as well as instinctive and to see lions hunting co-operatively is particularly enthralling. I once saw six lions in Mikumi hunt zebras in this way. The lions were lolling around on the track when I came across them. The track was raised about eight or nine feet above a seasonal black-cotton swamp or *mbuga*, to avoid flooding during the rains. Unable to pass the lions without disturbing them I parked my little Suzuki jeep a short distance from the nearest and settled down to watch and wait. A family of five zebras appeared some distance away, as if from nowhere, and began to graze out on the *mbuga*, beyond a drainage line marked by a thin stand of trees. The lions soon took interest.

One lioness slipped over the edge of the track and down the banking, into the wheaten-coloured grasses at its foot. The other five, including one full-grown male, soon followed. I could clearly see their heads and the give-away black backs to their ears. The heads were held back, noses horizontal, above the seed-sprays of the grass, to reduce their profile, eyes narrowed to slits, squinting down the nose to concentrate on the unsuspecting zebras. I watched in fascination as the lions edged out in line abreast, glancing at their companions at intervals like well-drilled troops "dressing from the right" on parade.

Their right-hand marker was the lioness that had first descended the bank. After what can only be described as an "approving" look along the line of her pride-mates, she left her post and stalked with slow deliberation through the swathes of grass. There was plenty of cover between her and the zebras but instead of approaching them directly she chose a more circuitous route with the obvious intention of outflanking them. She stopped frequently to watch them and to glance back briefly towards the other lions. Eventually I lost sight of the tell-tale backs of her ears. Her pride-mates, some five or six metres apart, waited.

Their eyes and mine were on the zebras. After some twenty minutes one zebra raised its head and stood motionless. This alerted a second zebra, and a third. Then the whole group exploded in a shell-burst of stripes. The single lioness, now behind them, revealed herself, her role complete, as the zebras raced in panic towards the banking and the open plain beyond. They did not see the waiting lions until the big cats rose to confront them.

Unable to turn in time the zebras had no choice but to accelerate even further and to swerve to avoid the nearest lion before hurling themselves up the steep banking. It was like watching a cavalry charge in microcosm. How the lions must have felt I cannot imagine, for to throw oneself at an oncoming zebra travelling at around 55 k.p.h. and weighing over 400 kg must be daunting even for the world's second-biggest cat. I braced myself for an "unstoppable force meets immoveable object" impact, hoping my small Suzuki would not be involved.

The foremost zebra was at the centre of the charge. Only instinctive reactions, adrenalin and good luck lay between it and a dramatic death. Directly in its path, a split second away, was the male lion, literally rising to the challenge. Just above them, on the track, was my Suzuki. The lion and the zebra and me, isolated in our own small world like individual infantrymen in the thick of battle. Perhaps conscious of the Suzuki, and certainly conscious of the lion, the zebra veered to its left and almost in the same motion leapt for the top of the bank. The lion swerved in mid-spring to intercept it, striking out with a fore-paw, claws outstretched. The zebra's hind hooves scrabbled for purchase as it landed, and I expected it to collapse and go skidding across the track in front of me in a storm of dust and stripes.

It didn't. Miraculously all five zebras escaped and were soon standing, flanks heaving, on the far side of the track, some eighty metres away, looking back for a few moments before bolting once again. They had been saved by their involuntary forward charge, for like all cats lions are hard-wired to chase rather than confront head-on. And by the momentary delay that occurred as each lion twisted from confrontation to pursuit. The lions, except for the one that had initiated the charge, were by now aligned along the track, all staring at the zebras yet striving, as cats do, to retain some self-respect, as if the thought of knocking down a zebra had been the last thing on their minds.

I have seen lions hunting many times in Mikumi. Hardly any of them were males. Females, for one thing, significantly outnumber males, but there also seems to be an evolutionary division of labour amongst lion prides. Male lions, like most other male animals, are physically dominant, their main duties, it seems, being to father offspring and protect the pride territory rather than to provide food. Being supreme opportunists all lions, whatever their gender, will hunt if the right occasion arises. Especially in areas where buffaloes, giraffes (or more rarely even small elephants) are hunted, when greater strength or greater numbers are needed. Generally though, lionesses are left to "bring up the kids" and do the shopping. And as the supermarkets in the bush tend to constantly relocate, bringing home the meat (which sometimes puts up a determined fight on reaching the check-out) isn't quite as easy as driving to the nearest Tesco's.

The division of labour within a pride is not just gender-based. For certain lionesses do most of the hunting, while others will often lie back and watch, joining in only if their pride-mates are seen to be failing – a situation we all recognize. My own experience in Mikumi, where over the years I got to know a few individual lionesses, tends to confirm this. Most of the hunts I witnessed were carried out by single lionesses or two lionesses working together, despite the fact that the prides in question would have included five or more adult females.

Not that such hunts were usually successful. Even when lions hunt in pairs or larger groups their rate of success is only around 30% and when hunting alone this falls to a mere 17-19%. This seems pathetic when compared with levels of achievement in human terms, when pass marks of 45% or fewer in important exams might doom individuals to failure. But considering that lions can often afford to spend up to 20 hours or more a day lolling around, eating, sleeping or fornicating, while many of us work our socks off for a take-away pizza, why would they need the protestant work ethic? Lions are cats and cats do only what is necessary. And it works.

But even when resting, lions are impressive. The outlines and contours of their underlying muscles are so clear that one feels that da Vinci could have made accurate sketches of leonine musculature without resorting to dissecting corpses. The thick-packed muscles of the shoulders and fore-legs are especially imposing, the latter culminating in paws as big as side-plates, capable of swatting a full-grown wildebeest or zebra to the ground with a single swipe. This mighty array of muscle and latent power is covered, in a healthy lion in its prime, by a supple pelt, often "hammer-marked" with faint spots, relict traces of the animal's juvenile years. Its basic colour is normally described as tawny, though it can be almost grey or gold, and in Mikumi I have often seen an unlikely hint of green in their otherwise grey-brown colouration. Manes among males can be blonde, brown, rufous or black, a combination of any of these or almost non-existent.

Lions' pelts are not always in prime condition. Those of older individuals are often punctured by canines or scarified by claws, in addition to missing tail-tufts and clumps of mane, lacerated cheeks and noses, and ears ragged from bites (not only from other lions but also from ticks, with which most lions are infested). Evidence of internecine confrontations and family squabbles attest to the true nature of the beast. Lions are killers. Even when resting they are no more docile than hired assassins between contracts. And their somnolence is deceptive; they can be on their feet in less than a second, and tearing apart some unfortunate animal soon afterwards.

As Anjum and I discovered one beautiful, typically calm Mikumi morning, when thoughts of death, had they entered our minds at all, would have seemed as inconceivable as razor wire fences in the Garden of Eden. Even when we came across fourteen lions, stretched out on the track like floppy toys, their languor was in keeping with the serenity of the morning. If anything the lethargy of the lions enhanced it. We were in a Land Rover and as I parked it nearby and switched off the engine one or two of the lions raised their heads, only to sink back into somulence soon afterwards. After that, as I took one mundane photograph after the next, the lions only moved to shift positions slightly or to switch a lazy tail at a bothersome fly. Eyes would open momentarily at the clunk of my heavy camera mirror, then slowly close, as if pneumatically controlled.

Normally I might have moved on after a few photographs but there was no one else around so we stayed, windows open, enjoying the cool breeze and the joy of being alive in such a place on such a morning. Then I noticed some movement across the *mbuga*. Raising my binoculars I saw a single female eland walking through the distant scrub. Soon afterwards I saw more urgent movements. And so did one of the nearby lionesses. She suddenly sat up as if powered by a spring-loaded switch, eyes narrowed. Following her gaze I saw three spotted hyenas running, close to the eland but away from her. Ahead of them bounded a tiny eland calf, Bambi-like, across the *mbuga*.

By now all the lions were alert, two or three standing, the others sitting upright, twenty-eight eyes on the faraway chase. The result of which seemed inevitable. Hyenas have great stamina and jaws that can crunch the thigh bone of a giraffe, or rip a tiny antelope to bloody rags. But suddenly the little eland turned, in a desperate effort to get back to its mother. The hyenas cut across to intercept it, forcing it to adjust its course. It was now heading directly towards the lions. And us. One lioness was already walking forward, head lowered in stalking posture but making no attempt to hide. The others, three full-grown males, five full-grown lionesses and five sub-adults, soon joined her. They stood in ragged line abreast and clearly exposed, a few metres apart, as if knowing that concealment was unnecessary. The baby eland bounced towards them. The hyenas, seeing the lions, pulled up warily.

One of the male lions smacked the calf to the ground as a man might swat a fly. The others rushed in. Quickly I started the Land Rover and drove over, stopping right alongside the viciously snarling scrum that the lions had formed around the eland. Assuming that the poor creature was already dead I looked down from my open window to find it not only alive but miraculously unmarked. It was bleating pitifully, its disproportionately large ears spread wide, its big, gleaming eyes staring up at me from between the legs of the lions, as if pleading for me to intervene.

I have been close to lions countless times but never in such circumstances. Their collective snarls and rumbling growls was like an orchestra from Hell, so deep and serrated with menace that the Land Rover's frame and mine seemed to vibrate in resonance. It was – and I use the word as it was intended to be used – awesome. What the calf felt, what unimaginably loud and unearthly noises were amplified by those great, leaf-like ears and converted to a screaming cacophony inside its brain was beyond comprehension. I have read that animals attacked by predators become anaesthetized by shock but it didn't look that way. My own adrenalin rush seemed to have frozen in mid-flow. All I could do was to look on as the eland's body, little bigger than that of a child, began to turn in torturously slow motion, like a chicken on a revolving spit. The bleating head stopped bleating and disappeared; I never saw it again. As the body turned, twisting now along its length, I saw the first large smear of blood on its haunch. The creature was being torn asunder.

Its tiny body, subjected to fourteen forces pulling in as many different directions, came apart. The lions were thrown back in a clawing, demented fury, each splinter group fighting over a leg or some other portion of an animal that less than ten minutes earlier had been trotting alongside its mother, full, no doubt, of the natural joie de vivre that characterizes most young animals. I quickly drove a few metres further away, aware that one wild swing of a forepaw could accidentally hook my door handle off its catch. Or even the door from its hinges. A long time ago, in Plymouth zoo, I saw a lioness batting a huge oil drum around her enclosure as if it was a ping pong ball. I was under no illusions about the power generated by the swipe of a lion's paw, accidental or otherwise.

The three adult males were now fighting so viciously over a single bone that one had ended up on another's back. While one of the adult females walked off, relatively calmly now, with a whole haunch. So much for masculine superiority. Every recognizable piece of what had recently been a complex living creature was gone within minutes, but for a few scattered bones and somewhere, the calf's head. The comparative quietude, after the brief uproar, seemed to shiver with silent waves of sound, as if the air still trembled with echoes of the demonic frenzy.

I drove off, into the usual tranquility of what was now mid-morning. Neither Anjum nor I spoke for some time, chastened by what we had seen, our impressions of the power and savagery of lions fundamentally changed. Some innocence, some naivety, had gone. Not that I had ever been deceived by lions in repose; it was not the transformation from the soporific to the savage that had shocked me, but the speed and scale of that transformation.

A few years earlier I had experienced a very different but potentially more dangerous leonine encounter. I was with Anjum and our two Californian friends, Bob and Karen, in my small Suzuki. Whilst driving around the Ikoya Loop we had come across a dead wildebeest close to the track. I drove over, stopping some distance from the carcase and switching off the engine. A single Hooded Vulture was perched in a small, dead tree, close to the kill. The grass in the vicinity, except for a few odd clumps, was as short as that on a golf course fairway. A mouse would have thought twice about crossing it. There were no trees or bushes in the area within sixty metres or so of the dead wildebeest.

Our friends, unused to the bush and hoping to see and photograph lions, plied me with questions. I felt sure, I said, that a lion, or lions, had killed the wildebeest. And as it was quite fresh and only partly eaten, the cat or cats would be close by. But where? I scanned around through binoculars. I could see nothing under or around the bushes and trees in the middle distance, and closer than that there was nowhere for a lion to hide. The only obstacle in the wide circle of short, open grassland surrounding the kill was the slender trunk of a long-dead fallen tree, half-buried in the ground, some thirty metres from the wildebeest. Only the tiniest lion cub could possibly have hidden behind this log, but I checked it out through the binoculars to make sure.

After some time Bob asked if he could get out and photograph the wildebeest. In the end I relented, and asking my friends to remain in the Suzuki I got out to reconnoitre. As I stepped out of the Suzuki the vulture flew off, causing me to pause. The fact that it was in the tree and not on the ground should have warned me. Again I scanned around and again I saw nothing to arouse concern. I walked over to the wildebeest and soon afterwards invited my friends to join me. Bob took several photographs, at one point asking me to hold the dead animal by the horns and twist the head towards the camera. Feeling like one of those triumphant hunters who pose with their trophies I reluctantly obliged.

Eventually we all returned to the car, Bob and Karen disappointed at not seeing lions but excited by the kill. Instinct, which should have alerted me earlier, now told me to stay around for a while, so we sat in the Suzuki, watching and waiting and conversing quietly. Soon the vulture came back, and soon after that, it flew down by the wildebeest. Almost immediately a full-grown lioness charged towards it, seemingly from nowhere. A lion can cover thirty metres in less than two seconds but she pulled up as the vulture took off in panic, and after giving the bird a glowering stare, reclaimed her kill and resumed feeding.

We sat shocked. "My God!" said Bob, "Imagine if that had happened when we were out there!" Imagine indeed. I felt extremely foolish, with every reason, and after we had watched and photographed the lioness for some time I drove slowly over to the half-buried tree trunk, from where she had charged. Although the nearer side of the half-buried fallen tree hardly projected above the ground there was a depression along the further side, in which the lioness had been lying. It was a lesson I would never forget.

That incident, like many potentially dangerous moments in the bush, became more frightening in retrospect than it did at the time. But one of my most unnerving experiences in Mikumi, also on the Ikoya Circuit, had nothing directly to do with animals. It was during the *masika*, the long rains that tend to occur between mid-March and mid-May.

I have always loved the long rains in Africa. Partly because they mark the end of the hot and humid season but mostly because rain – and especially thunderstorms – appeal to me. I have a theory that introverts like myself enjoy such things because they provide us with a good excuse not to be out and about, but ensconced in an armchair at home, or on the verandah of a safari lodge, revelling in the peace and privacy with little threat of being disturbed.

I especially loved the rains on safari, when we would often have what seemed like half of Africa to ourselves. When the bush becomes verdant almost overnight, humming, whirring, trilling, cooing and warbling with the sounds of insects, frogs, toads and birds, as if they had all awakened from some Rip van Winkle, dry season torpor. When the animals themselves (with the exception of the cats who in Africa hate getting wet) seem to rejoice in being drenched to the skin, or at least in the super-abundance of new leaves and shoots. And when a host – though rarely a super-abundance – of flowers springs up to add colour and delicacy of form to landscapes recently stark and drab.

The rains, however, can be a curse as well as a blessing. As they proved one afternoon in Mikumi. I had decided, foolishly considering the conditions, to drive around the Ikoya

Circuit. Anjum, who was with me, just as foolishly trusted my judgement. To begin with the track was quite passable but soon deteriorated into a linear skid-pan. Discretion is the better part of valour in the bush and normally I would have backed off, turned around and gone elsewhere, but we were in our second-hand but wonderfully robust Toyota GX Land Cruiser, in which I had great faith.

It was the best safari car I ever owned, with a 6-cylinder engine that had been designed for trucks, and of course equipped with 4WD and low ratio gears. It seemed able to cross rivers and climb mountains. But a big and powerful car, like everything else, is only as strong as its weakest link, which in slippery conditions is the lack of traction between tyres and track. Despite driving slowly ahead in 4WD we suddenly skidded off-track in a slither of black-cotton mud. For a few moments I lost all control as the Toyota slid sideways, coming to a stop on the short, greasy grass of the adjacent bank, having spun around completely. I switched off the engine, applied the handbrake and got out to investigate.

I didn't like what I saw. The bank on which we were now precariously parked sloped down increasingly steeply, terminating in a brief but sheer drop into a deeply flooded *korongo*, through which the water sluiced in a rolling, gurgling boil. I quickly found two suitable rocks to place behind the Toyota's rear wheels. With the car now reasonably secure I felt more optimistic but Anjum, small, not too strong and a non-swimmer, was eyeing the *korongo* and listening to the sinister surge of water with apprehension. Growling a few reassuring comments I decided to risk getting the Toyota back on the track, telling her to keep out of the way but to pick up one of the rocks as I moved away and to be ready to dump it behind a wheel should the car stop. Or – worse – begin to slide back. After selecting low ratio I started the engine and tried to manoeuvre the car up the bank.

For a few seconds everything was fine but suddenly the car slid to one side and then backwards. I heard Anjum's scream of alarm but somehow managed to stop the car moving until she was able to jam the rock behind a rear wheel. After switching off the engine and applying the handbrake (almost pointlessly in the circumstances) I climbed out. To my horror I saw that the Toyota was within a few feet of the edge of the *korongo*. Quickly I placed a rock behind the second rear wheel. It was only then that I began to appreciate how lucky I was to be still alive. And to imagine Anjum's plight had the Toyota, with me inside, slid into the torrent. Almost certainly I would have drowned, leaving her – panic-stricken – to face the night in an area often patrolled by lions, leopards, elephants and buffaloes, alone and on foot, without food, water or shelter and without hope of another vehicle passing by, perhaps for days.

By now the sun had sunk below the Vuma Hills and darkness was falling with tropical suddenness. Too scared now to risk another attempt at driving back to the track I decided to leave the Toyota where it was and spend the night inside it. Quickly I collected more rocks, and four or five tree branches, to make the vehicle as secure as possible. "Tomorrow morning at daybreak", I told Anjum, who was by now quite agitated, "I'll walk back to the main gate and get help".

"Don't be silly!" she retorted, "What if you run into lions or something?' I reminded her that lions were not as common in the Ikoya area as on the more open plains to the north. And conveniently disregarding my experience with the young lioness some years earlier – and in the same park – added that in any case lions, in the daylight, would run when approached by a man on foot.

Uncharacteristically she remained silent, as women sometimes do when faced with a man whose idiocy is unworthy of contention. Meanwhile there was little choice but to huddle sleeplessly through the night in the car, one window slightly open to provide ventilation and allow the local mosquitoes to enjoy a midnight feast. My greatest fear was that the heavy rains that had created the flash floods would return with a vengeance but in fact the night remained dry and ironically quite pleasant. A reassuring full moon rose high above the track before eventually falling into the tangle of branches beyond, its bright light shining in fits and starts through the windscreen of the steeply canted car. And through the partly open window came a familiar rainy season sound, like an orchestra of tiny elves drumming on tiny glass anvils with tiny glass hammers, the intriguing, tinkling sound of Common Reed frogs. Which sadly did little to drown out the daunting rush and gurgle of the waters coursing through the *korongo*.

When things turn disastrous a good night's sleep can work wonders. Not that we had such a sleep but by the time dawn broke we at least felt more optimistic than we had done the previous evening. Before the sun rose, after much hacking of branches and grasses, I created a friction-providing twin-track up the greasy slope. And then, with Anjum standing ready to do her stuff with a rock or two if necessary, I began to inch the car back on to the track. And to ease through its sloughs of mud to the drier conditions beyond. Ecstatic with relief Anjum tossed away her rocks and climbed in alongside me, and we headed for the exit. Some 6 km. from where we had spent the night we came across two male lions and a lioness, all in a state of excited, sexually-aroused unpredictability. "Good job you didn't walk", observed Anjum drily.

Lions, lodge elephants, buffalo-emasculating honey badgers and leopards that looked like Persian carpets were not the only animals to give us pause in Mikumi. Once, when returning from a morning game drive in the north of the park with my friend Kevin and his then wife Kate I was amazed, as we drove through a belt of *Commiphora/Combretum*, to see a black rhino. I stopped immediately. Even in the late 1970s, rhinos were rarely recorded in Mikumi. This was the first I had seen there.

It was nosing slowly towards us in a zig-zag, like a bloodhound following a scent trail. On arriving at the edge of the track it stared at us through the intervening shrubs. Kevin started to take photos but the rhino, alarmed at the click of the camera, moved off, parallel to the track but behind us. I reversed slowly until Kevin hissed "It's here! Right by the track!". Easing the Renault back a little further I suddenly saw the rhino poke its head through the screen of leaves just two metres from me. I stopped and switched off the engine as Kevin, using my shoulder as a tripod, as was his wont, clicked away.

We all expected the rhino to move off again, or to charge out and poke an exploratory horn through the Renault's biscuit box frame. But to our astonishment it sank down, lay on its side and fell fast asleep, its head sticking out from the undergrowth on to the trackside verge. After a few minutes, inspired by curiosity, I quietly opened my door and stood outside, ready to leap back should the rhino spring to its feet. It didn't. Kevin and Kate, not to be outdone, crept out to join me. We edged closer to the rhino, which slept on, until I could have touched its anterior horn with a walking stick.

I felt no threat whatsoever. On the contrary my overriding feeling was one of poignancy at the innocence of the animal sleeping at our feet when we, as human beings, represented its greatest threat. Where had it been heading? And why? Seeking a mate? Or just a soul mate, male or female, with which it could share a little time before local – and perhaps Africa-wide – extinction intervened? Greatly moved I soon said "Let's go – and leave the poor thing in peace". And we did. As we drove off we all took a last glance at what might easily have been Mikumi's last rhino. I murmured "*Lala salama!*" (Sleep peacefully!), knowing that its chances of a natural death were well beyond hope.

CHAPTER XIII

"Authority Forgets A Dying King"

As with all safaris I remember those in Mikumi by their most prominent event or sighting, as village Africans remember the "year of the locust" or "the year of the great floods". So it is in the bush. A bend in the track, a marker stone, a familiar tree can bring old memories immediately to mind. Half a lifetime after the sleeping rhino incident in Mikumi, I would remember exactly where it had taken place, and often say in passing, "That's where we saw the rhino". Just as I might say "That's where the lions killed the baby eland"; or "That's where we saw a cheetah climb that tree"; or "I call this place "Butter-flow Bend" (after a dead buffalo, its name mispronounced by a friend's child).

People feature in most of my safari memories: "Carole's Corner" or "Bob's Breakfast Stop", in Mikumi; "Anjum's Campsite" at Voi in Kenya's Tsavo East; "Vesey's Viewpoint", on the rim of Ngurdoto Crater in Arusha National Park. The list is long. Sometimes, however, inanimate objects are evoked; "Sunrise Baobab" near Msembe in Ruaha; "The Bell Rock" at Moru Kopjes in the Serengeti; the "Clatter-Clatter Bridge" in Mikumi.

Lions often dominate these remembrances of times past. Partly because I have seen many hundreds of them, partly because the excitement of seeing them has never waned. I have mentioned earlier the impact of leonine symbolism upon my childhood mind but one image in particular intrigued me. It was that of a lion depicted on the tins of Tate and Lyle golden syrup that my mother sometimes bought. Enclosed within a horizontal oval frame it showed a dead male lion lying on its side, with what seemed to be a swarm of bluebottles hovering around it. Which, when you think about it, was a very strange way to promote golden syrup.

The flies, I eventually discovered, were in fact bees and the picture represented the Bible story in which Samson, after killing a lion with his bare hands, returned to the body later to find bees nesting inside it, and ate the honey that he found there. This did not make the picture or its connection with golden syrup any less bewildering but it helped to explain the text below the picture, which read: "Out of the strong came forth sweetness."

As a child I would never have imagined, as I munched my way through a crust of bread smothered with butter and golden syrup, that one day I would see a lion almost exactly like the one on the Tate and Lyle tin. Yet more than thirty years later, in the famous Ngorongoro Crater, I did.

I was with my safari partner Barry, in my little Suzuki jeep, a new, 4WD replacement for the old Renault 4. Soon after descending to the Crater floor, out on the plains east of the Lerai Forest, I had stopped (rather charitably) so that Barry could focus his binoculars upon some "LBJ" ("little brown job"), as birds such as larks, pipits and cisticolas are known to the cognoscenti. Birders tend to wax lyrical about these nondescript little creatures, primarily, I believe, because it validates their avifaunal omniscience and keeps untutored hoi polloi such as myself at arm's length. I like birds but the "little brown jobs" rarely have me salivating with excitement. In fact, if accompanied by Barry and/or Kevin, the former a most knowledgeable birder and the latter a keen bird photographer, I would pretend not to notice anything less striking than a Lilac-breasted Roller, the "Technicolour Dreamcoat" of the East African bush.

That morning in the Crater I must have been feeling unusually benevolent and Barry took full advantage. As he focused on the bird, gasping endearments (towards – I hoped – the bird), I looked around for something more worthy of attention, and soon found it. Some distance away, its great shaggy head raised, lay a male lion. It was watching us. "There's a lion over there!", I murmured excitedly. Barry, binoculars trained on the somewhat smaller "brown job", kept his counsel, only responding (with a disapproving sigh) when I suggested that we should "drive over to take a look". Ignoring his implied disappointment I edged the Suzuki forward. Barry, with another sigh, lowered his binoculars and muttered something to the effect that big cats, unlike the utterly bewitching Little Brown Jobs, are hardly likely to fly away.

We drove towards the lion in strained silence. In those days you were allowed to drive off-road in the Crater and I drove across the short grass in a series of slow sinuous advances. Normally when approaching shy or nervous game in this way I would stop frequently, allowing the animal to adjust to the presence of the vehicle. But the lion looked on with apparent indifference.

The look in its eyes was serene, its face framed by a brown ruff, the mane beginning to darken at the crown and at the beard. Its head was tilted slightly back, allowing it to look down its nose at us in that supercilious way that comes so naturally to cats. I stopped the Suzuki some six metres away and switched off the engine. The lion watched as I placed a beanbag on the sill of my window and rested my camera upon it. Looking through the viewfinder and focusing on his eyes I was struck by their amber clarity, the pupils shrunk to black dots in the morning light.

Barry had murmured "Oh God..." as we had come to a standstill but I was concentrating on photographing the lion's head and his utterance scarcely registered. It was only as I zoomed out to photograph the whole lion that the reason for Barry's remark became clear. As my view broadened I saw dozens of black flies on the lion's forelegs. Then I saw the exposed ribs, furred black with flies. And then what Barry had seen. For the lion's waist was hollow and dark with dried blood. And where the underbelly and groin should have been was an even darker cavity, seething with maggots. A dense, restless profanity spilling from what, if anything, was left of the lion's innards on to the grass, like living, writhing grains of rice from a burst sack. The beast was in two halves, united only by a bloodied strip of hide and whatever bones and sinews might still have been intact beneath it.

It was not a lion but two halves of a lion. That the animal was alive at all, its eyes and face so remarkably normal, showing no signs of the horrors and agonies being played out behind, was almost unbelievable. Its head had now slumped to the ground, though the eyes remained open. Its rump, I now noticed, had been punctured by large canines. The tip of its tail had been bitten off and the paw of its left hind-leg savagely mauled. It had obviously lost a fight with a rival male, which had bitten it across the small of the back, perhaps dislocating the spine, for the hindquarters and tail seemed immobile.

I wondered how long it had lain there, on that pastoral, almost lawn-like greensward littered with pink-and-white "paper flowers", in this idyllic caldera. And how much longer it would lie before dying of thirst or loss of blood. Or before the spotted hyenas, so numerous and bold in the Crater, moved in, whooping with eager anticipation, to commit regicide. I have seen, in this same crater, three spotted hyenas chase a healthy, full-grown lioness from a kill and pursue her for half a kilometre. A near-defenceless lion would not keep such creatures at bay for long. Nor would the stinking, crawling cesspit of maggots take the edge off their appetites. Moved by such thoughts, perhaps, and by our own helplessness, Barry quietly – and quite rightly – said "Let's go". As I started the engine the lion raised its head, as fine and healthy a head as you could imagine, the golden eyes devoid of self-pity.

Lions might not pass unchallenged as "kings of the jungle" but as kings of our folk-lore they reign supreme. Yet even kings are mortal. Surprisingly, in all my days in the East African bush, where the big cats were plentiful and death so commonplace, I never saw a dead lion. And only once, in a land where skeletal remains often lie scattered on the plains in eye-catching isolation, have I ever come across a lion skull. To see a dead lion would be rare. But to see a lion dying violates the senses. It is like witnessing the passing of something over which death should have no dominion.

CHAPTER XIV

With the Anti-poaching quad in Ngorongoro

In the early 1980s an Australian teacher at the International School of Tanganyika, where I worked, had a live-in Maasai boyfriend who went by the unlikely name of Fred (his more traditional surname being Ole Uho). She had met him when the overland truck on which she was travelling passed through the Serengeti, where Fred was a ranger. He was a likeable man with many friends still working in the Serengeti and Ngorongoro and knowing that my friend Kevin and I were passionate about safaris and wildlife he arranged for us to spend two days camping in Ngorongoro Crater as guests of the anti-poaching squad.

Thrilled at such an opportunity Kevin and I drove north some time later. At the N.C.A. (Ngorongoro Conservation Area) headquarters we checked in with the Chief Conservator, a big, bluff Tanzanian with a dead-pan sense of humour. When I attempted to introduce ourselves he interrupted, saying "No point in telling me who you are. You *Wazungu* (Europeans) all look the same to me", neatly turning the old white stereotyping of black Africans inside out. It was said tongue-in-cheek and he went on to be extremely helpful, assuring us that the anti-poaching unit's Land Rover would pick us up at 9 a.m. the next day from "Forest Hostel", our regular stop-over whenever we passed through the Crater Highlands.

"Forest Hostel" (now "Rhino Lodge") was as unfashionable as its name. An estate agent would have described it as "rustic". Unlike its upmarket rival, the Crater Lodge (later entitled the "Maasai Versailles" because of its opulent décor) and the state-owned "Wildlife Lodge", the only other Ngorongoro lodges then in existence, it was set back from the Crater rim. But we liked it, not only because it was much cheaper but also for its simplicity.

In my imaginings it was always Christmas there, though we sometimes stayed there in July or August. Such skewed recollections are due to the hostel's location, which at 8,000 feet was far more conducive to Christmassy sentimentality than sweltering Dar es Salaam. Even in mid-December, at the height of the southern "summer", Forest Hostel could be refreshingly cool and the mornings misty. And with log fires in its dining room and bar in the evenings, Christmases there were as near as we ever got to the sleigh-bells-in-the-snow stereotype. To enhance the myth a wispy cypress tree, festooned with the usual flashing lights, tinsel and brightly-coloured baubles, would be set up in the dining room. While the gravelly voice of Jim Reeves, immensely popular throughout East Africa, crooned songs from his *Christmas Album*. And from beyond the grave.

Across the lawn from the main complex stood the bar, with a fireplace of Dickensian dimensions though the log fire itself was usually Scrooge-sized. What the bar lacked in physical warmth, however, it more than made up for in congenial atmosphere, for it was popular with the safari companies' African driver-guides and N.C.A. rangers as well as passing expatriates like ourselves. Most tourists, other than back-packers, sought greater comfort and better views in the posher lodges along the crater rim.

Few clients at "Forest Hostel" considered sobriety a virtue and as every habitual drinker knows a straight line is the shortest distance between two pints. Consequently most of us, when commuting between the accommodation block (or the communal toilets that were situated there) and the bar did so in the most direct way, by crossing the intervening lawn. As the lawn was regularly grazed by several wild buffalo bulls (regarded by many old-time hunters and present-day park rangers as the most dangerous of all big game), this expediency had its drawbacks. Especially after a few beers on a moonless night.

On such an occasion I almost literally collided with one of these beasts. Which as the animal in question weighed almost 600 kilogrammes and I about 70 would have been unwise, leaving aside the question of its huge spread of horns. I only became aware of its presence at the last moment, as I could barely see where the night ended and the buffalo began. With a startled (and startling) grunt it lurched heavily to one side, presumably to confront me, arousing two other near-invisible buffaloes into irritable demonstrations of their own. I dodged, like a nippy fly-half breaking from a ruck, between the three of them and down the path into the adjacent bar. The buffaloes had no doubt seen it all before, and were not about to interrupt their grazing for too long just to follow me up and pitchfork me on to the roof of the bar.

But it was "Forest Hostel's" birds that provided many of our happiest memories. The hostel's dining room had a small balcony at one end, its low wall abutting a small flower garden. Here we would sit in the relatively warm afternoons or early evenings, enjoying a glass of lager and admiring an intermittent pageant of brilliant sunbirds. The most striking were the relatively large Bronze and Tacazze. These highland species look almost black in dull conditions but are transformed by sunlight, the foreparts of the former into a gleaming, metallic bronze-green, with copper highlights, the Tacazze to a scintillating metallic violet. Their restless forms, shimmering with each movement, fluttered and twisted and probed as they and other sunbirds sipped nectar from the red-hot pokers and moon-flowers that contributed their own beauty to a bewitching little cameo.

Kevin and I were sitting on this balcony after breakfast when the anti-poaching people arrived to collect us, precisely on time. This took us by surprise as schedules, in Africa, are normally designed, like trousers with elasticated waists, to conform rather than impose. Grabbing our bags we hurried out, to be met by a handsome, smartly uniformed ranger. He had just stepped down from a Land Rover bearing the Anti-poaching Unit logo. Moderately tall, his small, slender moustache and serious demeanour enhanced his air of quiet authority. "I am William", he declared, offering a hand as we confirmed our own names, before introducing us to the driver, Anton, and a fellow ranger, Charles, whom we were invited to join in the back of the vehicle.

We were soon driving the wrong way down a one-way track, the ascent road that leads from the crater floor to the crater rim. This was slightly unsettling as I knew from experience how narrow and tortuous it was, with cliffs on one side and precipitous drops on the other. The thought of meeting a vehicle going the other way wasn't comforting. William, sensing my unease, explained that the anti-poaching unit was allowed to use it as a descent road as it is much quicker and much closer to the anti-poaching headquarters than the regular Seneto Descent Road. He also assured me that the calls he had recently made, over the vehicle's radio system, were to his colleagues at the foot of the Crater wall, to confirm that no one was coming up the other way. "I hope they got it right", remarked Kevin, as we bumped around a hairpin bend to find ourselves gazing down a steeply declivitous drop into the caldera.

Over the next two days we were to see twelve of the approximate twenty-two black rhinos then thought to inhabit the floor and lower slopes of the Crater, thanks to the eyesight of an old Maasai guide, Elias. African rangers, game scouts and guides usually have astonishingly good eyesight but Elias's verged on the supernatural. On one occasion he not only pointed out but identified a cow and calf rhino that to me were little more than blobs even through binoculars. Of course he knew where to look and he knew every rhino in the Crater, but it was still extraordinary. Among the rhinos that we encountered was a closely assembled group of four, to the west of the flat-topped Engitate Hill, named after the girdle that Maasai women wear. The rhinos were flaky-white from rolling in alkaline mud, now dry, and standing almost hock-deep in whippy-looking grasses that shone silver in the morning light.

I took photographs, aware, thanks to the ruthless greed and incomprehensible ignorance that blights our planet, that I was most unlikely, ever again, to see four black rhinos together. "Prehistoric" is a word that comes too easily to mind in the presence of these animals, as if they are left-overs from the age of dinosaurs, a species that has reached the end of its evolutionary shelf-life; it is said that rhino evolution peaked with *Indricotherium*, the great hornless rhino that died out about 10 million years ago. But it is Man, not time, that is hustling the species into extinction. Until recently the Black Rhino was extremely successful in its preferred habitat. There might have been a million as late as 1900 though some biologists think that their numbers have been falling since about 1700, when they estimate an Africa-wide population of 850,000.

Killing a rhino is a simple business, requiring little courage or skill if you have a modicum of bushcraft and an automatic rifle. Rhinos have small brains and poor eyesight, they are scarcely able to see a Land Rover at more than thirty metres, though their sense of smell and hearing is good. Their "charges" are mainly explorative, aimed at making an intruder reveal itself, and hopefully back off. And though they can move with surprisingly speed and agility, few confrontations result in injury or damage, let alone death. Frederick Selous, famous hunter and frontiersman, said he had never heard of a single white hunter being killed by a rhino.

To put the matter into a more damning perspective, the biologist John Goddard, when studying rhinos in Ngorongoro in the 1960s, often worked alone, on foot and unarmed. He identified 110 rhinos on the Crater floor, yet today, more than three decades after the mass slaughter of the 1980s, there are still only around 26. In the early 2000's I asked the N.C.A's Tourism Officer, Asante Melita, why population growth had stalled. A bespectacled, studious and polite man (his given name means "Thank you"), Asante told me that it wasn't due to poaching, which was then, he assured me, more or less under control in Ngorongoro. But slow reproduction rates, inbreeding, high mortality rates among calves, which are sometimes killed by spotted hyenas or lions, competition for browse due to elephants, and a tenfold increase in buffaloes in the caldera since 1986, which might be responsible for an increase in tick-borne diseases.

Whatever the case, the Crater rhinos are up against it, as are rhinos generally, for they carry a formidable price on their heads. One rhino might carry three kilogrammes of horn, representing a staggering $300,000 at 2018 prices, more than the price of gold and easily enough to keep the average African in beans and *ugali* (maize porridge) for a lifetime.

For four days we scoured the Crater for rhinos, but we saw much else, including mating lions (the lions in the Crater seem exceptionally libidinous or exceptionally bored), and the customary abundance of other animals and birds. Some of the most interesting interludes for me, however, had nothing directly to do with wildlife. I was surprised, for example, when at one point William indicated something ahead and I saw a line of Maasai cattle wending its way across the central plains, led by a young boy and followed by a Maasai elder. The Maasai were forced out of the Crater in 1976, generations after they themselves had probably evicted their former enemies the Datoga. But they are still allowed into the Crater under licence, so that their cattle can lick the soda that they covet and seem to need.

This particular Maasai elder had no licence, William told me, long before he challenged the elder and remonstrated with him, but he let him off with a caution. The old man, face weathered by countless suns and the winds that blow without let or hindrance across the grasslands, strode off in a red-shawled huff, spear and cattle stick in one hand, bald pate gleaming, the cattle-bells clanking again as the herd moved on. William watched them go with professional detachment. With less detachment, a single male lion also watched, from the edge of the Mandusi Swamp. It could easily have brought down one of the cows but not with impunity, as it must have known. It confined itself to window-shopping.

That evening after dinner William invited Kevin and I to accompany him and Charles on a night drive across the Crater, to deliver diesel fuel to the village of Nainokanoka, just outside the caldera at the foot of Ol Moti. I suspect that the two of them were also a bit bored. It was a cloudy, moonless night and we saw none of the nocturnal animals we were hoping to see. We did, however, see spotted hyenas on the prowl, looking far more sinister by night than by day, and great gatherings of wildebeeste or smaller scatterings of gazelles, spectral in the near-darkness, their eyes, when caught in the sweep of the headlights, glittering like stars in a series of minor galaxies. The drive back was just as uneventful.

But Nainokanoka itself had its own excitements, with the transfer of diesel from a large drum to a smaller one, in almost complete darkness. The whole village had turned out to watch, and a small number of men, murmuring instructions, manoeuvred the drums into place and supervised the transfer. One of them was smoking a cigarette, which was poised just above the flow of fuel and the smaller drum, with little clumps of hot ash falling down, from time to time, into the fuel.

Kevin and I watched the glow of the cigarette like birds hypnotized by a snake, until I tugged Kevin's sleeve and said "Let's get out of here". Kevin needed no further encouragement and we backed off into the darkness. "At least here", Kevin murmured, as if speaking in a library, "we'll only be blown to bits, not vapourised". We didn't know then that diesel fuel has to be heated to around 62° C before it becomes inflammable, and as the ambient temperature in Nainokanoka at the time would have been well below 15° C, we would have been quite safe. Ignorance is not always blissful.

The next morning after breakfast William, perhaps thinking that we had seen enough rhinos, said "Today we will go to the old farm". Soon afterwards we found ourselves back in the northern sector of the Crater, crossing the Munge. A little further on, Anton brought the Land Rover to a standstill. "Old German farm", William announced, getting down and inviting us to do likewise. Some thirty metres or so up the slope I saw several tall stands of sisal by a scattered pile of stones. William picked up a few rocks and lobbed them, as if they were hand grenades, into the ruins. "Sometimes there are lions", he explained.

Which is ironic, for Adolph Siedentopf, who had built the farmhouse in the dying days of the 19th Century, after he and his family had lived there for some time in tents, was a cattleman, with dreams of expanding his herd to 5,000. Like most settlers he regarded lions as vermin. Eva Wenkel, who lived with the Siedentopfs for more than a year, didn't see a single one, though she heard them in the distance. Yet soon after the First World

War, Sir Charles Ross, who bought Adolph's farm from the custodian of enemy property, recalled that: "Lions were to be seen every morning on this side of the crater if one went to look for them". They still are.

Ross was another eccentric East African "character". Ninth Baronet of Balnagown, Scotland, and to the manner born, he employed a chauffeur in Ngorongoro Crater at a time when cars could get no closer than Arusha, 190 km. away. He also designed the "Ross rifle", which saw action in the trenches of Flanders, though the Canadian infantrymen obliged to use it were not impressed. They threw the rifles away in disgust and grabbed Lee Enfields from dead British troops. Nevertheless, Ross made a lot of money out of his firearms. To thwart the British tax authorities he declared his Scottish estate American territory, causing the British Government to proclaim him an outlaw.

Meanwhile William's "hand grenades", clattering among the ruins of the farm that Adolf Siedentopf had built and that Ross had acquired, caused a stir among the local lizardry but little else. After a few moments grace, to give lurking lions a chance to show themselves, we walked over. The farm that had once covered a third of the Crater floor was now reduced to rubble, reminding me of Shelley's lines from *Ozymandias*, "Look on my works, ye Mighty, and despair". Adolph was no "Ozymandias, king of kings", but he had been king of all he surveyed and mighty in the physical sense, six foot four inches tall and "immensely strong". Nor was his little thatched farmhouse an illustrious ancient monument but its location, just north of the Munge and below the slopes that run down in such fluid splendour from Ol Moti, was surely more beautiful than that of any royal palace or its gardens.

I stood thoughtfully among the stones, moved by the sweet sorrow that certain ruins evoke. Not that I mourned the loss of the Siedentopf farm, I was glad that it had gone. But what a fine thing it must have been to stand there, on your own verandah, and look south across the Munge and your pastures patterned with cattle, towards the gleaming, white-rimmed Lake Magadi and the dark spread of the forest at Lerai. Or north towards the Olkaria Hills and the mass of Ol Moti beyond, the slopes dappled green and gold, as I have seen them, with grass and daisies, sunlight and shadow.

If this was an African Eden to Adolph Siedentopf, it was not because of its wildlife. He was, after all, a farmer. Apart from the lions that were probably shot on sight, he and his workers, some of them Nderobo hunter-gatherers, are said to have "killed thousands of wildebeeste in order to can the tongues, which were carted out on the backs of porters all the way to Arusha", presumably as part of the war effort. But Eden, as Genesis reminds us, was not without its bad days. A Dr. Hans Reck wrote that Adolph, "single handed in the wilderness, had to fight a lot of battles with the surrounding Maasai, and his increasing herds were again and again the target of theft and pillage". It was even alleged that Adolph "wound up dead with a Masai spear through the abdomen".

The truth, though just as tragic, seems rather less romantic. He allegedly committed suicide by poisoning in Alabama, USA, in 1932. If so it must surely have been due to a broken heart, for as British forces had approached Ngorongoro in 1916, Dr Reck

"…saw his wonderful cattle, fifteen hundred head of mixed breeds, being driven under a cloud of dust towards the South. They were approaching the slopes of the mountain in an almost endless train, and disappearing into the jungle on the slopes.

A few years later, Siedentopf had lost everything, the change of climate having killed the animals off in hundreds. Siedentopf returned to his defeated homeland, after being a prisoner of war, as poor as when he had first arrived twenty years before."

There had been two farmhouses in the Crater. Adolph had set up his brother, Friedrich Wilhelm, in a second one thirteen kilometres south of his own, between the foot of the Crater wall and the Lerai. In my impressionable, misguided youth, when I had dreamed of becoming a hunter in East Africa, I had read a book by a man who had realised a similar dream long before. Appropriately named "J.A. Hunter", he was a man of his time, famous and popular in the Kenya of his day but remembered now for slaughtering no fewer than 1,600 rhinos, half of them within two years. In 1923 "J.A.", as he was widely known, had visited the Crater for the first time, with American clients. They had travelled on foot from Arusha, and were not to see another white person for almost three months.

Arriving in the Crater they had found Adolph Siedentopf's old farm abandoned. Travelling south they had called at his brother's "little thatched cottage" by the Lerai, where they discovered that its new owner, Captain George Hurst, had recently been killed by an elephant at Kilwa, on the Tanganyikan coast. After seeing off his clients at Tabora John Hunter had returned to the Crater to spend a few days at the farmhouse, hunting and killing five lions with the aid of Hurst's "kangaroo hounds".

"It never occurred to me", he wrote, "that the day would come when lions would be carefully protected as valuable game animals. In those days we regarded them simply as a dangerous nuisance."

His description of Friedrich Wilhem's home by the Lerai had fascinated me. I would never have believed then that thirty years later I would stay at this same farmhouse, or at least just outside it, but this is where Kevin and I now pitched our tents, on the old farmhouse lawn. On our return from each day's foray into the Crater I would walk with William down to the Lerai (the Maasai word for the yellow-bark acacias that dominate the forest) to look for firewood among the disorder of its understorey. It was a short but eagerly-anticipated walk, for we never knew what to expect. In fact we saw little but waterbuck, vervet monkeys, a bull elephant with a single, slender scimitar of a tusk and a small variety of birds, but the elegant trees and the abiding silence were blissful. Things might have been a bit more lively two decades earlier, when John Goddard recorded 23 rhinos living in the same forest, a ratio of seven per square kilometre.

After dinner each evening, cooked on yellow-bark logs from the Lerai, the fire was re-vitalised. William, Charles and Kevin and I (Anton and Elias had gone to stay at the rangers' quarters at the foot of the ascent road) sat around it, enjoying bottles of lager from what William called the "fridge", the little stream that gurgles through the grove of trees behind the farmhouse, in which the lagers had been left to cool. We would talk long into the night, Kevin and I seated astride rhino skulls (minus the horns, of course, and surprisingly comfortable). Our conversations would be punctuated from time to time by explosive cracks, as the stones encircling the fire, exposed to heat on one side and falling temperatures on the other, split in two. Before retiring to my tent I would walk behind the old farmhouse into the darkness of the woodland to urinate among the trees, watched with disapproval, no doubt, by the ghosts of Captain Hurst and Friedrich Wilhelm. And who knows what else.

CHAPTER XV

An Eventful Night in the Crater

A few years after our stay with the anti-poaching squad I camped on the Crater floor again. I was with another friend and colleague, Patricia. We didn't camp at Friedrich Wilhelm's old farm, which was reserved for the anti-poaching unit, but on an officially designated site nearby, known as "Fig Tree Camp Site" after the great strangler fig that dominates the clearing. No longer a camp site, "Fig Tree" is now reserved as a picnicking stop-over for day-tripper tourists.

Patricia had arranged to meet her Egyptian boyfriend, Ibrahim, in Arusha, I was going north to spend a little time alone on safari. The detour to Ngorongoro had been a last-minute idea when Patricia, who had never seen the Crater, realized that she would have two days to spare before Ibrahim's arrival. Fortunately, with such a possibility in mind, I had brought along a tent borrowed from my other friend and colleague, Kevin, and his wife Claudia. One of those family-style affairs with two separate sleeping compartments and a large "living space".

Kevin, normally easy-going, had not been too keen on the idea. "It's Claudia, Gray", he had explained, "you know how *Swiss* she is…" Claudia, whom Kevin had recently married, was and is a lovely, elegant lady, and she and I got on well. But she *was* Swiss. She didn't yodel, at least not in my presence, nor did she have a cuckoo clock but she *had* worked in a Swiss chocolate factory and she was scrupulously clean and orderly and "proper". In the end Kevin had agreed to lend me the tent "as long as you bring it back in *pristine* condition". I promised that it would come back "as spotless as a Swiss chalet".

With the precious tent and much else in the back of my little Suzuki Patricia and I had set off from Dar heading west to Dodoma in central Tanzania and then north towards Arusha. The journey was long but as enjoyable and entertaining as journeys with Patricia always are. Apart from having been a wonderful teacher she is well-travelled, well-read and a talented embroiderer, conjuring all kinds of fabric scraps and haberdasher's rejects into the most beguiling compositions.

Physically she defines the word "bonny", which in her native Scotland means "pleasing to look at" but which in her adoptive Lancashire means "well-rounded". The word can also mean "extremely good". All three are appropriate and if the term "well-rounded" has too much Lancastrian candour about it I would argue that if Patricia was much thinner she wouldn't be as "pleasing to look at". And she wouldn't be Patricia, for her personality is as bonny as her build. She laughs a lot, often irreverently, occasionally with an explosive derision capable of shattering egos, as more than one pompous international school administrator has discovered. And she talks as much as she laughs, almost always with an engaging joie de vivre.

North of Dodoma, at Kola, near Kondoa Irangi, we stopped off to see the nearby rock paintings, believed to be the work of hunter-gatherers a millennium-and-a-half ago. A local guide of indeterminate age (the difference between chronological and biological age often being hard to pinpoint in a continent where life is often harrowing) had conducted us to the nearest site. It wasn't just the wear and tear of a harsh existence, however, that had prematurely aged him. He was given, we soon realised, to a passion for *pombe*, the traditional African "moonshine". In fact, to borrow a Naval expression, he was "pissed as a handcart". Stumbling erratically after us through the open bush he shouted incomprehensible directions from time to time, pointing the way ahead with vigorous if unhelpful flourishes of his arm.

By chance or foggy-minded design we eventually reached the first of the many rocky outcrops where the paintings are to be found. Our guide, incapable of accompanying us up the steep slope, exhorted us, in a slurred mixture of Swahili and broken English, to make our way to an overhang half-way up the kopje. On reaching it we found the rock embellished with several faded, elongated human figures and various antelopes, depicted in ochre. Our escort, some distance beneath us and obscured by the intervening rock and vegetation, treated us to a distractingly unintelligible commentary on these ancient representations, which no doubt, in his younger, more abstemious days, he had got to know by heart.

After seeing and photographing the paintings we climbed down little wiser. We knew that there were more interesting paintings on more distant kopjes but we also knew that our guide had already reached his limits. Disappointed, and aware that we would probably never pass this way again, we retraced our steps to his simple base, paid him more than he deserved and drove off up the dusty dirt track.

After driving through the Irangi Hills and the little town of Babati we turned off to spend two days in Tarangire National Park, where we saw 800 elephants in a single morning. And none the next. It was in Tarangire that Patricia, realizing that she would have two days to spare, had suggested taking a little detour to Ngorongoro before her boyfriend arrived. I had immediately agreed and soon after leaving Tarangire we were hammering over the rocks and corrugations of the Rift and up into the Crater Highlands.

After booking the Fig Tree campsite we set off around the southern crater rim and down the Seneto descent road. The word "road", to anyone unfamiliar with African conditions, is a little misleading, though the Seneto track, by African standards, is a fairly straightforward drive in a well-maintained 4WD. In our case it was made less straightforward by the fact that the little Suzuki jeep was seriously overloaded. Had it been a boat a responsible harbour master would have prevented it from proceeding to sea. Apart from ourselves, with all our camping equipment and baggage, we were required by N.C.A. regulations to take a ranger with us, despite the fact that it is impossible to get lost in the caldera and that the ranger we had with us, Faraji, was unarmed.

As the Suzuki's rear seats had been folded forward to make space for the luggage Patricia had volunteered to lie on her back on top of the cargo, allowing Faraji to occupy the front passenger seat. And incidentally his birthright, for "Faraji" means "comfort". This left the supine Patricia with her face only a few inches below the car's roof. Not the happiest of situations on a rough dirt track that is quite rocky in places. There were times when Patricia's nose, had she not squirmed quickly to one side, would have come into unwholesome contact with the Suzuki's mild steel roof, the "mildness" of which might well have been lost on Patricia. "Ibrahim won't recognize me after this," she giggled, somewhere behind me. "I'll look as if I've done fifteen rounds with Mohammed Ali…"

Meanwhile, from the driving seat, I looked down into the celebrated caldera and in the excitement forget Patricia's situation. "Ant-eater chats on the right! The dark birds with white rumps!" I enthused, followed by "Look at that fantastic candelabra euphorbia! The sap is poisonous, but the rhinos eat them, I'm told". Throughout this outpouring of received wisdom Patricia maintained a most uncharacteristic silence. Until, bouncing down a particularly uneven stretch, I enjoined her to "Look out for Chandler's Mountain Reedbuck! Little greyish antelopes found on rocky slopes like these!" Appropriately in these volcanic landscapes, Patricia erupted, her voice amplified, in a tinny, robotic kind of way, by the imminent presence of the bare metal roof. "FUCK Chandler's Mountain Reedbuck!" she snorted, "I can't see a bloody thing except the car *roof*, you pratt!" Risking further explosions I pointed out the practical and moral disincentives implicit in her exhortation, and its almost certain illegality under Tanzanian law. Then she and I and Faraji (though he had no idea why) burst out laughing.

Thankfully we soon reached the level caldera floor and soon afterwards the Fig Tree Campsite, close to the southern fringes of the Lerai. The site is sacred as well as beautiful, the burial place of Gitangda, a Datoga leader killed in battle with the Maasai in the mid-nineteenth century. The graves of distinguished Datoga elders (invariably men) are marked by trees that have sprung spontaneously from the burial mound, an earthen pyramid known as a *bung'ed*. In Gitangda's case the tree is a fig though not, it seems, the monumental strangler fig (*Ficus thonningii*) that dominates the site. Each tree that has grown from a *bung'ed* is known and revered by the Datoga. Strangler figs, in the Crater and elsewhere, are also acknowledged by the Datoga's former enemies the Maasai. In passing they will tuck tufts of grass into the figs' aerial roots, in deference to their god *Engai*. He, they believe, gave them all the cattle on Earth, exporting them from the Maasai Heaven via the aerial roots of a legendary fig.

Initially we wanted to pitch our borrowed tent under the huge tree in the centre of the campsite. Its great, elliptical green umbrella looked inviting in the heat of the Ngorongoro afternoon. As a one-time aspiring Boy Scout I should have known better; "Never camp on a slope or under a tree" was one of scouting's best-known commandments. In the event it was Faraji who dissuaded us. And with good reason. As we had entered the campsite I had been obliged to steer around a smaller fig tree, one that had, Faraji told us, recently crashed to earth during a violent thunderstorm. And in doing so crushing to death a young German woman who had been camping beneath it.

It was a timely warning. Later, having set up our tent well away from the nearest tree, I wandered over to the fallen one and mused upon the lottery that is life. Morbidly, I wondered what that young woman would have thought as a girl, had she been told by some fortune-teller that she would die a few years later, killed by a fallen tree in Ngorongoro Crater during a thunderstorm. She would surely have laughed at the absurdity.

Having unloaded our things we drove off for a late afternoon game drive. Soon after leaving the campsite Faraji pointed out a dark-maned lion at the foot of the Crater wall. He urged me off the track (permissible in those easy-going days) and across the short-grass plain towards the lion. As always in the bush, except in really dusty conditions or heavily-infested tsetse-fly country, the windows of the Suzuki were fully open. In fact my driving seat window could not be closed in a hurry, as my camera bracket was clamped to the sill.

As we approached, the lion, which had been sniffing the ground, looked up. I was anticipating some good photographs of a prized "black-mane" but when I saw this one's face I couldn't help smiling and reminding Patricia of her comment about doing "fifteen rounds with Muhammed Ali". For the lion looked like a punch-drunk fairground bruiser, with "cauliflower" ears and features that looked as if they been hoofed and clawed in a hundred confrontations with desperate zebras and ambitious rivals. His jaw was distorted, perhaps broken, and he was blind in one eye. I have never seen a less photogenic lion. But I stopped alongside him and switched off the engine.

As if affronted by my comments he ignored us and resumed his sniffing. Faraji then drew my attention to two more dark-maned lions jouncing over the greensward towards us in that heavy, leonine way, bow-legged and bellies swinging. Excitedly, and a little anxiously because of the open window, I expected a battle royal, and another mauling, or worse, for the battered old bruiser. But the three must have been brothers or pride-mates. They were soon indulging in the usual feline greeting rituals, rubbing heads and pressing along each other's flanks. Absorbed by this bonding display I almost forgot to take photographs, and when I remembered I was frustrated (in those pre-automatic focus days) by the constant writhing and inter-weaving of the lions.

Fortunately I hadn't fixed the camera to the window bracket. Lost in their rituals the three lions gravitated towards the Suzuki. To my amusement, the nearest of them, the badly battered one, aroused to a high state of excitement by the familial fuss, began to include the car in his greeting routine, rubbing himself against it. Patricia gave a little cry of alarm as the car rocked sideways, but there was little I could do without making the situation worse. I then had to lean quickly to one side as the lion rubbed itself against my open window frame. I watched his great head come alongside me. The dark mane blocked the frame completely, spilling inside the cab. Had I remained upright it would have brushed my face. More worryingly, underneath that haystack of half-matted hair was the camera bracket, with its angular projections. I held my breath, praying that the mane wouldn't get entangled.

It didn't, and after I had taken more photographs we left the lions to celebrate their reunion. Faraji wanted to show us something else, and directed me to a low rise just north of Lake Magadi, one of the Crater's main features. He asked me to stop by a flat outcrop of rock at the crest of the rise. On getting down we saw that the rock was pock-marked with shallow holes, the cups of prehistoric *bao* boards, ground into the rock, in later years, by the pointed hafts of Maasai spears. Each set of holes was arranged in double-columned rectangles.

Bao is an ancient game, probably spreading throughout Africa from the north, and still popular. It is normally played on wooden boards (hence the name *bau*), and is as complicated, I am told, as chess. Faraji invited me to play but I have little patience for board games. Patricia, more accommodating, obliged, and sat down cross-legged with the ranger to learn the basic rules. The Maasai are enthusiasts and the stakes can be high. Many a head of cattle has been won and lost at *bau*, perhaps here in the middle of the Crater. Patricia, having no cattle to lose, was giggling softly at her own incompetence as I left them and I wandered off, thrilled to be alone and on foot in a place known as the world's "Eighth Wonder".

Except for a few Grants and Thomson gazelles, and further away a small group of zebras and three buffalo bulls, the area was devoid of animals. But I was lucky enough to see something that I had never seen before or would ever see again, the remarkable mating "dance" of a pair of ostriches. *Struthio camelus* is a most unusual bird; even its specific name means "camel-like". Often, when compiling my list of birds after a safari, I would forget to include it, as if it was a mammal, not a bird. Apart from being unable to fly, it can run at 70 km. per hour and has a kick like a rodeo horse. And as if that was not enough to reclassify it as mammal the male ostrich is also one of a very few birds that possess a penis. As I, and its mate, were about to find out.

Male ostriches, as with many male birds and mammals, enjoy the privilege, if such it is, of being responsible for a number of females. In this case the male was either a serial divorcee or just embarking on his marital career, for he had only one hen to contend with. But even a single female is capable of leading her mate a more-than-metaphorical dance. Ducking and weaving with near-political expertise, and ruffling her otherwise redundant wings, this one cleverly kept just ahead of her ardent pursuer. I was reminded of the Irving Berlin classic *A Man Chases a Girl until she Catches Him*, as she danced her erotic way across the short-grass, the male red-faced and red-necked with frustrated passion.

I then became aware of another crimson accessory, some thirty centimeters long, jiggling flaccidly between his legs. It is something of a shock in a bird, and just as surprisingly I saw no evidence of an erection, which apparently is brought about by "a burst of lymphatic fluid" rather than an expansion of blood vessels as in mammals and reptiles. Discounting the possibility of erectile dysfunction I concluded that the required stiffening of the male's resolve was achieved in a matter of moments during the brief final flurry. Certainly the hen eventually crouched in submission and allowed the cock to mount, and after a momentary orgasmic flutter rose to her feet again. What she thought of it all is a mystery but the male seemed contented enough, strutting around triumphantly, penis still swinging gently. "And I missed it all!" complained Patrica, still sitting, cross-legged and confused by her *bau* board, when I told her about it later.

It was dusk by the time we got back to the campsite but we soon had a small fire crackling. Darkness comes early in the crater once the sun sinks beneath the rim and the air cools quickly. Pulling on sweaters we cooked a simple meal and sat by the fire to eat and to enjoy a few lagers. The night, quite eerily, was almost silent. Faraji was silent also, unless we spoke to him, content to eat and drink and pleased, in his hospitable African way, that we were happy. "Just think", said Patricia at one point, "we are in Ngorongoro Crater, at night! Just us and all these wild animals... isn't that wonderful?". As it was. How many people can say that they have shared the caldera of an extinct volcano, at night, with 20,000 or so large herbivores, 60 or 70 lions and almost half-a-thousand spotted hyenas?

It was also thought-provoking. Patricia's pronouncement had caused us to lapse into a long silence, broken only when she added, rather more seriously than is her habit: "It's like being a Christian in the Coliseum". Which, though something of an exaggeration, was, in the circumstances and after several lagers, excusable. We were not tied to stakes but we were not lolling around in a 5-star lodge either. And in case we had doubts, just as we fell silent again the hyenas began to whoop and from somewhere beyond the Lerai a lion moaned softly. I imagined its great soughs of breath condensing in the cold night air. We remained silent, as our hunter-gatherer ancestors might have done, not out of fear but out of instinctive respect. Soon afterwards, tired but contented, we decided to go to bed.

I invited Faraji to sleep in the "living room" sector of the tent, outside our own two cubicles, but he chose to sleep sitting up in the Suzuki. "Maybe he knows something that we don't?" said Patricia after we had bidden him goodnight. She was only half-joking, I suspect, but laughed it off, retiring into her tented cubicle and I into mine. For a while we lay in our sleeping bags, talking through the fabric walls of our respective "rooms". We then fell silent, listening to the occasional noises of the night. Eventually I heard Patricia snoring lightly, then not so lightly. Then I too must have fallen into that deep, dreamless condition that the sleep research people know as "N4".

To be awakened from an "N4" is almost (though I cannot speak from experience) like being awakened from the dead. So when this happened some time later I felt completely disorientated. Patricia's snoring brought things into focus but it wasn't that, I knew, which had awakened me. I had been shocked from sleep by an unearthly scream. I lay still, wanting to believe that the scream had been part of a nightmare but knowing that it hadn't. And yet, had it been real, Patricia would surely have woken up?

In the aftermath of the scream the silence of the night, broken now only by Patricia's snores, was a threat in itself. I listened anxiously for sounds from the Suzuki, just outside. There were none. How come Faraji not heard the scream? I was now fully alert. The scream was real. And human. No animal could utter a noise like that. Night noises on safari are common, and if you are camping, sometimes worrying, but this was different. Far more ominous than the call of a nearby lion or the stomach rumblings of a bull elephant, close to the tent, or even the maniacal cackling of excited hyenas. It was sinister. Once again the memories of the two expatriates murdered while camping on the crater rim, and more recently the murder of two Danes, camping down by Lengai in the adjacent Rift, came to mind. Both incidents perpetrated, allegedly, by disaffected Maasai *moran*.

I was now sitting upright, listening intently. Suddenly the silence was broken again. Not by a scream this time but by sounds that were vaguely familiar. Sounds from my youth. The croaking, clicking sounds made by the ratchet of a large fishing reel being wound back, deliberately and very slowly. Except that these sounds, increasing in tempo, terminated in a second chilling scream. Followed by a sepulchral silence disrupted only by Patricia's snores. We were being tormented, I realized, by wandering young Maasai. Motivated merely by mischief? Or far worse? I felt very much alone. How could Patricia and Faraji sleep through all this? Meanwhile the creaks and clicks began again, and I braced myself for the next unearthly screech...

Suddenly, amid the confused complexities of my brain, came another, less literal "click". I remembered a passage I had read in one of my field guides. Describing the call of a nocturnal animal that "begins as a soft groaning and rises to (about 150 repeats at short intervals) an ear-splitting climax (heard up to 3 km away)… " The call of the Tree Hyrax, a creature no bigger or more dangerous than a rabbit. I was overwhelmed with relief. And chastened by my own foolishness. It is astonishing, and worrying, how the human mind, even one not given to superstition or alarm, can so easily be deceived, for my fears had been genuine. Recently, still bemused by my absurd suspicions so many years ago in the Crater, I looked up rock hyraxes on the Internet. "At night", I read, "Tree Hyraxes emit a scream that chills the blood of even the hardest man".

I am not the hardest man. My blood was as chilled as blood ever gets outside a hospital freezing unit, Patricia's as chilled as a glass of mulled wine. She, and presumably Faraji, the "Comfortable One", were sleeping through screams that can be "heard up to 3 km away". It was like sleeping through an air-raid warning in the London Blitz. Once the screams had ended, and I knew what had caused them, I too fell asleep. But at a time when the human spirit is said to be at its lowest I was awakened yet again. This time by an animal much larger and more threatening than a rock hyrax.

I could hear its loud, snuffling grunts and the sounds of carnassial teeth chewing something flexible but tough. Not Patricia's legs, thank God, for astonishingly she was still snoring. Whatever it was, it was chewing its way into the tent. At least I knew that I was dealing with an animal this time and not some resentful young Maasai armed with spear and *simi*. Too tired and angry now to be afraid I unzipped my cubicle and peered into the "living room" section beyond.

A bloated moon must have been shining above the Crater's cloud cover, its twice-diffused light weakly illuminating the tent's interior. The grunting and snuffling had stopped at the sound of the zip but it soon resumed. I saw the far corner of the tent being nuzzled and chewed by invisible but clearly powerful jaws. I could make out the form of the animal's snout, broad and powerful beneath the cotton-canvas and rubberised ground-sheet. Too large for a honey-badger (which would have been bad enough), too small for a full-grown lion. It must, I thought, be either a young lion, messing around playfully or, more probably, a hyena. Neither possibility was comforting. A single spotted hyena can bring down an adult wildebeest and its jaws can reduce (it has been recorded) a galvanized iron bucket into pulp. And not too many years earlier a hyena had dragged a sleeping camper from his tent by his head, up on the crater rim.

Whatever it was, I had no intentions of sharing a tent with it. Grabbing a heavy safari boot I crawled into the living space and whanged the boot as hard as I could at the bulge in the corner of the tent, which was already in shreds. I once dreamed of playing cricket for Lancashire and though my career petered out at club level I was quite a good fielder at mid-off or point. All those years of play and practice now paid off, for the boot caught the mystery beast on the snout with a fearful "Clump!". "Fearful" because I had no idea what would happen next. In the event there was a loud grunt of surprise and pain and the welcome sound of a fairly large animal legging off to the safety of the Lerai.

Incredibly Patricia snored on. I spent the rest of the night listening to her wheezings and waiting for the next incident. The hours passed slowly but uneventfully, the hyraxes having abandoned their manic commotion. As soon as the orange fabric of the tent began to lighten with the dawn I crawled out. Patricia was still asleep and so was Faraji, flopped back in the Suzuki's front passenger seat as if he had been shot. I inspected the corner of the tent, now a masticated lump of torn canvas and saliva-slippery strips of rubber. My mind fast-forwarded to the time when I would have to return the tent to Kevin and (more worryingly) to Claudia.

Much later, Patricia emerged, as Faraji slept on. Walking over to where I was brushing my teeth by a water stand-pipe, she stretched out her arms, yawned and with a great sigh of sleepy satisfaction, rubbed her eyes and said "I feel great! I slept like a *log*! – How about you?" Just above our heads in the branches of a thorn tree the hyraxes were settling down for the day.

A week or two later, back in Dar, I plucked up the courage to return the tent, rolled neatly in its duffle bag, to Kevin, after first making sure that Claudia was out.

"Ah", said Kevin, "I was wondering when you would bring it back – I hope" (his eyes narrowed) "that it is *spot*lessly clean? I mean *Swiss* clean…?"

"Spotless…", I replied. Quite honestly, for I had brushed and sponged the dirt and dust and dried saliva away long before. "Better had be", Kevin muttered, "or Claudia will…" (he predicted excruciatingly painful consequences involving a sensitive part of my anatomy and a Swiss Army knife). "The tent", I insisted, is perfectly clean… it's just that…"

CHAPTER XVI

Tarangire
–
The Park No One Knew About

To say that no one knew about Tarangire National Park, even in the late 1970s when I first went there, is untrue. But at that time, and throughout much of the 80s, relatively few people were aware of its existence, and far fewer knew exactly where it was. Even John Williams, that much-respected authority on East Africa's bird-life and wildlife sanctuaries, showed Tarangire, in his popular *Field Guide to the National Parks of East Africa*, as being 100 miles north-east of its actual location. Which might explain why few people ever found it. Including, I suspect, John himself.

I have always blessed him for this atypical lapse. While dozens of other safari vehicles were presumably grinding around 100 miles to the north-east, looking for a national park that wasn't there, my safari partners (at that time Barry and Kevin) and I had the actual park more or less to ourselves, a glorious corner of the Maasai Steppe in which to wander at will. It quickly became a favourite.

Topographically it is pleasing rather than dramatic and in terms of animal numbers relatively quiet for most of the year. But its panoramic landscapes have a rolling and restrained beauty, fairly uniform from afar but at closer quarters varied, and studded with great baobabs, those most African of trees, which impose an African grandeur and scale upon this otherwise unassertive land. Through these landscapes winds Tarangire's eponymous river, in braided sweeps of sandbar and sun-reflecting shallows, flanked by dessicated dry season grassland and bush or terraces greened by the seasonal rains.

As the surface water on the Simanjiro Plains east of the park begins to dry up in June, herds of eland and oryx file into the sanctuary to seek sustenance from the saline waters of the Tarangire and its adjacent grasslands and bush. Followed in July by large congregations of zebras and wildebeest and other big game, including certain lions, which like the Maasai with whom they share an uneasy truce, commute between wet and dry season grazing areas.

Elephants also migrate in and out of Tarangire, to be transformed into toys by the giant baobabs under which they often seek shade. Not that the baobabs dwarf them into complete insignificance, for Tarangire's elephants can be striking in number as well as size. My friend Patricia and I, as mentioned previously, once saw 800 in a single morning, two herds of around 300 and several smaller family groups. One of these groups of 300, after milling around on a riverside bluff below the old "Tented Camp", had eventually set off in line ahead across the long-grass plains of Lemiyon, northwards through the Rift towards the Maasai "Mountain of God", *Ol Doinyo Lengai*. I can still see those elephants, strung out across the plains in a line that stretched and diminished into the distance. There was a purpose about them, as if they were making for the sacred mountain to petition *Engai*, the Maasai God, in person. They were certainly in need of divine intervention, though I am told that Tarangire's elephants, for now, are holding their own in a relentlessly hostile, ever-encroaching world.

Sadly the park's rhinos haven't fared so well. The only rhinos you will see today are the black metal ones that adorn the park gates. Yet when my early safari partners and I first went to Tarangire in the late 1970s at least two, sometimes four, would be visible from the terrace of the "Tented Camp" itself, suggesting that many more were hidden away throughout the park. By the early 1990s numbers had dropped so drastically that we no longer expected to see any, a situation that seemed to mirror the wider picture, for it was estimated that the numbers of black rhinos in Africa fell from 65,000 in 1970 to 2,300 by 1993.

We were privileged, in those early days, to see Tarangire as it must have been long before it was gazetted as a Game Reserve in 1957 and later as a national park in 1970. And privileged too in having the place pretty much to ourselves. We also had access, in effect, to our own private campsite. It was known as Campsite No. 3 but its fine location belied its typically pedestrian designation. It was situated on the edge of the escarpment overlooking a broad bend of the Tarangire River, with the long swells of the Maasai Steppe and distant, isolated hills to the south and the mosaic of grassland and bush and stands of palm beyond the river to the west. The campsite itself sloped gently down to the escarpment edge, where moderately high cliffs fell steeply to the river. A twin-trunked baobab (until it disintegrated) stood at the upper end of the site on an old termite mound, with a water stand-pipe at its foot, and away to one side, like a sheepish-looking sentry box, was the usual long-drop lavatory.

The campsite, like that of its "Fig Tree" counterpart in Ngorongoro, is now reserved as a picnic site for the safari companies and their clients. I have only been once since its transformation and I hardly recognized the place. The long-drop lavatory had been replaced by a smart toilet block that even had gob-stopper-sized naphthalene balls, in various pastel colours, in its urinals. And (an unthinkable luxury in the old days) there was toilet paper in its cubicles. The cliff edge by which we used to pitch our little tents had been fenced off, presumably to prevent those tourists who don't know a cliff edge when they see one from falling headlong into the river 40 metres below. Much of the rest of "No. 3" has been designated as a parking area, each allotted space marked out neatly with white-washed stones to spare drivers the difficulties of parking five or six 4WDs in a space large enough to house an Airbus A380. Such is progress; Man cannot resist imposing his will upon nature. Woman neither, for the culprit in this case was a female Chief Park Warden.

Long before this well-meaning lady came along with her revolutionary plans and a sack filled with multi-coloured naphthalene balls, Tarangire and Campsite No. 3 were uppermost in our list of safari destinations. Even the tyres of my Renault 4 would break into a high-pitched hum, as if with joy, as we cruised along the smooth dirt track towards the Tarangire entrance gate, often after the punishing drive across the Rift. Had I been a passenger and blind I would still have known, when I heard those happy tyres, that we were approaching the park gates. Arriving at Tarangire was like arriving at Paradise. Better, in fact, as almost certainly much more is expected of you in Paradise.

And arriving soon afterwards, at Campsite No. 3, was even more pleasurable. For apart from the wonderful views from the escarpment edge it was, unlike its No. 1 counterpart in Mikumi, a relaxing place, even at night. The only time I felt vaguely threatened there was on emerging from my tent one morning to be immediately "mock-charged" by a bull elephant. Even then, had the charge been serious, I could have slithered off the cliff-top to the comparative safety of a protruding ledge just beneath. Birding was also excellent on and from "No. 3". But one of the campsite's main attractions was that we were allowed to drive after dark between it and the "Tented Camp", at that time Tarangire's only lodge. A much-appreciated concession, as driving at night was strictly forbidden to other visitors, and in other national parks.

Sometimes on these nocturnal commutes we would encounter lions, ghostly and far more sinister in the headlights of a car than in daylight. More often we would come across elephants, and a variety of other big game, including "animals of the night" such as spring hares, porcupines, genets or civets. But our greatest pleasures on the campsite itself came at the end of the early morning game drive, when we would sit by the campfire enjoying a long and lazy late breakfast. Or in the long afternoons before the evening drive, when I would sit by the edge of the cliffs on my tin trunk, scanning the watercourse and neighbouring bush for whatever wildlife I could find.

Even when lions were absent from their favourite ambush stations amid the riverside bushes there was always something to see. Reedbuck, appropriately among the beds of reeds that fringed the far side of the river directly beneath; a herd of buffalo scattered like a broken necklace of blackwood beads on the green baize of the river terraces; giraffes browsing among the acacias; olive baboons foraging among the open bush or plucking nuts from the graceful doum palms; elephants, ears flapping like punkah louvres in the shade of a baobab or fig or stand of palms, or cruising by, at cooler times, in a silent grey convoy.

If Barry or Kevin or both were present, birding (and in Kevin's case bird photography) would occupy much of our time. The campsite had its own bird populations, many habituated to human presence. Not being confined to cars we could walk around at will and still get close to certain species, among them Red and Yellow Barbets, which Barry once described as being "tame to the point of exhibitionism". They would almost take food from our hands, a risky inclination here on the fringes of Maasailand, where the pastoralists often use colourful barbet feathers for decoration.

Barbets, as Barry would remind me, are related to woodpeckers. Which always struck me as odd, as in some ways they are very different. They breed in termite mounds or riverbanks rather than trees, for one thing, and woodpeckers, unlike barbets, can be as coy as Bollywood heroines, sliding coquettishly behind a tree just as you focus on them through your binoculars or camera lens. After which they will make their way up the far side of the tree until you almost dislocate your neck trying to find them again. The brassier Red and Yellow Barbet has an appropriately brazen call, a repetitive "toogle-di-doogle" that sounds like a discordant toy trumpet, often made by two or more birds in concert.

Ashy Starlings, endemic to Tanzania, were also common on the campsite. Evolution, like God, sometimes works in mysterious ways, and as Barry was fond of pointing out, the only other member of the Ashy Starling's genus is the Golden-breasted Starling. Which is almost identical in form yet brilliantly coloured, unlike the uniform grey-brown of its "twin". The two are allopatric (not found in the same areas) but another brilliantly coloured starling, the aptly named Superb, was also a frequent visitor to the campsite, as were White-headed Buffalo Weavers. I have long thought the latter name, like so many others, poorly chosen. Not because I have never seen the birds weaving buffaloes, but because, although they do have white heads, their most noticeable feature is their strikingly red rump. But then birding is an esoteric pastime, the avifaunal equivalent of train-spotting. With similarly esoteric adherents.

Casual (i.e. inept) birders such as myself tend to prefer birds that are either very colourful or big and barbaric, another reason why I loved Tarangire, for it has plenty of both. Raptors are particularly well represented and even I would get excited at seeing an African Hawk Eagle or the magnificent Martial Eagle. I must confess, however, that after a lunchtime beer on the terrace of the "Tented Camp", with various swifts and swallows weaving invisible cat's cradles overhead, and with dizzying speed, I would sometimes leave my companions to their avifaunal obsessions and drive back to the campsite in the hope of seeing lions. It wasn't just a case of birds versus large mammals; long safaris can be like long marriages, all the better at times for periods of self-imposed separation.

The "Tented Camp" (now Tarangire Safari Lodge) was, like Campsite No. 3, superbly situated along the edge of the escarpment. Its spacious terrace overlooked a sublime swathe of *Acacia tortilis* parkland that shelved gently down to the river. We would sometimes sit for hours there in the afternoons, discussing the morning's events and sightings while the swifts and swallows zipped around overhead and elephants, buffaloes, giraffes, zebras, wildebeest, impalas and whatever else came and went in the valley below. George, the "Tented Camp's" cheerful Chagga barman, would moved in unobtrusively from time to time to top up our glasses of cold lager. On Sunday afternoons, when we were often the only visitors, George would refuse to take payment for our drinks, a unilateral declaration of independence that would have displeased his boss, a Mr. Patel who lived in Arusha, but that we were never allowed to question. Neither George nor his colleagues (all Chagga) would let us buy them drinks in return.

The predominant atmosphere in Tarangire, as with all the parks and reserves, was one of tranquility charged with an undercurrent of exciting expectation, of being intensely alive and "at one with the moment". When I think about the park now, years after my last visit, I think in disconnected little cameos, as if clicking at random through an online archive crammed with old photographs and video clips. A dull brown squacco heron by the river, seen from the campsite above, bursting into snow-white effloresence as it took flight; an African Wild Cat kitten hunting grass-hoppers along the fringes of the track, at night; Fringe-eared Oryx coming in to drink one idyllic evening at the waterhole that Barry and I knew as "The Lily Pond".

The "Lily Pond", in a sequestered corner of the park by a little-used track that led to Lake Burungi, was one of Barry's favourite haunts. A dedicated birder, predisposed by nature and by the nature of his interest to long periods of observation in one particular spot, he loved the stillness and the melancholy silence that evenings in such places often bring, and that we always found there. My own inclination was to move on, to see what lay around the next bend. But I made an exception for the "lily pond". There, in the shade of a spreading fig, we would sit from late afternoon until sundown, watching birds or merely sitting in the car, doors wide open, in a beatific, almost transcendental state. From time to time elephants, zebras, wildebeeste, giraffes, impalas, eland and oryx would come down to drink and bring us back to earth. They always came to the far side of the pond, wading out into the shallows among the bright green lily pads.

In all the hours we spent there we never saw another human being. Nothing dramatic ever happened, though we saw the occasional python, never very big, and I was once alarmed, whilst trying to photograph such a snake, when a sudden crash behind me caused me to freeze. Half-expecting to see a big cat launching itself towards me I saw, instead, a monitor lizard about four feet long, leaping headlong from the thick bush. Not at me but past me, sailing into the water with a spectacular belly-flop. Such distractions were rare and generally the peace and solitude were reason enough to be there, as the evening sunlight picked out the sky-blue stars of the lilies and was shattered into splinters by the ripples of the distant shallows.

Most of our time in Tarangire was spent in the park's northern sector. Partly for practical reasons, for the tracks in the south were poorly developed and often poorly maintained, partly because the northern areas, quiet of tourists and even travellers in those days, seemed to have everything we could wish for. Splendid *Acacia tortilis* parkland; red earth hardpans where baobabs and elephants and termites imposed in different ways their will upon the land; bleak black-cotton grasslands and silent belts of *Combretum/Dalbergia* woodland, in the dry season attractively "autumnal". It was an ecosystem large and varied enough to provide us with most of the park's species of mammals and birds, the adventure that we craved and the aesthetic pleasures that are to be found in the wild disorder of the bush.

Some days were better than others. On one occasion, after the customary evening game drive, Barry and I were sitting on the cliff edge at the campsite sipping lager and looking forward to a simple dinner. The sun had dipped below the distant Rift wall, bringing a greyer unity to the bush but not yet to the river, its plaited streams reflecting the soft orange of the sun's afterglow. Suddenly Barry drew my attention to the broad river bend some three hundred metres away. Looking out and down I saw a small-headed, long-legged silhouette against the orange panels of reflected light. The unmistakable form of a cheetah. It was the first cheetah we had seen in Tarangire and we were thrilled. But it was the setting as well as the sighting that would be filed away in the photo albums of our minds, one of many award winning pictures never to be taken.

After the cheetah had disappeared I speculated as to where it might be heading. With luck, I thought, we should be able to find its tracks early the next morning, follow it up and photograph it. Failing that I could at least familiarize myself with its footprints and make sketches for future reference.

We set off the next day before the strengthening light bled colour into the monochrome landscapes. Barry, not known for leaping from his sleeping bag and bursting into song, or for the clarity of his enunciation, was murmuring, quite logically, about the illogicality of looking for cheetah tracks before the sun was up. In fact we soon found a few promising scuff-marks, though nothing conclusive. And then I lost the trail completely.

A little while later, however, as the light strengthened and we were motoring across the Englehard bridge with its powdering of fine sand, I saw cat prints, though none were distinct. A little further up the track, beyond the kopjes where we would often see klipspringers, I picked up the trail again and saw more promising prints. Stopping the car and grabbing my note-book and a pencil I got out. I had to walk back some distance to find the most suitable pugmark, the tell-tale claw marks of a cheetah clearly visible. Kneeling down, I began to sketch it.

I had only just begun when Barry, from the Renault's front passenger seat, called out in his characteristically low mumble.

"Graham!".

"Yeah?"

"Lion"

"What?"

"Lion".

"Lion?"

"LI-ON!".

I was busy sketching. "No", I responded, without looking up, "Cheetah!".

"LI-ON" he repeated.

Barry can be argumentative and so can I. A little irritated I called back "It's a bloody CHEETAH print! I'm not stupid! I can see the *claw* marks!"

"GRA-ham", came the distant voice, adding, in the kind of staccato tone that infant teachers sometimes adopt with particularly dumb children, "I-am-not-talking-about-the-cheetah-prints!. There-is-a-LI-ON!. WATCH-ING you…"

I stiffened, raising my eyes to look up along the track. Close to the car but between it and me was a lion cub, sitting on a fallen tree in the trackside scrub, staring at me. For a moment I felt relieved, even excited. Until I remembered that lion cubs have mothers. Very possessive, protective mothers. I then saw, beyond the cub, the lowered head of a lioness. She was watching me through disapproving eyes. Uncoiling slowly I stood up, knowing that Barry couldn't reverse the car as I still had the keys. I then became aware of two other, larger cubs. All eyes were now on me. Keeping my own eyes on the lioness I began to inch my way back to the car, stopping after every little step and trying to look as inoffensive as possible. Which wasn't difficult. It was a long 50 metres. Such situations are rarely dangerous but that is not how it seems at the time.

The story doesn't end there for a little further on we found the cheetah, in the most ludicrous of situations. It was on the far side of the river, lolloping away from a large male baboon that was charging after it, one of a troop that was foraging across the riverside meadow. It was like watching a Ford Fiesta chasing a Ferrari F 12. Needless to say, the cheetah, without sacrificing too much feline self-esteem, kept just far enough ahead to avoid being overtaken.

I never saw another cheetah from the campsite but in the dry season lions were never far away. After leaving Barry and Kevin birding at the Tented Camp one afternoon I arrived back at the deserted campsite to find long lines of zebras and wildebeeste edging down the nearby wooded defile to the river. A route to water – and sometimes slaughter. Among the low bushes at the far side of the river several lionesses and their adolescent young were lying in wait. The zebras were nervous, holding back, while the wildebeeste, more thirsty or less cautious, filed closer to the river. The lions watched them come.

And so did I. Now and again the leading zebras, perhaps catching vague whiffs of lion on the light, capricious breeze, wheeled around, causing the procession behind to dissolve into temporary whorls of panic. Then the need to drink would reassert itself and the stop-start procession would move forward again. Eventually the wildebeeste at the head of the column spilled out on to the grassy flats by the river. Some then stepped out on to the sandbanks in midstream. All herbivores can be unwary at times but wildebeeste sometimes seem driven by a death wish. And death wishes, in the African bush, are readily granted.

Despite the fact that there was plenty of water in midstream some of the wildebeeste, lured by a slightly deeper pool by the far bank, wandered over to satisfy their thirst. Within 20 metres or so of the lions, now crouching like coiled springs. With each passing second I expected the predators to come bursting from the bushes. It didn't happen. Experienced lions, especially females, know that a moment's impatience can make all the difference between feast or famine. After a few brief drinks the wildebeeste, perhaps growing instinctively uneasy, moved back to the greater safety of midstream, where many of their counterparts were now gathered. The zebras had stopped a little way up the declivity, frozen into a suspicious stillness.

The patience of cats is well known but when you are watching lions stalking prey, or close to ambushing it, time seems to pass with glacial slowness. Their self-control at such times is astonishing. So much so that I have often felt, after watching an unsuccessful hunt, that more impulsive tactics might have proved more productive. On this occasion, after long minutes of tension and expectation, I risked putting down my binoculars in order to pick up my note-book and pen from my nearby tent, so that I could scribble a few observations. In those few moments two of the lions must have charged from cover. I heard a commotion and looking down saw the wildebeeste surging back up the slope in great scallops of dust, causing the zebras to charge off also. The wooded defile drummed with hoof-beats.

Out on the sandbanks where the wildebeeste had been drinking a solitary lioness lay panting. A few metres away the body of a wildebeest calf lay motionless. Then I saw a second lioness, lying some metres away from a second lifeless calf. Neither lion seemed interested in eating and more surprisingly none of the younger lions had broken cover. Through my binoculars I saw that both calves were unmarked, as if merely sleeping in the sun, the lionesses like innocent bystanders. Yet in less than thirty seconds, two living beings, their blood still warm, their flesh no doubt still trembling, had been swatted into eternity.

Lions often featured in our most exciting moments. On one of my first safaris to Tarangire I was with John, in the Renault. Feeling adventurous one morning I had chosen to drive south to the Gursi Swamps. Few people, even park rangers, ventured so far south in those days, and we were probably the only visitors in Tarangire at the time. So when we broke down in the late morning, close to the Gursi (and a pair of mating lions), I was worried. Not because of the lions but because the clutch cable had snapped and we were a long way from the park headquarters, the Tented Camp and the campsite.

Walking forty kilometers, unarmed in big game country, is far less dangerous than many people might think but it wasn't a pleasant prospect either, especially in the heat of the day. So I was relieved when John, the most practical by far of my safari partners, revealed that a car can be bump-started without engaging the clutch. The secret, he said, was push-starting it in first or second gear and turning on the ignition at the critical moment. The problem then was that changing gear whilst on the move was practically impossible. Nonetheless, driving back to the campsite in first or second gear was better than walking.

John was not too keen to get out and push with the two lions looking on. They were about eighty metres away and like most love-lorn creatures, self-engrossed. John eyed them warily from the safety of his seat. "They might go away soon", he murmured, his knowledge of mating lions more limited than his knowledge of cars. "They won't", I assured him. He mulled on this for a few moments then, with some reluctance, said "Right. But first we need to turn the car around". This made sense, as a three-point turn without a clutch was out of the question and to drive off the track in order to turn would have resulted in four flat tyres, for the bush was spiked with young thorns.

We slid outside, causing the lions to snap into red alert mode. Lions treat people in vehicles as if they don't exist, but step outside and they react at once. This pair was too far away to be menacing and after giving them time to adjust we began to manoeuvre the car around. Once it was facing in the right direction John, with a quick glance towards the lions, said "Right – get back in and put it in first and I'll start pushing. Switch on the ignition once it's moving but don't get carried away and go racing off!"

The Renault started more easily than I had expected and in my excitement I forgot John for a moment and the Renault surged forward. I heard him yell out and almost braked, which of course would have stalled the car. He soon came running alongside and, throwing open the front passenger door, flung himself into his seat, growling something about me "charging off like Niki fucking Lauda" (then a top formula one driver). Laughing inadvisably I suggested that a Renault 4 in first gear was hardly comparable to a 3,000 cc Ferrari, before adding, just as inadvisably "And incidentally, you should never run away from lions – cats are programmed to chase moving objects". This elicited a predictably profane response. Glancing in the rear view mirror I saw that the lions had leaped to their feet, more from alarm than murderous intent.

Once we had left the lions far behind John told me that it *is* possible to change gear without a clutch, if you choose the appropriate moment, but I was in no mood to experiment. First gear was fine with me in the circumstances though I had to drive as slowly as I could to avoid overheating the engine. Eventually, at the top of a downhill stretch, John asked me to stop and put the Renault into second gear, while he push-started it again. The car, with gravity on its side, started without a hitch. An hour or so later, still in second gear, we reached the Tented Camp, dehydrated and tired but exhilarated. So much so that we decided to stay around, have a few celebratory drinks and treat ourselves to dinner. By 8 pm, after a good meal and more drinks than intended, we got the friendly camp staff to shove us off, again in second gear, and bloated with lager and the optimism it inspires, set off cheerfully into the night, towards the campsite.

The Renault's headlamps were pathetically weak and corroded into permanent misalignment. The nearside one shone upwards and to the left, as if designed to highlight nocturnal birds or animals that might be perched in roadside trees. The offside lamp projected a broad cone of light that dimmed alarmingly as it expanded, leaving me to guess what lay beyond. So I almost braked and stalled the car when a civet, its silver-grey coat heavily spotted with black, suddenly dashed across the track ahead of us. Civets, predominantly nocturnal, are beautiful creatures and incidentally surprisingly plucky (I have seen one successfully defend itself against two full-grown lionesses) but their sense of self-preservation on the roads at night is abysmally poor. Most of the civets I have seen have been pasted to the tarmac like little oriental rugs. To have been flattened by a Renault 4 travelling in second gear, however, would have been unthinkable even for a civet and this one made it safely across before vanishing into the adjacent bush.

Soon we were cruising down the long slope towards the Englehard Bridge. It was a moonless night but ahead we soon saw the shadowy forms of two more love-lorn lions. The male was plodding hopefully down the slope behind the female. Unable to stop without John having to get out and push me into a restart we motored past. The lions, now ghostly grey in the pale headlights, gave us a sidelong glance as we cruised by. "Thank God for that" said John, "But I'm bursting for a pee. Can you stop once we get well away from these buggers? It'll be easy to start again on this slope".

I too badly needed a pee but the choice of a convenient stopping place was soon out of the question. For ambling up the middle of the track towards us was a large bull elephant. To have tried to squeeze past it, with inches to spare, could have been disastrous. "Oh fuck!" moaned John as I braked and stalled the engine. We were now stuck. The elephant, as often happens with bulls encountered on the track, seemed determined to be as awkward as possible. He now turned sideways on, blocking the track completely, and toyed apathetically with the roadside grasses, like a child playing with food he no longer wants. Somewhere behind us in the darkness and the silence the lions were padding down the slope towards us.

Lions mean little to a swollen bladder. "To hell with it", said John, opening his door, standing with his back to the car and directing a jet of processed lager into the darkness, hopefully to leeward. I followed suit on the other side. The side, I couldn't help thinking, on which the two lions would soon show up. Meanwhile the elephant was still blocking the track ahead, some thirty or forty metres downhill. The capacity of the human bladder can seem amazing, and we were out of the car for much longer than either of us thought prudent.

The lions must have been close. Being cats, predisposed to choose the most comfortable of options, they would not have left the track. The elephant, being a bull with stubbornness embedded in its D.N.A, now made a troubling situation worse by advancing slowly up the track with a macho elephantine swagger. Still outside the car, feeling physically relieved but uneasy with our dilemma, I asked John if we should try to start the car and risk slipping past the elephant or get back inside and sit it out? "Let's give it a go", I said, before he could respond. "It won't take much to start it on this slope..."

"It isn't you who does the pushing!", muttered John, "And with lions (he gave a searching glance behind him) breathing down my bloody neck for the second time today!" But the lager had inflated our self-confidence as well as our bladders and ordering me to get back in he soon began to push. The car started at once and John raced up and jumped in. The elephant was now almost upon us but I had no choice but to keep going. The big bull, stopping to confront us, swerved and recoiled into pre-charge mode as we squeezed between him and the roadside bush. With a great shake of his head and flapping of ears he turned and crashed into the undergrowth, rounding on us again to scream his displeasure. The full-bloodied scream of an elephant, at close quarters (and especially at night), can be terrifying but it is has its lighter side; elephants intent on trampling you into the dust tend to do so in silence. "My God!" gasped John, "What next?"

We soon found out. For as we approached the Englehard bridge and swept off on to the secondary track that led to the campsite we ran into a whole herd of elephants, of which the lone bull had been a mere outrider. Forewarned by the enraged bull and furious at our intrusion they crashed and screamed on either side, largely disembodied by darkness. In their panic and outrage (there were several young calves) they charged back and forth across the track, trumpeting as if hired to herald the Day of Judgement and strike fear into the souls awaiting retribution. Half expecting to be smashed to pulp but high on adrenalin and alcohol I could only keep going. Soon, engine straining in second gear, we were climbing up to the top of the escarpment. As the track levelled off again, with the hullabaloo some way behind us, John said "I'll sleep tonight".

Two brushes with mating lions, and two with angry elephants, was enough excitement for one day. But a few years later I had yet another interesting encounter with mating lions in Tarangire. I was still driving the Renault 4 but my companion on this occasion was Kevin. His main interest on safari was photographing birds but he wasn't a man to pass a pair of mating lions without reaching for his camera. So when we came across them, resting side by side close to the track after their latest copulation, he urged me, quite unnecessarily, to stop.

He had a photo-journalist's (i.e. ruthless) approach to his pastime and as the lions were on my side he leaned over, his robust frame pressing me back against the seat as he used me as a human tripod, his elbow lodged in the crook of my neck. His jostling movements annoyed the male lion as well as me. Its body language, unwelcoming to begin with, became threatening as it crouched, ears flattened, canines bared, face wrinkled with menace.

The female seemed to find her consort's aggression sexually arousing, for she immediately "propositioned" him, as lionesses do, rubbing her flank seductively along his in tail-curling anticipation. The male needed little encouragement and was soon astride her, pumping away with that absurd combination of absent-mindedness and concentration that transfixes male faces, like those of infants on potties, when their basic bodily needs are being gratified. Kevin, with similar self-absorption, clicked away.

On reaching a climax the male, as male lions do (no one seems to know why) lowered his head to grab the female's nape, as she, again characteristically and just as bewilderingly, rounded on him with a snarl and a vicious show of teeth, causing him to dismount and leap to one side in a most undignified way. He redirected his resentment at us, and for a moment I thought he might charge. But after growling and grimacing he stalked off a little way and collapsed in a feline flop. The lioness, meanwhile, walked towards us, passing by my open window with nothing more than a cursory glance.

Kevin heaved himself back into his own seat, and thrust his head through his open window to follow her progress. "Hey!" he called out softly, "She's climbing the tree behind us!" And then, with even more excitement, "She's going out on a branch! Right over the track! Back up! Back up!" In the rear-view mirror I saw the lioness standing on the hefty branch under which we had recently passed. I switched on the ignition, causing the male lion to sit up and snarl. Waiting until he had flopped again, with Kevin growing increasingly impatient, I slowly began to reverse. Kevin, eager for an unusual photo-opportunity, directed me. "Left a bit – bit more – back a bit – back a bit – another yard…". And, in a final flurry of exclamations, "That's it! Perfect! Hold it there! She's lying down now! I'm *right* underneath her! I switched off the engine as Kevin squeezed his head and enough of his shoulders through the small window space to allow him to point his lens vertically upwards. "Great angle!" he whispered. The lioness, now invisible to me, must have been about ten feet above his head. In those pre-automatic days Kevin was not the fastest gun in the west when it came to focusing. Seconds seemed to stretch into minutes. Then I saw him stiffen, bracing himself for the first of many shots.

Just as he whispered "This is *fan-TAS-tic!*" there was a great, splintering detonation as the heavy branch above us cracked. I instinctively ducked, expecting the roof to be crushed as the branch and the lioness crashed on to it. Kevin yelled out in alarm, somehow yanking his head, shoulders, arms and camera back through the small window frame in one highly-motivated movement.

Physics was my weakest subject at school but it didn't take an Isaac Newton to know that the branch and the lioness were about to hit the car's roof with catastrophic (the first syllable quite appropriate) kinetic energy. Something had to give, and that something was the Renault's roof. This was confirmed a moment later by a mind-numbing crash, followed by a dense flurry of falling leaves and other debris, and the inevitable, dry season cloud of dust.

Fortunately the lioness had flung herself to one side in mid-air, almost combing Kevin's hair with her flailing paws before hitting the ground with a thump. More fortunately the heavier and lower end of the branch must have hit the ground a split second ahead of the rest, absorbing much of the impact. The lioness, more interested in saving face than in Newtonian physics, sprang up growling with fury, amid the falling leaves and choking dust, directing her anger at the innocent Renault. This triggered off the male, who had also leaped up and was now approaching the car in a snarling, tail-thrashing temper.

The lioness, remembering that cats were created to give dignity a living definition, suddenly recovered her composure. I could almost hear her saying "Pull yourself together, woman!" as she shook herself off and walked past us as if we and the Renault and the fallen branch didn't exist. She rejoined the male, distracting him from his own undignified antics and the two of them withdrew a little and settled down to lick themselves back into a better mood.

Meanwhile the shallow dome of the Renault's roof had been pushed inside out by the impact of the falling branch. Miraculously it hadn't split. The fallen branch was still in place, however, but with some pulling and heaving through the car's open windows we were able to manoeuvre it backwards until it fell to earth with a thud, bringing the male lion momentarily back to his feet. We then pushed against the downward-bulging roof and it popped back into its former shape with a loud metallic "boink!", bringing the male lion to its feet yet again. "Could have been worse, Gray", said Kevin, "We could have been in a convertible".

Soon, with the Renault's roof and bonnet still adorned with small branches and leaves, we decided to press on, arousing the male lion to yet another show of anger. Leaping to his feet he faced us with an "enough is enough!" kind of growl, tail-tip twitching. Our path was now blocked but in the end I drove off the track, intending to outflank the lions and hoping that I was not driving over any thorns. The lion stood his ground but we bounced around him, tyres intact.

Despite such incidents, and despite the fact that once away from the lodge and the park headquarters we were usually entirely out of contact with the outside world, my companions and I always felt at home and secure in Tarangire. Campsite No. 3, as I have said, was rarely visited by big game and as our safaris to Tarangire were almost always in the dry season, when the park is at its best, we never got bogged down in mud. The "Tented Camp", with its friendly, helpful Chagga staff, was another comforting factor, for more often than not it was within an hour or two's drive or, had we ever broken down completely, an uncomfortable but manageable five or six hours' walk. Of all the East African parks Tarangire was the most relaxing. And amongst the most rewarding.

CHAPTER XVII

In Grandmother's Garden

The huge Selous Game Reserve, its nearest point a 250 km (155 miles) drive south-west of Dar, via pot-holed tarmac and sometimes rough dirt track, was a very different prospect. We only ever visited its northern sector but even this, in the late 1970s and the 1980s, was relatively little-visited. Its sparse network of tracks, unmapped and unmarked, wound through woodland and thorn-bush, black-cotton grasslands, green river terraces and the delightful plains that rise and fall like a gently billowing sea beneath the Beho-Beho hills. Through all of which the Rufiji River writhes in sinuous sweeps to its mosquito-ridden, mangrove-matted delta. This sprawling wilderness, bigger than Denmark or Switzerland, is paradoxically known in Swahili as *"Shamba ya Bibi"* – "Grandmother's Plot (or Garden)".

Some garden! When I first went to live in Tanzania in 1977 I was given an old Shell map of the country. I remember being astonished at the area taken up by the Selous. But I was also intrigued by a tiny black cross printed in its north-eastern corner, labelled "Selous' grave". I love maps and would often pore over this one, my eyes always drawn to that little cross. The grave that it symbolized, I thought, might now be overgrown with bush or buried under the silt of the Beho-Beho River, but "One day", I told myself, "I will go there and find out".

Two years passed before I did. Two colleagues, Rebecca and Fiona, had been invited to Beho-Beho Safari Camp by its white Kenyan manager, Alex. The camp was otherwise closed for renovation and Alex had suggested that the girls join him for four days during the long school holidays. Rebecca, knowing how keen Kevin and I were to go to the Selous, had asked Alex if we might go along. He had kindly agreed, on condition that Kevin and I brought our own tents, as most of the camp's cabins had been dismantled. We and the girls were to travel down in Rebecca's Land Rover.

Kevin and I, true to our independent, sometimes chauvinistic spirits, had been a little wary. Alex had the reputation of being a "Kenya cowboy" (white Kenyan adrenalin junkie with abundant machismo and accountable, at least in colonial times, to no-one). "KC's", as they were known, could also be extremely hospitable and friendly, as Alex proved to be, but in any case the opportunity to spend four days at Beho-Beho, a splendid synthesis of hill and savannah, lake, river, sand-rivers and streams, was too good to turn down.

Two young Australian men had also been invited and had travelled down ahead of us, along with a young Brit, Guy, the son of the couple that managed the Oyster Bay Hotel in Dar, part of the parent company that owned the Beho-Beho Camp. Agatha Christie could hardly have invented a more disparate set of characters, brought together in a remote and unique location by unforeseen circumstances. And cut off completely, in those pre-mobile-phone, pre-internet, pre-tourist-saturated days, from the rest of the world in typical Agatha Christie tradition.

Rebecca and Fiona were part of a small set of fellow-teachers that Kevin and I knew, uncharitably, as "The Aunties", for their perceived bourgeois sensibilities. The Australian boys, Matt and Ryan, were happy-go-lucky back-packers and keep-fit fanatics who spent most evenings doing pull-ups from a beam by the camp bar. Guy, the Brit, was an intelligent, serious-minded young man, a cricket enthusiast and amateur astronomer who amused himself during the day by playing "Owzat", a cricket-orientated table game, and after dark by scouring the heavens through his telescope. Sadly his passion for cricket was largely passive as he had been a victim of the thalidomide scandal of the late 50s and early 60s, growing up with a badly malformed leg and epilepsy but without self-pity. His disabilities had driven rather than daunted him and he had matured into a likeable, erudite young man. His knowledge of astronomy was profound. It had led to Guy becoming a friend and protégé of Sir Patrick Moore, a well-known and well-loved (if rather wacky) astronomer and TV personality.

Lastly, of course, there was Kevin and I, with our own idiosyncrasies, interests and prejudices. And of course Alex himself, the stereotype "Kenya Cowboy" with his personal (and very "KC") pastimes. One of which was to sit at the back of the bar at night armed with a .22 rifle, taking pot-shots at the spotted hyenas that loped in to sniff around for what they could find. Not what one would expect of a safari camp manager but exactly what one might expect of a "Kenya cowboy".

Much to everyone's amazement we passed four enjoyable evenings together, playing darts, eating and drinking, telling safari stories, following the progress of Guy's "cricket matches" and exchanging inevitable Anglo-Australian insults with Matt and Ryan whilst scrupulously avoiding their gymnastic activities. Guy had also, with the aid of his telescope, entertained us from time to time with little lectures on the topography of the moon's visible face and on the southern constellations.

Star-gazing was only possible before the moon came up. On our first night it was perfectly full and bright enough to read by. Through Guy's telescope it was transformed into a crisply detailed, 3D lunar map, rather than a merely enthralling thing of sublime, ethereal beauty. When we all retired to bed on that first evening, Kevin and I to go to our tent, the others to their *bandas*, we were stopped in our tracks on the verandah by the scene that the moon had engendered.

Beyond the dark, meandering riverine woodland bordering the stream below the camp the grasslands and hills, bleached by dry season suns and winds, gleamed ghostly white, as if, whilst we had been indoors, they had been blanketed by an impossible fall of snow. To the south shone the Beho-Beho Hills, defined at their eastern extremity by the broad bulk of Kipalala. To the west stood Hatambulwa, also named Mt. Johnston after the Scottish explorer who died and was buried at Beho-Beho in 1879 (his expedition taken over by his 22-year-old countryman Jospeph Thomson, soon to acquire fame for his crossing of Maasailand). Beyond Hatambulwa rose Fuga Hill and in the distance the roller-coaster peaks of the Ulugurus. It was like walking into a noiseless, cavernous Christmas grotto.

The silence would soon be broken in a most unearthly way. Werewolves, said to be greatly affected by the full moon, do not figure in the long list of mammal species found in the Selous, but their earthly representatives do. After bidding the others goodnight Kevin and I walked off to our little tent a short distance away. To be awakened soon afterwards by the kind of sounds that surely welcome newly-arrived souls to the far bank of the Styx.

At least the sounds, unlike the dreadful calls of the tree hyraxes that I had heard when camping with Patricia in Ngorongoro, were familiar, though no more comforting. Being close to a pack of spotted hyenas in one of their frenzies, when their whoops and howls dissolve into a cacophony of hysterical giggles, is disconcerting enough when you are in a vehicle. Lying in their midst in the dead of night, protected only by the thinnest of fabrics, is very different. We huddled in our sleeping bags, wondering aloud, in low voices, if they were merely protesting against our presence or slavering with excitement at the thought of the vacuum-packed human flesh so close at hand. It didn't help to know that thanks to Alex, some of them probably had .22 bullets lodged in their backsides. Or to remember that a single spotted hyena had been known to drag a camper from his tent. By the head. There was little that we could do but "lie back and think of England". Or Papua New Guinea. Or anywhere other than Beho-Beho. As it happened the hyenas must have dispersed at some point, allowing us to fall back into an uneasy semi-somnolence.

Alex laughed about this over breakfast the next morning. But eager to please us, and assuming that Kevin and I were looking for what "Kenya cowboys" tend to call "a bit of fun", he suggested that we might go off on a foot safari along the little tributary that flowed below the camp. We could, he said, follow it downstream to where it joined the Beho-Beho, close to Selous' grave. And then, after visiting the grave, walk back to camp across the old battlefield where Selous had died. We immediately agreed.

At the time there were two game scouts at the camp, Omari, based there semi-permanently, and Edwin who was passing through. But Alex, to our surprise, insisted that we didn't need to take either of them along. "You're my guests", he said. Dismissing our uncertainty about the probability of breaching game reserve regulations he added: "It's OK, just go. Take the path down to the water pump at the valley bottom then follow the valley downstream. You'll pass through a ravine – an old male leopard hangs out there so keep your eyes peeled…" It was just what we wanted. To experience the Selous on its – and our – own terms. And the prospect of bumping into a leopard was exciting rather than discouraging.

As we were about to leave after breakfast Alex came over with his .22 rifle and handed it to me. "Take this", he said, "just in case. It's loaded so keep the safety catch on. There are nine more rounds in the magazine. I wasn't new to firearms, having, in my Naval days, become a good marksman with the Lee-Enfield .303, a rifle virtually unchanged from the model used in the First World War by British "Tommies". I had also owned a Winchester .22 and a Spanish 12-bore shotgun, with which, I regret to say, I had dispatched a small number of rabbits and hares. Thankfully this phase had passed, but I was well aware that shooting at a leopard (or any other potentially dangerous game) with a .22 was far more dangerous than not shooting at all.

But the rifle was psychologically reassuring. As we set off down the slope to the valley bottom, with me carrying the gun, I assured a sceptical Kevin that "At least the noise might scare off the leopard or whatever…"

"And if it doesn't?" he enquired from a few paces behind me.

"We die a romantic death", I replied, "With our boots on".

"I'll settle for a care home in Cleethorpes", came the response, "wearing my bedroom slippers…"

Thus uplifted we strode on. After reaching the water pump we picked our way through the steep-sided, heavily wooded ravine, proceeding in single file along the narrow strip of sand that bordered the stream, in the shade of the over-arching trees. The shallow watercourse (officially the Msini River though in the dry season hardly worthy of the definition) gurgled and swirled over and around the smooth stones and boulders of its shingle bed.

Brilliant red dragonflies hovered in the dappled light above the water, and butterflies, mostly whites, flickered past or clustered around patches of moisture on the stream's sandy banks. Among them were a few citrus swallowtails, their blue or green wings panelled like cellophane-thin stained glass. Adrenalin crackled through our nervous systems like static electricity, heightening awareness to fever pitch, all senses alert to the delights and potential dangers of the bush. The old male leopard, if around, was keeping a panther-like low profile.

After a while the high, forested banks tapered to much lower, more open levels, where we were soon faced with a dilemma. The exposed, largely sandy stream-bed on either side of the tributary thinned out completely as the stream widened. The right bank was broad and flat but cluttered with geological rubble, making walking difficult and frustrating. The left bank was thick with *Hyperhennia* grasses, almost as high as an elephant's back.

With the hubris of the relatively young and inexperienced we chose to push through the grass, following an obvious game trail, heavily stamped with the spoor of buffaloes. The high, stiff grasses and the pungent smell of buffaloes closed around us, the narrow trail littered with dark, fresh "cow pats". We could see nothing but grass on either side and little more ahead. Neither of us needed reminding that we were following a herd of large animals that experienced rangers, armed with rifles, normally treat with great respect.

"This is a pretty dumb thing to do, isn't it?", muttered Kevin behind my sweat-stained back.

"True."

"So – er – why are we *doing* it, Gray?"

"You tell me… Adventure? Death wish?"

"Trampled into two strawberry trifles, by 600 buffaloes. Is that what you call a romantic death?".

"Better than a care home in Cleethorpes…"

"Speak for yourself", said Kevin, before lapsing into what is often referred to as a meaningful silence. Within the thicket of grass the air itself was ominously silent, no hum or buzz of insects, no murmuring of doves, no thud of hoof or snort of alarm, only the muted rasp and rattle of the grass as we brushed through.

We didn't realise how tense we had become until we finally emerged into pleasant riverine woodland, when we both instinctively stopped to heave sighs of relief. Reassuringly, there were no signs of the buffaloes other than their tracks and droppings though what we did see, soon afterwards, was even more worrying. At the foot of a large, riverside fig was a great heap of dung, with two parallel scrape marks at its base. Stopping, I informed Kevin, with due gravity, as to its origins.

"Rhino".

"Shit!" exclaimed Kevin.

"Exactly, my dear Watson. And fresh shit at that – look…" I kicked the latest droppings with my safari boot.

"Whose idea was this?" demanded Kevin petulantly.

"The rhino's, I suppose. They have to shit somewhere…"

"I mean this fucking foot safari, you silly bugger…"

"Alex's", I replied, eager to shift the blame.

"Typical Kenya cowboy!" growled Kevin.

We pressed on more warily now, scanning every bush, every shadow. Expecting, at any moment, to blunder into a much-persecuted rhinoceros, eager to get its own back. As soon as the sides of the Msini's stream-bed broadened again we scrambled down the low bank and walked out towards the water-course, immediately feeling much safer. Some time later we found ourselves in a broad, flat sector of the stream, just before it bottle-necked between high cliffs, off-white and crumbly as Cheshire cheese. Between us and the cliffs the broad shingle banks on either side of the stream were scattered with bulky black boulders, presumably of volcanic origin.

Suddenly nightjars, one by one, began to rise beneath our feet in startling inflorescence, to flutter short distances, awkward as autumn leaves blown on the wind. On coming to earth they became part of it, relying on stillness and superb camouflage to escape detection. One was so reluctant to fly that it allowed

Kevin to kneel within a few feet of it, its soft colouration and cryptic markings moth-like against the shingle, eyes closed to slits to avoid betrayal by reflected light.

It didn't fool Kevin. He clicked away with his Canon, sending Kodak shares soaring. In the end the nightjar (Gabon, we had hesitantly decided) gave up its pointless pretence and fluttered off towards the bank. But soon I found another subject for Kevin's restless lens, a dead but far from faded butterfly. We discovered later that it was in fact a moth, named after Croeseus, the fabulously rich king of Lydia. Also known as the African Sunset Moth because of the Turneresque flare of orange and gold on the lower extremes of its hindwings. One of the few moths to fly by day, and as splendid as most other moths are sombre. Its predominantly black velvet wings are banded and spotted with apple green, the "sunset" flares at the tail set off by streaks of black. The colours produced not by pigment but by refracted light, which might explain why the moth was as striking in death as in life.

Kevin, enraptured, knelt down yet again to further improve Kodak's market value. I meandered on alone, in search of the next exciting discovery. And inadvertently found one. Fortunately I had proceeded slowly, stopping here and there to focus on a colony of White-fronted Bee-eaters that were wheeling and clamouring outside their nesting holes in the cliff face a little way ahead. Even as a casual birder I had always loved East Africa's bee-eaters, both resident and migrant, for their slender forms and attractive colours, though I didn't know then how intriguing their lives can be. White-fronted bee-eaters, for example, are co-operative breeders, with non-breeding individuals helping with every aspect of the nesting process, from digging the nesting holes to incubating and feeding the chicks. But there is, it seems, a darker side to this ornithological socialist idyll, for we are told that "Female white-fronted bee-eaters leaving their nesting burrows must avoid pursuit by unmated males who may force them to the ground and rape them".

Unaware of all this at the time I watched in wonder as they dipped and ducked and circled across the face of the cliffs before advancing further across the shingle. Kevin had by then completed his "Croesus portfolio" and was following me. Which was just as well. For suddenly he called my name in one of those chilling stage whispers that on an African foot safari cause you to freeze in an instant. I felt his hand on my shoulder, pulling me back. Had he not done so I would have walked into an African buffalo bull.

For several moments I stared at the buffalo, almost in disbelief, shocked to have come so close to such a large animal without it, or I, realizing it. It was hunched on the sand at the edge of the shingle bed, its huge black back towards me, its head curled in towards its body, one horn projecting outwards in a thought-provoking curve. I hadn't noticed it because at a casual glance it would have looked like one of the large black boulders by which it was surrounded. All our instincts were now concentrated on getting away. Stepping over the shingle as if tip-toeing through a minefield, we edged towards the far bank, eyes fixed on the slumbering beast, hearts thudding.

It is a common misconception that wild animals, even when resting, remain alert enough to notice the approach of a human being. But the buffalo dozed on as we moved away, hardly daring to breathe until we reached the steep bank and climbed to its crest. Looking back down we saw that there were in fact three buffaloes, amongst the scattered black boulders that, at a casual glance, they so resembled. Many more buffaloes were grazing amidst the scrub on the opposite bank. "Good job you stopped me", I said to Kevin, "I'll buy you a beer when we get back".

"*If* we get back", said Kevin.

The pessimism, facetious as it was, was not unjustified. We now found ourselves at the edge of a broad expanse of young

Hyphaene palms, which start their lives as huge rosettes of leaves. They were densely distributed and above head height. Reluctant to retrace our steps I climbed a nearby tree to plan a less adrenalin-charged route back to camp, and was pleased with what I saw. A five-minute walk through the *Hyphaene* grove, I informed Kevin from my perch, would bring us into lovely, gently undulating short-grass plains, where small groups of impala were grazing peacefully. "Five minutes is a long time in the bush, isn't that what Harold Wilson said?" Kevin responded, before reminding me that Wilson had been Member of Parliament for Huyton. "Damned sight more dangerous there than here...", he added.

Remembering my second teaching practice in Huyton (once described as "Godless" by an ex-police sergeant that I knew) I was inclined to agree. And having seen what lay beyond the grove of palms I felt relieved. Climbing down from my perch I took two slabs of *kashata* (peanut brittle), one of our safari staples, and our two water bottles from our haversack. After quickly disposing of the former and taking a few long swigs from the latter, we began to push through the palms, clapping our hands to warn off whatever might be lurking there.

We passed through without incident and were soon strolling in much more relaxed mood through the open grassland. Our adventure was not over, however. The grassland led us back towards Beho-Beho far more quickly than we had come, and we were on the high bank just across the stream from the camp when we came across a honey badger. The last time I had encountered one on foot was in Mikumi at night, wearing only my underpants and carrying a Maasai spear. At least I was now fully clothed and carrying a .22 but the honey badger's reputation for emasculating bull buffaloes and tearing car tyres to shreds was still uppermost in our minds as the creature approached.

It quickly became apparent that the animal was sick and seemingly blind. If anything this made it seem even more threatening, as it writhed a tortuous course across the grassland, wheezing and snuffling harshly. As a precaution I raised the .22, flicked off the safety catch and trained the gun on the animal, just in case. It seemed drawn to us but passed by a few metres away, its frightening array of teeth bared in pain rather than anger. It continued on its erratic course, wheezing and rasping.

"That's quite enough excitement for one morning", said Kevin, as we watched it go, "Let's get back and play "Owzat" with Guy, it's a bit less stressful…" As he said this 5,000 kilogrammes of further stress heaved itself into view over the edge of the hill. A large bull elephant, presumably after drinking from the stream below, now confronted us. Alarmed by our presence, it wheeled to face us and began to charge, ears spread and trunk tucked into a tight spiral.

Elephants can cover the ground with deceptive speed and there was nothing we could do to escape. Such "charges" are almost always bluffs but you never know this until the last moment, by which time every blood vessel in your body is fizzing like shaken-up champagne. Pathetically I raised the .22 and aimed it at the elephant's forehead. It was like trying to stop a 5-ton truck with a rubber band and paper pellet. The famous hunter Karamoja Bell shot 800 elephants using a .275 Rigby Mauser, but a high velocity .275 is very different from an ordinary .22. And Walter Dalrymple Maitland Bell, to give him his full name, was very different from me. Leaving aside the question of calmness and courage, he could apparently shoot fish dead as they leaped from the waters of a lake.

At least I had enough presence of mind not to fire the .22 and the elephant stopped, standing tall and shaking its great head with a mighty flap of ears. It gave out a piercing trumpet before hastening off, tail raised, and disappearing down the opposite side of the hill. We listened as it crashed away through the undergrowth. When all had fallen silent we breathed out for what seemed like the first time in minutes and headed down the steep-sided ravine below the camp. "All we need now", said Kevin, "is to bump into that bloody leopard…"

What we did bump into, on arriving back at camp, were two very angry game-scouts. Alex was standing with them, sheepishly. Omari and Edwin, both wearing their official uniforms, had seen us walking back. They had even witnessed our encounters with the honey badger and the elephant through Guy's telescope. They were not pleased. Omari spoke little English but Edwin informed us, quite rightly, that by walking unaccompanied in the bush and being in possession of a gun we had broken two serious Game Department regulations. The elephant, he said, could have killed us and he and Omari would have been blamed for allowing it to happen.

We deserved the dressing down and apologised. Tanzanian officials, like officials everywhere, can be bloody-minded and bureaucratic but Tanzanians, by nature and when shown respect, are quick to forgive. Edwin's prominent lower jaw and brooding disposition, however, suggested that he was in no mood to compromise. He ended his terse lecture by warning us that he would report any further transgressions to his headquarters at Matambwe Gate. This might have resulted in heavy fines and expulsion from the Reserve in the case of Kevin and I, and in Alex losing his job.

The game scouts' anger, though we didn't realize it at the time, was directed more at Alex than at us, as the young Kenyan regularly flouted Game Reserve rules. Alex now aggravated the situation by dismissing their accusations and exaggerating his authority as camp manager. The two scouts kept silent but were seething with humiliation and resentment. Alex's overbearing "Kenya cowboy" attitude, we discovered later, had been antagonizing them for months. We were now guilty by association, as well as by our own thoughtless actions, and Omari and Edwin were determined to make us pay.

They soon got their chance. Kevin and I, despite the morning's adventures, could hardly wait to go walking again. And I soon identified an objective. To the south-east of the camp, towards the eastern extreme of Kipalala Hill, rose a smaller hill, gently conical and noticeably greener than the sun-bleached grasslands that swept around its lower slopes. It had caught my imagination for reasons that I cannot explain except that it was different, and that human curiosity is a strange, unfathomable thing. Between the hill and the camp, beyond the ravine, lay the kind of African landscape that I always feel like dancing across, arms outstretched and singing with joy, like Maria in *The Sound of Music*.

Skipping through cool Alpine pastures starred with edeleweiss is one thing; cavorting across the African plains another. But I persuaded Kevin that the inviting green hill had to be climbed. "As long", said Kevin, "as we take Edwin or Omari. Armed with something more powerful than Alex's popgun..." Edwin was hovering moodily out on the terrace at the time and after summoning up some courage and contrition I approached him, pointing out the "green hill" and revealing our ambition to climb it.

The game scout, his prognathic lower jaw a perfect symbol of his stubborn nature, gazed at the hill as if he had never previously set eyes upon it. A hill, to most Africans, is an obstacle to be circumvented. Why *Mzungus*, white men such as ourselves, would want to go there, let alone climb it, was beyond his comprehension. His jaw seemed to jut out even further as he looked. But then, perhaps seeing his opportunity to teach us a lesson, he relented. "Tomollow", he announced (like many Tanzanians he pronounced his "r's" as "l's"), "we go to gleen hill. After bleakfast..."

He was back on the terrace the next morning when Kevin and I, having breakfasted early, walked over, binoculars around our necks. Kevin was carrying his camera bag and I had a haversack containing our water bottles and simple snacks. "*Twende!*" ("Let's go!), ordered Edwin, picking up his rifle, a Rigby .416. An old hunting firearm but a serious piece of kit. Gladdened by this we followed him down to the Msini in single file.

On reaching the stream Edwin turned to head through the ravine. But instead of keeping to the stream-bed as we had done the previous day he chose to follow a game trail a little way up the opposite bank. This puzzled us as it was much easier and safer to walk alongside the watercourse. It was the first sign of Edwin's quirky, obdurate mind-set and of the conspiracy, as it later transpired, between him and Omari, to punish us for our earlier misdemeanors. And for whatever humiliations they had suffered at Alex's hands.

If Edwin's tactics were intended to wrench us out of our comfort zone they soon succeeded. As we pushed through the luxuriant undergrowth I suddenly became aware of a familiar bovine smell. Moments later Edwin snapped the Rigby to his shoulder. Kevin and I froze, braced for the crash of the gun. None came. Looking over Edwin's shoulder, along the line of the rifle barrel and through the intervening foliage, I saw a dark, amorphous patch, too dark for shadows, amid the faded greenery. The neck of a buffalo. I saw the swing of its head and the spread of its horns as it turned. And then we were engulfed in an maelstrom of sound as it and the rest of the small herd, disturbed whilst coming down to drink, wheeled and crashed in panic, hooves scrabbling as they struggled to haul themselves up the forested bank.

When the clatter subsided Edwin moved on, without a word, though now with the rifle in both hands, in front of his chest. Soon we were out of the ravine and pushing through the "adrenalin grass" that Kevin and I had walked through the day before. Reassured by Edwin's gun and his readiness to use it we passed through the tall grass without incident and before long were walking through the gallery forest where Kevin and I had seen the rhino midden. Edwin marched past the pile of dung, saying only "*Kifaru* – Lino", with the indifference of an English park ranger pointing out an offending dog turd on the path.

We descended to the broadening stream-bed, where Kevin and I had seen the dead Croesus moth and the nightjars. This time I took better notice of the large black boulders, relieved to see that none of them had horns, and once again we climbed the far bank and stood at the crest, confronted by the dense thicket of immature *Hyphaene* palms, a dwarf forest of great, spiky green fans. Almost immediately, too quickly for fear or for Edwin to bring up his gun, there was a heavy jostling sound among the nearby sworls of palm and a thudding of feet.

A rhino crashed from the thicket. Had it charged towards us Edwin might just have had time to fire a shot, but the animal, blindly or knowingly, pounded past sideways on. It quickly vanished into the thicket, smashing through the young palms as if through a cabbage patch. Hardly breathing, we listened to the receding sound of its passage until all went silent. "Get the peanut brittle out, Gray", murmured Kevin at last, "I hate the thought of dying on an empty stomach".

Peanut brittle (*kashata za karanga*) and sesame seed brittle (*kashata za ufuta*), both popular in East Africa, were two of our safari stand-by's. Rich in protein and sugar they were sustaining, easy to carry and ideal during our frequent breakdowns in relatively remote areas. Right now they served as comfort food and as a distraction from the rhino. After giving one of the small, square blocks to Edwin and sharing two others among ourselves we followed the game scout (and the rhino) through the palm grove. On reaching the open grassland we scanned around for it, though Edwin, who like most game scouts and rangers had much better eyesight than ours, had already said (with some disappointment I thought) "Lino gone".

Gone – yes. But gone *where*? Back into thick cover, I would have guessed. And the only cover I could see beyond the palms was a wooded depression about half a mile away, towards which, to our astonishment, Edwin now headed. On reaching the depression he strode down into it without hesitation or the slightest rational motive. Like goslings imprinting themselves upon the nearest moving object we followed him. In the midst of the depression, choked as it was with stunted trees and tangled undergrowth, Kevin asked Edwin what we were doing there and why.

"We go to the gleen hill", the game scout answered, cryptically.

"It's a funny way to get there" remarked Kevin.

If the rhino had indeed taken refuge in the depression we were grateful not to coincide with it. Emerging unscathed, if completely baffled at this Edwinian master class in orienteering, we strode on towards the "gleen hill". After our encounters with the buffaloes and the rhino this turned out to be an anti-climax. The grass was much longer than it had seemed from afar and the hillside was strewn with dark, half-hidden rocks, making the climb to the summit, which should have been simple, frustrating in the increasing heat. On reaching the top Edwin soon banished our disappointment by pointing out two more "linos" in the valley between the hill and its higher neighbour, Kipalala.

Looking through my binoculars I focused on the area of long grass that Edwin had indicated and saw the pale grey backs of the two animals shining in the sun. Then one of them moved and I saw that it had a reddish mane. And suddenly the two rhinos became two warthogs. Edwin wouldn't believe it until he borrowed my binoculars and saw for himself. He handed back the binoculars without a word. Not that we thought any less of him; in the elastic distances of Africa and the shimmering distortions of the noon-day sun size can be deceptive and forms are often compromised by intervening vegetation. Even the best rangers and game scouts are sometimes fooled. I myself have mistaken warthogs for lions, lions for patches of grass and (many times) patches of grass and dead tree branches for lions. But Edwin, feeling that he had lost face, retreated behind his sulky facade.

From the top of the green hill we could see the camp clearly through binoculars, and the route back, across the intervening, gently quilted grassland, seemed straightforward. But our escort, whom with heavy irony we would come to know as "Edwin the Pathfinder", had other ideas. Just as he had led us, perplexingly, into the wooded depression, he soon led us up to the top of another hill, that we could easily have walked around, and back down again, like an African version of the grand old Duke of York. By now Kevin and I were tiring and becoming irritable.

"Edwin", Kevin demanded, why are we walking *over* hills when we could walk around them? *Kwa nini*?"

The game scout didn't answer but his lower jaw locked into an attitude of defiance.

"And why", I asked, "are we going *this* way when the camp (I pointed towards it) is over *there*?"

Exasperated by Edwin's sullen silence we both stopped, causing him to stop also.

"Edwin", said Kevin, "we would like to go back to the camp. Over there".

"We are going to camp", said the game scout, tetchily.

"We *are*?".

"*Ndio* – we are going camp", Edwin insisted.

"But why", I insisted, "are we not going straight to the camp, *moja kwa moja*?"

"First we go Selous' glave" he replied, with a doggedness that didn't encourage further debate. "Evlybody go Selous' glave", he said, as if it was the Taj Mahal. But sensing an impending mutiny he added "*Sio mbali sana*" ("It is not very far") and, before we could argue, led us off.

"Not very far" in Africa is much the same as "not very far" in Ireland, except that in Africa there is far more scope for exaggeration. And in Ireland, as opposed to the African bush, one is unlikely to bump into anything more threatening than an imported Aberdeen Angus bull or a native tractor driver giddy on poteen. By the time we reached the riverine woodland alongside the Beho-Beho, close to which Selous' grave is situated, Kevin and I were wilting, and though grateful for the shade and ready for a rest, longing to press on and get back to camp. Only to find that a family of elephants, as keen as we were to get out of the sun, was now blocking our path, raising querulous trunks as the acrid scent of three sweaty human bodies drifted their way.

With a shake of her head the matriarch registered her displeasure but immediately led her group off in that deceptively fast, gliding way that elephants sometimes adopt, their progress as smooth and silent as that of passing cloud shadows, even through a landscape littered, as this was, with fallen vegetation. Edwin watched them melt into the grove of doum palms before saying a quiet "*Twende*" and escorting us through the rest of the woodland, across the broad sand river and through the corresponding belt of palms beyond.

As we emerged, eyes narrowing in the noonday glare, Edwin again motioned us to stop. Using the Rigby as a pointer he indicated another elephant, this time a lone bull, a short distance away in the open bush. In fact Edwin was pointing not at the elephant but at something nearby, a flat stone slab that we hadn't noticed, half-hidden by dry grasses. "Selous glave", he said, with all the enthusiasm of a Southern Rail guard announcing Clapham Junction.

I was thrilled. For over two years, since I had seen the little black cross on my old Shell map, with the legend "Selous' grave" alongside it, I had wanted to go there. And there it was, at the lower edge of a gently shelving swathe of short-grass plain, as accessible as a grave in an English country churchyard. Except of course for the bull elephant. I watched it grazing beyond the stone slab, thinking how appropriate it was that the old hunter and soldier was buried here, on the battlefield where he had fallen, and where elephants still wander. This particular elephant, however, was not wandering as quickly as we would have liked, and it was some time before we could walk safely over to the grave.

I was struck by the monument's simplicity, a modest tribute to a modest yet intriguingly ambiguous man. I had expected a headstone or marble cross, though on reflection the elephants would have used such things as a rubbing post, with predictable results. Instead, towards the front of the plain, horizontal slab, was a stone prism bearing an engraved bronze plaque. The plaque was badly oxidised and I was obliged to lean close to it to decypher the inscription:

"CAPTAIN F. C. SELOUS D.S.O.
4TH. ROYAL FUSILIERS
KILLED IN ACTION 1917"

By the plaque was a small, dust-clouded jar, filled with the dessicated stems of what had once been wild flowers, and a few dead insects.

Selous had in fact died close to the gravelly knolls some distance away, from where the ground falls away towards the Beho-Beho. His company, having come upon members of the *Schutztruppe* (Germany's colonial army) as they retreated towards the Rufiji, had entrenched among the knolls, outnumbered by the German officers and their African *askaris* (soldiers) by about four to one. Despite this numerical superiority the German-led troops, knowing that more British forces were closing in, were beating a strategic retreat, occupying the riverine woodland along the Beho-Beho and assisted by comrades on both flanks. Selous, concerned by enfilading fire, had left the safety of the trenches to try to pinpoint the snipers responsible.

He should have known better. According to an eye-witness he had "gone forward down the slope about fifteen yards, and was just raising his glasses…when he received his first wound…". In his right side. In an attempt to regain his trench, or because of the impact of the bullet, he half-turned. A second bullet smacked into his head, killing him instantly. For a few moments the troops in the trenches behind him stopped firing, shocked at the death of such a well-known, much-loved man.

Only four days earlier, on New Year's Eve, Selous had celebrated his 65th birthday. At a time when British men over 41, despite the enormous losses on the Somme the previous year, were neither compelled nor encouraged to join the armed forces. Born in Regent's Park, London, into an aristocratic family, Selous was partly of French Huguenot descent, hence the surname. Although famous as a hunter-naturalist and a "Boy's Own" hero and role model, and a close friend of such eminent contemporaries as Theodore Roosevelt and Cecil Rhodes, he was an unassuming man with a strong undercurrent of melancholy in his make-up. One of his sisters, Annie, later wrote that he had often told her that he "would not mind dying at all, or would as soon die as live." And so, perhaps "half in love with easeful Death", he had walked out to shake it by the hand, here in this glorious big game country that was his spiritual home.

He was buried under a tamarind tree (now gone), his new helmet on his chest. And was now just five or six feet below us, for Kevin and I, out of weariness, not disrespect, had sat down on the grave. After a short time I picked up the little jar with its crumbling contents and replaced them with an inch or so of water and a posy of tiny, sky-blue *Commelina* flowers. It was to become a habit of mine over the years, though one that might not have met with Selous' approval for my funereal vases were usually empty lager bottles. An old teapot would have been more suitable, for Selous, a rarity among "old Africa hands" in being near-teetotal, had an English passion for the "cups that cheer but not inebriate".

Each to his own, though we would have welcomed a mug of tea at the time. Edwin, by now, was just as ready as we were to get back to camp, and did not demur when we insisted on doing just that. Crossing what had been a no-man's land on January 4th 1917, we must have walked close to the spot where Selous had fallen, before taking a quick look at the trenches, still perfectly recognizable though choked with dry grass. From there it was a relatively short walk to the camp.

Notwithstanding Edwin's less than magical "mystery tour" Kevin and I were still keen to go out walking, and the next morning, after breakfast and with Alex's agreement, we set off again. This time Omari, in full uniform, accompanied us, carrying a rifle and a very obvious grudge. We had not yet atoned, it seemed, for our misadventures two days earlier, as Omari was determined to remind us. His English was even more limited than our Swahili, which in the circumstances hardly mattered as he made Edwin's taciturnity seem garrulous.

His intentions, however, were clear. He was young and exceptionally fit and soon led us off down the slope towards the Msini at an uncompromising pace. And in a grim mood, like a corporal in some elite special forces unit who had been ordered, on his day off, to take two soft, would-be recruits on a route march to break their will. Kevin and I struggled to keep up with him, a disparity that had advantages as a full-grown lioness suddenly sprang from the grass, almost literally beneath Omari's boots. She raced off down the slope. Omari didn't break stride or raise his old Lee Enfield .303. "*Simba*" he growled, as casually as if he had started a hare.

"I know a fucking lion when I see one", muttered Kevin, as we watched the lioness bound across the stream below us and disappear into the bush. "But why are we *following* it? And why are we running as if we're chasing the last bus back to *Battersea*?" I had a question of my own: "*Omari, wapi tunakwenda?*" "Where are we going?" Without slowing or turning he called out:"*Labda bwawani wa viboko*" ("Maybe to the Hippo Pool"). "*Labda?*" I asked, hoping for something a little more certain than a "maybe". Getting no response I asked "Where *is* the Hippo Pool? "*Wapi?*" Omari, again without slowing or turning, waved an arm in the air with vigorous ambiguity, as irritated Tanzanian traffic policeman sometimes do in the rush hour. The gesticulations might have meant that the Hippo Pool was just this side of Hatambulwa Hill, towards which they were vaguely directed, or anywhere between it and Lake Tanganyika. "This", said Kevin prophetically, "is even worse than yesterday".

Ignoring our protests Omari splashed across the Msini exactly where the lioness had bounded over, as her paw prints in the streamside sand confirmed. Again without breaking stride Omari led us into the dense bush on the far side, following the same game trail that the lioness must have taken. Kevin and I had already assumed the kind of fatalism that comes with helplessness in potentially perilous situations, when natural fear gives way to a most unjustified insouciance.

This insouciance didn't last long for as we followed Omari through the bush and into a glade amidst a grove of palms we found ourselves hurrying towards a most unwelcoming herd of buffaloes. We were not, at first, unduly alarmed, for despite their size and fearsome reputation a herd of African buffaloes will almost always charge off when challenged, even by a single, unarmed person on foot.

And so it initially proved. As Omari marched unwaveringly on the buffaloes blinked first, wheeling and charging off with a great drumming of hooves. One small calf, however, was left behind and seeing the danger I stopped immediately. Kevin stopped behind me but Omari strode on. Predictably the calf's mother came pounding back from the forest. Omari, with no obvious fear, stopped and brought up the Lee Enfield. For the second time in two days I braced myself for the crash of a heavy bore rifle and whatever mayhem might follow. And for the second time in two days it didn't happen. The buffalo had stopped by the calf, perhaps ten metres from Omari, bristling with body language. The game scout backed down, calmly lowered his rifle and turned. "*Twende*", he commanded, leading us off at an angle to our approach route, backs to the buffalo.

The buffalo cow followed. Whenever I looked over my shoulder, which was often, she was there, keeping her distance. In situations such as this you look around instinctively for climbable trees, and somehow, in Africa, there are none. We were surrounded by trees, but trees without branches. The buffalo trailed us to the very edge of the palm grove. Even when she stopped she stood watching us, full of menace. She was still watching when I last saw her, a quarter of a mile or so behind us.

Our relief was short-lived. Omari had led us into an upward sloping expanse of *Hyperhennia* grassland. The grass was well above our heads and quite dense, but the whole hillside was also scattered, like the shingle banks of the Msini two days earlier, with large black boulders that looked like dozing buffaloes. And dozing buffaloes that looked like large black boulders. Those that were buffaloes, and they were many, rose in alarm, stampeding unseen through the grass and across the game trail. We were surrounded. Omari pressed on like a man intent on suicide. The upheaval gradually subsided as the buffaloes outstripped us, though Omari, determined to put the fear of God into us, strode after them.

And then, as if relenting, he called back "Hippo Pool *karibu sana*", pointing up the slope with his rifle, "The Hippo Pool is very close".

"Thank fuck for that", said Kevin.

The high grasses phased into more open bush and thankfully the buffaloes had vanished. At the upper extremity of the slope Omari stopped, for the first time on the trek except when confronted by the buffalo cow in the palm grove. We joined him, legs muscles aching, shirts dark with sweat. "Hippo Pool", he said, motioning downwards with the rifle barrel. Moving closer we found ourselves at the edge of a steep-sided cliff. Below us lay an oxbow bend in the Msini, where the stream, much deeper and wider than elsewhere, curved around a thickly bushed promontory, forming a large pool. Five or six hippos blew and snorted their annoyance, edging away to the far side of the pool from where they watched us distrustfully. A Green-backed Heron skulked in a bush overhanging the pool, and a Malachite Kingfisher embroidered a brilliant blue thread from one side of the pool to the other, to perch directly beneath us. Overhead a Wahlberg's Eagle rode the thermals in easy, side-slipping spirals. Kevin was already reaching for his camera. Omari, his mission to put us in our place accomplished, sat down in the shade of a small tree, his rifle on the grass beside him.

I offered him a drink from my water bottle. He refused, as African game scouts and rangers often do, no matter how hot the day or how long the walk, but he accepted a Sportsman from the packet I always kept on safari for such purposes. He was soon drawing contentedly on the cigarette and gazing in a dreamy, unfocused way towards Hatambulwa and Fuga, oblivious to the activities in and around the pool below. The tensions that had existed between us quickly eased and we were soon conversing as best we could in poor Swahili on our side and almost non-existent English on his.

Despite the language problems it soon transpired that Omari and Edwin, as we had suspected, were angry with Alex and his contemptuous attitude towards the Reserve's regulations and their own authority. Kevin and I, perceived as Alex's good friends, had unwittingly exacerbated the situation by going off unescorted on our first foot safari, two days earlier, armed with the .22. Now, it seemed, our sins had been absolved.

"The quality of mercy" did not exactly "droppeth like the gentle rain from Heaven" but here in this soothing, sequestered place, with Omari relaxing at last and no large and threatening animals to disturb us (the hippos by now as placid as poached eggs in their pool) it was conciliatory enough. Kevin and I sat down on the lip of the cliffs, legs dangling, enjoying the transformation from rigorous route march to rest and recuperation. I am not one, however, to sit still for long and after a little while, with Omari's agreement, I strolled down the slope with my binoculars to do some casual birding. "*Jihardharini viboko!*", Omari called after me, "Watch out for the hippos!", though his voice wasn't too heavy with concern.

Nonetheless, as the hillside levelled out by a narrow stream-bed, sandy except for a weak flow of water that emptied into the pool just around the corner, I proceeded cautiously, scanning the thick vegetation that crowded in on both sides of the watercourse. Normally when walking in the bush I gave such places a wide berth, clapped my hands or tossed a few rocks ahead of me to forewarn any sleeping or dozing animals, thus minimizing the risk (I hoped) of any "fight or flight" encounters. But because I was looking for birds I had remained silent.

The hippos – and hippos kill more people in Africa than any other mammal species – were aware of our presence and therefore unlikely to leave the safety of their pool, and after remaining motionless for a few minutes, eyes examining the tangles of vegetation, ears alert for the slightest disturbing sound, I relaxed. Before stepping cautiously out into the bed of the watercourse, to gain a more extensive view. A flickering movement in the bush opposite stopped me in my tracks. A grayish bird, about the size of a babbler or thrush, was flickering amongst the leaves at the base of a shrub.

Raising my binoculars slowly, for the bird was only seven or eight metres away, I began to focus in on it. For a second or two I could only see grayish patches between the sage-green leaves. Then the back of the bird sharpened into a curve but a curve that was edged by hair. I realized, with that mixture of excitement and alarm that sooner or later surprises anyone who ventures into the African bush on foot, that I was looking not at a bird but at an ear. The ear of a large animal. Too grey for a buffalo, and too close to the ground, for resting buffaloes would never lie on their sides in such thick bush. As I shifted the binoculars slightly to try to see more of the animal's head, I saw the curve of a horn against the leaf litter. The anterior horn of a sleeping rhino.

I then became aware of a movement behind me. I half-turned slowly, fearing the worst. Thankfully it was Kevin. "What have you got?" he whispered, as birders do, anxious for a glimpse of an unusual species or better still a "tick", a new one.

"A rhino's ear", I whispered.

"Bollocks!", said Kevin.

"No. Can't see *them*. Only its ear. And a horn. And (I spelled this out syllable by syllable) I-am-not-jo-king"

Kevin raised his own binoculars. "Jesus Christ your'e right…", he murmured.

"Better get out of here", I whispered, already backing away slowly and turning to climb up the slope. Kevin, after one more look at the rhino, followed. For the second time in our lives he and I had been within a few metres of a sleeping rhino, this time accidentally.

"What next?" I asked Kevin when we were far enough up the incline to speak openly, "Ripped apart by wild dogs? Strangled by a leopard?". "That's tomorrow", he said, "haven't you read the itinerary?" On reaching Omari I told him that we had "almost walked into a sleeping rhino – just down there!". He grunted his acknowledgment and took another puff at the stub of his cigarette, still looking out dreamily towards Hatambulwa and Fuga. He didn't actually say "Been there, done that, bought the T-shirt…" He didn't need to.

CHAPTER XVIII

Goodbye to Our Past,
Hello to Someone Else's...

With the onset of the new millennium came a seminal change in my life. In 2001 I retired officially from teaching to concentrate on writing and photography, and though neither led to fame or fortune they provided Anjum and I with some wonderful opportunities with regard to life on safari. After decades of driving around in mainly old and unreliable vehicles and living in small tents or cheap lodges, we bought the best safari car I ever owned, a second-hand Toyota GX Land Cruiser. And my writing and photography provided us with a few "fringe benefits" if not hard cash. Our safaris became much more upmarket.

Not immediately, for our first "New Age" safari was almost as simple as the old ones. In 2002 I was asked, by an energetic and enterprising American lady called Jeanette, if I would like to take photographs of the various ethnic groups that live around the Serengeti for a proposed book of hers. We had known Jeanette and her English husband David for some time. As trained biologists they had studied lions in the Serengeti for four years. Jeanette, widely known as "Mama *Simba*", had written a book, *Lions Share*, about their experiences and together they had produced smaller books, all illustrated by David, an artist as well as an authority on African wildlife and a dedicated conservationist.

The financial incentives for my photography were small, and as far as I know Jeanette's proposed book, *People of the Greater Serengeti,* was never published, but I jumped at the challenge as it promised great adventure. Anjum and I drove north in our recently-acquired Toyota GX and met Jeanette and David in Mto wa Mbu, by Lake Manyara. They had arranged a little excursion to Engaruka, 42 km. to the north along the western wall of the Rift Valley, so that I could photograph the intriguing ruins there.

The drive up the Rift was nostalgic as well as interesting, as the last time I had been down that way was with Vesey and my old shipmate Lofty 35 years earlier, though we hadn't gone quite as far as Engaruka. I was pleased to see that the Rift, once away from Mto wa Mbu, was still refreshingly wild, surprisingly green in places (it was April) though much drier as we drove further north. To my delight we encountered scattered groups of game, Grants gazelles, zebras, giraffes and ostriches. And surprisingly few people, though there were WaArusha settlements here and there and once, high on a bluff overlooking the track, we saw a lone Maasai herdsman watching us go by.

David had been a little wary about making the trip as "bandits" had been reported along the route in recent months and the young Maasai *illmurran* can be a law unto themselves at times. But we drove on unhindered, the dirt track narrowing and becoming more rugged as we approached Engaruka. The village lies at the foot of the escarpment beneath Empaakai and its beautiful caldera in the Crater Highlands. It was, at first sight, nothing more than an isolated, nondescript settlement, causing me to wonder why anyone would still live there, let alone why people had lived there for hundreds of years.

David drove on through the dreary huts and we arrived at a large school, in itself unattractive but beautifully located by a pleasant stream, overhung here and there by mature shade trees. And this is when Engaruka began to come into its own. We were greeted by two of the school's teachers, Israel and Vincent, Mission-educated Maasai who had agreed to act as guides. Both mild-mannered and in western-style clothes they were soon leading us slowly up the slopes in single file, following the stream.

Suddenly the screening streamside vegetation opened up, where the stream broadened into a wide pool. Beyond the pool was a sight that brought us to an abrupt halt. At the foot of low cliffs, in the shade of a great spreading fig, a large number of Maasai elders and "warriors" sat on the tree's roots or on the sloping ground, like spectators in a natural grandstand, reddish tunics standing out in the shadow, the odd spear or cattle stick gleaming silver or yellow where a stray beam of sunlight touched upon it. Many of the men held "wands", slender bare branches cut from some shrub, with their terminal leaves intact. Israel told us later that the sticks are used to "beat those people who do not come to meeting" (presumably ritually and, knowing the Maasai, with some hilarity on both sides).

I have seen tens of thousands of Maasai but never anything quite like this. It was the African equivalent of blundering into a Sioux Indian pow-wow by a tributary of the Rosebud or the Tongue in late-nineteenth century Montana, with Sitting Bull or Gall or Rain-in-the-Face addressing a hundred or so warriors. The reality was less romantic, as realities tend to be. The Maasai, we afterwards learned, were arguing about water rights. But I stood transfixed. All my instincts demanded a photograph but Israel, anticipating my intentions, murmured. "Do not take picture – they will make quarrel".

"Making a quarrel" with a hundred well-armed Maasai was the last thing I wanted. They had in any case seen us, and just as predictably ignored us, as if we were no more substantial than a whirl of dust, raised by the wind. Just for a few moments, as I looked on through a gap in the bushes and they seemed absorbed in their dispute, I was half-tempted to risk a quick shot, for the record. But prudently I let the moment pass and we moved on up the slope towards to the ruins.

The history of Engaruka has puzzled archaeologists for over a century though the ruins themselves, like many others, have little visual impact. To anyone familiar with British upland farm country they recall the dry-stone walls and sheep pens to be found on certain hillsides and fells. Except that the walls and circular enclosures at Engaruka are made of dark volcanic stone and many of their boulders have been scattered or taken for other purposes.

Such water-channels and irrigation furrows and partial enclosures that remain are to be found on once-terraced slopes above the settlement, among the coarse grasses, straggling euphorbia and stunted figs and thorns that grow on these wild hillsides. It is thought that they go back 3 – 600 years, possibly founded by the Sonjo, a small tribe now living just west of Lake Natron, who were later displaced by the Sukuma. The name Engaruka is said to be a Sonjo greeting, corrupted by the Maasai, who now dominate the region. Whatever their origins, a community of several thousand people almost certainly flourished on these irrigated inclines while Shakespeare was writing his plays, perhaps long before. They grew sorghum as a staple, though cattle, perhaps stall-fed, were kept in the once-circular pens.

I photographed the ruins with Jeanette acting as a somewhat eccentric model, sitting inside one of the pens or standing by an irrigation ditch. She was wearing a colourful shawl over her jaunty hat like some bizarre mediaeval queen, bright eyes gleaming from a face lined and tanned by the suns and winds of the Serengeti and yet somehow, despite the tufts of grey hair showing from under the hat, still girlish, still glowing with curiosity and still in love. With life, with the natural world, with Africa and, I suspect, with David.

Some time later, on the way down, we passed the spot where we had seen the Maasai. The meeting had broken up and the old men had gone. Most of the *ilmurran*, the young "warriors", were making their way downstream ahead of us. But in the pool, two of them, splendidly built and completely naked, bathed unselfconsciously in the cool waters, like statues sculpted from blackwood by an African Michelangelo. Again, I was tempted to photograph them, but I didn't need Israel to warn me of the consequences. Nearby, two *ndito*, unmarried girls, were cleaning cooking pots in the stream, and chatting, as they worked, with the two men.

It was an enchantingly innocent cameo, the late afternoon light near-perfect for photographs, but fearful of a "quarrel" we moved on. On reaching a pleasant meadow upstream of the school, we thanked and paid and bid goodbye to our guides, while we stopped to rest and enjoy a late picnic lunch in the shade of a huge fig. As we were standing by our friends' Land Rover eating our sandwiches and drinking our tea a group of about twenty *ilmurran*, coming down from the meeting, swung into sight, and being Maasai came over to confront us.

They all carried spears and looked as wild and healthy and excitable as young lions. Facing us on a broad front, two metres away, they stared at us eye-to-eye with typical *ilmurran* self-assurance. David greeted them in Swahili and invited them, in the African way, to share our food. They dismissed our puny sandwiches with a collective glance and without comment, as if we were offering them dog biscuits. One could speak a little English, and demanded that we photograph them. David asked how much and the young man came up with an absurd fee. We laughed, and so for a moment did he, before interpreting what was going on for the benefit of his friends.

For some minutes we haggled, unsuccessfully – the Maasai know their value. The spokesman stared at us for a few long moments, then without even a shrug turned and jogged off, followed by the others, hurling their spears ahead of them in long arcs, partly for the hell of it, partly, I suspect, as a show of contempt for our *Wazungu* values. Of all the traditional Maasai I ever encountered these were the most authentic, the closest I ever came to the Maasai that Joseph Thomson first encountered by Kilimanjaro in 1883.

We were soon to find ourselves among two other fascinating ethnic groups that live along the southern shores of Lake Eyasi, south-west of Ngorongoro Crater. David and Jeanette had built a house, with a studio for David and a simple outbuilding for guests, on the banks of the lovely Chem-Chem stream by the village of Mang'ola, a two-and-a-half hour drive from Karatu in the Crater Highlands. We were now to spend a few days with them there, before heading off by ourselves to Ngorongoro and the Serengeti.

Mang'ola lies just south of the lower slopes of Oldeani, "Mountain of Bamboo" and close to the north-eastern corner of the seasonal Lake Eyasi, in a branch of the Great Rift Valley. I had been there twice before, once on a day trip with Anjum and once on a short expedition with a low-budget safari company, when I had camped alone in a small tent by the Chem-Chem. These trips had given me a brief introduction to the Datoga people, a pastoralist cluster of clans that, like their former enemies the Maasai, were devoted cattle herders. And to the very different Hadzabe hunter-gatherers, the most interesting, in my opinion, of all East Africa's tribal groups.

On our first trip a local Datoga guide, Momoya ("Locust") had accompanied Anjum and I to his uncle's *gheida* (family homestead) out on the wind-swept plains, where I had photographed the women, some of them strikingly good-looking, at their morning milking. Later I had photographed some of the girls in their exquisitely beautiful, beaded ceremonial dresses and necklaces fashioned from concentric rings of polished brass. That afternoon Momoya, without going into detail, invited us to another, more distant *gheida* "to see a ceremony".

Anjum declined because of the sickening heat but Momoya and I set off. We arrived when the sun was at its highest, reducing shadows to a minimum and reflecting from the hard-baked earth with suffocating intensity. The *gheida* seemed deserted. It consisted of a few huts, haphazardly placed alongside an irregular open space. In the centre of the open space was a large, conical structure made of heavy logs and hard-packed earth. I would normally have asked Momoya about this but the heat had sucked my curiosity dry and in any case Momoya had gone over to the nearest hut to converse, from the doorway, with someone inside. In his absence I set up my tripod in the hope of getting some photographs.

I heard women's voices, excited and angry. Looking up I saw the heads and shoulders of three older women, clothed in black tunics and peering at me resentfully round the doorposts of the hut. Without taking their eyes off me they were mouthing their obvious disapproval at Momoya. He, with a rueful smile, shuffled over to explain. "They are afraid of your tripod", he said. They think you are making magic, that you will put a spell on them. It is best to put it back in the car".

I immediately dismantled the tripod, returned it to its case and took it back to the car, watched by the women. At Momoya's bidding I then sat on the ground by another hut, keeping my camera out of sight and drawing up my knees to squeeze as much of me as possible into the hut's scant shade. Momoya returned to the three women and began to talk to them quietly. After some time he came over. "They have agreed", he said. They will sing for us. You can take photos but only from here". He sat down alongside me.

And soon the women, after vanishing into the hut, reappeared and stood side by side in the doorway. They began to sing a dirge-like chant in thin, mournful voices. As they chanted they swayed backwards and forwards from the waist, rubbing the heavy brass bangles on their wrists together in rhythmic, off-key accompaniment. A fourth woman joined them, beating time with a stick on a stiff piece of cowhide or goatskin. And cautiously I began to photograph them.

It was more like a funeral than the wedding that I was expecting. Momoya had never said what the ceremony was about so now I asked him directly. "It is for this man", he said, nodding towards the cone-shaped structure. "Which man?" I asked naively, staring bemusedly at the conical mound. "The man inside this thing, this *bung'ed*", replied Momoya solemnly. It was only then that I realized that the ceremony was a kind of wake. The man that Momoya was referring to was dead. And buried under the *bung'ed*.

"He was a *bwana mkubwa*", Momoya explained, "A big man". "When such a man dies among the Datoga there is no ceremony as with your people. He is buried in a shallow grave and a *bung'ed* is built over his body, with stones and wooden poles and earth. Just as you see it. During this time people put milk and beer through holes in the side of the *bung'ed*, for the dead man After about six months all the man's relatives and friends and all the Datoga from many miles around come to celebrate. There will be *ngomas* [dancing and drumming[and much *pombe* will be drunk. A black bull and many other cows and goats will be slaughtered, there will be lots of meat. Near the end of the ceremony the eldest son of each of the dead man's wives will climb this *bung'ed* one by one and place honey beer and tobacco in a hollow at the top, for the dead man. Also grass, which to pastoralists like ourselves is – how do you say?"

"Sacred?"

"Yes, sacred. They will also place the dead man's stick and sandals there, for his use in the next world".

I stared at the *bung'ed*. Its pyramidic form and the provision of food and drink and material goods to sustain the dead during the afterlife brought to mind the burial ritual of some minor Pharaoh. Except that the *bung'ed* is not expected to last. "After the ceremony", Momoya continued, "these huts will be destroyed and the dead man's family will move and build a new *gheida* somewhere else. Slowly the *bung'ed* will be worn away until it is like an old termite mound. But always, as with a termite mound, a tree will grow from the old *bung'ed*. All over our lands there are trees growing from the graves of important men. They are known to our people. This is how we remember our important men – our…" He seemed to be searching for the right word. "Ancestors?"

"Yes", our ancestors".

It was, I thought, a wonderful way to be remembered. As long as you were important, that is, and, in this very male-dominated society, a man. This thought reminded me that in this semi-deserted *gheida* we had so far seen only four women. Just as I was about to ask Momoya where the men might be one appeared, as if from nowhere. Like the women he was clothed in a black shift. In one hand he held a cattle stick. He was standing erect, as if at attention, at the far side of the compound, and without preamble he began to leap stiffly up and down, as the Maasai *ilmurran* sometimes do, though unlike the Maasai he leaped alone and in silence. It was as if he was rehearsing for the ceremony, completely oblivious of Momoya and I.

A fifth woman had also materialized, squatting on the ground beyond the leaping young man, her black robes drawn up over her head to shield her from the sun's ferocity. Even from a distance she looked impossibly old, the skin of her face and hands stretched over the underlying bones like vellum and patterned with lines so fine that they might have been drawn in ink with an architect's pen. She was neither looking at the young man nor at us, staring, it seemed, into time rather than space. Her lips were drawn open as if by pain or scarcely bearable grief, exposing what remained of her teeth. "She is the dead man's first wife", said Momoya.

The four women had stopped singing and vanished into their hut. The young man who had been dancing also disappeared as he had come, without a word or gesture. Only the very old woman remained, one claw-like hand closed over her necklace of twisted yellow beads like a despairing nun clasping a rosary. Neither she nor anything else moved, including, it seemed, the sun, for the shadow of the hut by which we sat was as narrow as ever and the heat acute.

"Where is everyone?", I asked Momoya. For a few seconds, perhaps feeling that he had let me down, he didn't reply. Then he said "They will come. Many people. There will be dancing and singing and feasting, maybe for ten days. Special huts will be built for them when they arrive. They come from far, many miles". He might have added "But this is Africa..." and left it at that, but he didn't. "Perhaps they will come soon", he said. "Or maybe this evening". Or maybe, I thought, tomorrow or the next day or... But to please him I sat by his side, hunched in the inadequate shade, and lapsing into an unquestioning, African-style state of acceptance we waited. And waited. And I knew that I would never photograph or see the ceremonies and that in the end it didn't matter. Eventually, still without speaking, we got up and stretched and Momoya went to thank the women who had sung, and pay them. And then we drove back to Mang'ola.

The next day Momoya took us to Ghorofani, a low hill a little way outside Mang'ola, to see the local Hadzabe hunter-gatherers. Away from the Chem-Chem River that waters the area the land has a stark, semi-desert quality. As we walked up the stony, scrubby hillside after parking our car we found ourselves entering an expanse of dessicated open bush enlivened by greener thickets of wild sisal. It wasn't until Momoya stopped and said "We are here" that I realized that some of the vegetation had been woven into simple, dome-like shelters, almost indistinguishable at first from the living bush from which they had been created. And that we were being watched.

We had stepped not only into a different world but into a different age, and a lifestyle that had changed little in 10,000 years. As we stood, half-astonished, half-entranced, a short, sturdily-built man appeared from the bush to greet Momoya and speak with him in Swahili. The Hadzabe, or Hadza as they are often known, have no hierarchical system but this man, whom Momoya introduced as Onwas, was obviously the unofficial leader of his group. Probably because he was respected but also because he spoke fluent Swahili and a little English at a time when the Hadzabe at Mang'ola were becoming, for better or worse, a tourist attraction.

For the next few hours we were introduced to the Hadzabe way of life. Some of the men and older boys showed off their archery skills using longbows so powerful that I could hardly draw one back more than a few inches, and with an accuracy that would have had Robin Hood whistling with approval. Later some of them made arrows and arrow-heads and twisted bowstrings from buffalo tendons that had been teased, by a woman using her teeth and palms, into workable threads. We watched Onwas create fire, within a minute or two, using only an arrow shaft, a small block of wood and a little dry grass. We were shown arrow-heads daubed with a black, tar-like poison boiled and rendered down from the thick white sap of the desert rose and wrapped, for safety's sake, with strips of antelope skin. And later, as they sat on the ground in a circle and relaxed, we saw the men smoking *bhangi* from a single, spindle-shaped pipe of light stone that was handed from one to the next, two of the men breaking out in a fit of almost ritualistic coughing.

None of them, when standing, were much taller than their bows, which were about five to five-and-a-half feet long. The men looked strong and healthy though many are said to suffer from tuberculosis and some from AIDS. All were bare-chested, clad only in old shorts or more occasionally a loin-cloth, and sandals cut from old car tyres. They carried hunting knives at their belts. The only woman we saw was sitting straight-legged by a fire under one of the primitive shelters, cooking onions in one pan and melting down coloured plastic bottles in another, from which she would later make beads. She was wearing a simple, ochre-coloured shift and a necklace of home-made blue and green beads. Just outside the shelter two very small, naked and pot-bellied boys were firing arrows into a wild sisal root with tiny bows.

The Hadza are believed to number at most only 1,500, split into semi-nomadic kin groups of 20 – 40 that live along the southern shores of Lake Eyasi, with a smaller outpost just north of the lake. Their traditional homelands, where they have lived perhaps for more than 40,000 years, have diminished since the late 1950s by as much as 75% due largely to the intrusion of the more aggressive Datoga pastoralists and their cattle. Initially we only saw about 15 or 16 people in Onwas' group though later they were joined by five or six other women and a few girls, who had been out gathering *kongolobe (Grewia bicolor)* berries from a drainage line further down the slope. The pea-sized orange-yellow berries, fibrous and to my palate almost tasteless and with hard pips, disappeared within minutes. It was like watching ravenous children shoveling down popcorn.

The ripening of the berries at Ghorofan must have brought countless generations of Hadzabe to the area and still does, though it is tourism now, and the ever-encroaching tide of "progress", that helps to sustain (and to corrupt) Onwas and his people. And that will ensure, no doubt, that their encampment becomes a semi-permanent, yet paradoxically doomed, fixture. I knew, as we watched these peace-loving, stoical and remarkably independent people demonstrating their various skills and way of life, that I was witnessing the beginning of the end of their time on Earth. Inevitably they will be absorbed into "more advanced" ethnic groups, and become one of us.

I was as fascinated by what the Hadzabe had to say as much as what they were doing and as soon as I could I sat with Onwas and questioned him. Momoya, wherever necessary, acted as interpreter. When I asked Onwas if he and his people ever envied other Tanzanians or people such as ourselves he said "No. We have everything we need. Our bows and arrows, our knives, the clothes that we wear and the few pots and pans that the women carry. Everything else is *takataka* (rubbish)". I believed him. And I believed him when he said that the Hadzabe have no fear of the wild animals with which they share the land. "Sometimes the lions come at night while we are sleeping", he said, "but they do not trouble us".

The Hadzabe sleep, he told me, on the bare ground in the dry season, or in caves or under rocky overhangs such as those at Sonai, not far from Mang'ola. "Sometimes", he said, "we sleep in trees, like the baboons". It is the baboon that provides the hunter-gatherers with much of their bush-meat, though they will kill and eat almost anything that moves, from tortoises and rats to giraffes and buffaloes and, until they became scarce or locally extinct, elephants and rhinos. Onwas had killed all of these species and many others. Not always with impunity, for his right knee was still crudely bandaged after being dislocated by a wounded buffalo.

Their main quarry along the Chem-Chem is the baboon. Not only because larger game has mostly been shot out in the region but because the meat of the baboon is much relished by the Hadza. "It is sweeter than chicken" murmured Onwas dreamily, "We never get tired of eating baboon". In the old days elephants were highly prized, for a single bull or cow would keep seven or eight families in food for a week or more. The whole camp, he told me, would walk for miles to where an elephant had been killed and camp around the corpse until it had been reduced to skin and bones. He had, he said, even eaten lion and leopard ("This is the best part", he told me, slapping his forearm). But even the Hadzabe draw the line when it comes to snakes, which like most Africans they hate with a passion. And according to Onwas they won't eat hyena, fish or crocodile.

On our later visit to Mang'ola as guests of David and Jeanette I got to know Onwas and his group more intimately. In fact one of the household helpers, Onkay, was Hadza and another Hadza, Jegela, seemed to have attached himself to David and Jeanette's multi-ethnic "family" as an unpaid, uninvited but not unwelcome "hanger-on". Our hosts were busy during the day and, knowing that I needed to get out to take photographs of the Hadza and Datoga, left us to our own devices. Jegela, who spoke a little English, adopted us.

He was in his thirties, I would guess, short and quite slim but muscular like most Hadzabe men and quite good-looking, with a ready smile and a dark fuzz of moustache and beard that gave him the air of a friendly piratical rogue. He carried a bow and a handful of arrows (I never saw a Hadza hunter with a quiver) and dressed in typical Hadza style, wearing only shorts and rubber sandals. His only concession to fashion was the usual necklace of plastic beads. This was soon upgraded, for on our later safaris we always carried beautiful Sindhi beads with us that Anjum had brought from Karachi. These we used in much the same way as the old explorers and missionaries had done, as bargaining chips, in my case in exchange for photographs. Jegela was thrilled with the ornate beads that we gave him. He turned them into a necklace overnight and is probably still wearing it, perhaps to the surprise of the anthropologists and researchers who have since descended upon Mang'ola.

From the moment Anjum gave him the beads Jegela was determined to please us. Not always successfully as like many Hadza men he enjoyed a puff at the *bhangi* pipe and a swig from the "*tembo*" (fermented sugar-cane juice) pot, as a consequence of which he was not the most punctual or reliable of guides. When he did turn up he was a most engaging companion and we spent fascinating hours together. On one occasion in David and Jeanette's gloriously natural "gardens", while David and Jeanette's cook Athumani was preparing dinner. A short distance away the Chem-Chem swirled through a sequestered pool overhung by tall figs, tamarinds and graceful yellow-bark acacias and bordered, on its far side, by large rafts of dense papyrus. Despite the nearby Hadza and their lethal weaponry a troop of vervet monkeys often looked watchfully down from the treetops and once I disturbed a bushbuck just 20 metres from our guest house. Hadada Ibis, Green-backed Herons, Grey-headed Kingfishers and various other birds were to be seen by the pool or among its wooded margins.

On the greensward outside our guest-house, kept slashed into the semblance of a lawn by Massay, the Datoga gardener and odd-job man, stood a solid wooden picnic table. It was here, in the shade of a smallish tree with hanging panicles of white flowers, that Jegela and I spent the evening. The tree, Jegela told me, pointing out its straight shoots, was used by the Hadza for making arrows and firesticks. Bows, he said, were made from another tree (of the *Dombeya* species, I learned later). As we talked, partly in English, partly in Swahili and partly by body language, we were joined by a tiny dik-dik antelope, a half-tame creature known to David and Jeanette and their household simply as "Dik-Dik". It would pick its way around us and under the table with precise, exaggerated steps and on legs so slender and delicate that they might have been blown from strands of molten glass.

Had it known what Jegela was talking about it might have given us a wider berth, for at my prompting he had shown me his bow and arrows, naming the various parts in his language, Hadzane, and explaining their purpose. Un-barbed arrows, or arrows with a wooden barb, were used for smaller game or birds such as guinea-fowl, from the flight feathers of which Jegela's arrows were fletched. And after which he was named, he informed me, though whether "Jegela" meant "feather" or "guinea-fowl feather" or "guinea-fowl" I was never sure. Nor did it seem to matter as the Hadzabe change their names at will; when I talked to David about Jegela later he looked puzzled and said "Oh, he called himself Kampala until now, you just can't keep up with them..."

One of Jegela's three arrows was noticeably shorter than the others, its flight feathers cropped very short. Jegela told me that this type of arrow flew faster and was used for larger game. Which is why its barbed steel head was plastered with poison wrapped around with strips of impala skin. In my notebook I drew a rough sketch of a zebra and Jegela pointed out the critical target areas (heart, lungs or stomach) that needed to be hit in order to kill big game. A zebra or large antelope, he told me, would fall within about 50 metres if struck in the heart, twice as far if struck in the lungs and perhaps three times as far when pierced in the stomach. Larger arrow heads were used for elephants, he said, which were shot in the stomach, the animal taking "about two hours to die", though it is doubtful that he, unlike Onwas, had ever killed one.

Over breakfast the next morning David told us that he had heard a piercing scream during the night and that "Dik-Dik" was now nowhere to be seen. "Probably taken by a python", he said, "We've seen a big one by the pool". Uncharitably I couldn't help remembering "Dik-Dik's" rather trusting presence the evening before, as Jegela was showing me an unbarbed arrow, notched with tiny knife cuts near the point. "This", he had explained, "is for small animals". Adding, with what now seemed like dramatic irony, "Like this dik-dik". The mystery was never solved and soon after breakfast Jegela turned up, red-eyed but knowing nothing, he said when David questioned him about Dik-Dik's absence.

As if to shift the focus he asked if we wanted to "go hunting". He was planning to look for baboons along the Chem-Chem. The idea of seeing a baboon spitted by an arrow didn't appeal to me but the opportunity to see a Hadzabe hunting was too good to miss. Soon we were following him along the outer edge of the riverine woodland, keeping twenty metres or so behind him so as not to interfere. He was carrying a new bow and three arrows, all with barbed wooden heads.

He walked at an easy lope and in silence, scanning the crowns of the taller trees and their tangled under-storey to his right. Suddenly he stopped and in one fluid movement fitted an arrow to his bow and assumed a stooping posture. Slowly he stalked forward, eyes fixed on something hidden from our view, for we had also stopped. Then, still crouching, he drew back the bow. Even as he did so we heard a baboon's loud bark and the sounds of it and several others crashing to the ground and racing for their lives through the under-storey. Jegela uncoiled, releasing the tension on his bow and staring into the bush. Standing upright, he waved goodbye to the departing animals. "Bye bye, Baboon!" he called in English. And then in Swahili, "*Rafiki ya Hazabe!*' (friend of the Hadzabe!).

The baboons along the Chem-Chem have very different ideas about this "friendship" and all those in the immediate vicinity would now have bolted. Jegela, knowing this and smiling ruefully, waited for us to catch him up and walked on alongside us, his hunting over for the day. He would not, of course, go hungry, for he would never be refused food at David and Jeanette's. "But tomorrow", he said, "we will go walking again, with my friends. On the hill".

Early the next morning Anjum and I drove out to Onwas's camp at Ghorofani. Jegela had slept at Ghorofani overnight and so our arrival was expected, and with some enthusiasm, for at David's bidding we had brought along seven or eight large containers of water from the Chem-Chem spring, thus saving the women and girls many laborious treks there and back. The older women, bare-breasted with short, beaded skirts or *khangas* around their waists, eagerly took the water and decanted it, with great care, into lots of smaller vessels, in the skimpy shade of their various shelters.

And then suddenly Jegela, red-eyed from *tembo* or *bhangi* fumes or whatever else, called me and we were off into the bush, to hunt and forage, as my ancestors had hunted and foraged. No other signal as far as I was aware, no apparent leader, as the order of the march changed constantly, no concessions to my ageing, civilization-softened self. Or to Jegela's mighty hangover. There were eight of us, four men, three women and myself, Anjum having opted to stay behind. My companions were a quietly cheerful bunch, walking with their easy pace up the hill, chattering incessantly in their click language. The chattering surprised me, until I realized that they were not hunting seriously, just casually foraging.

The Hadzabe, like their kind around the world as far as I know, are mainly gatherers, hunting systematically only at the very end of the dry season, in certain areas. They are, of course, opportunists, and all the men carried their bows and arrows, but without urgency. Which doesn't mean that they went hungry, as in appropriate places they stopped to feed on *kongolobe* berries. Jegela showed me how to rub a handful of these between my palms, to de-husk them, before stuffing the inner fruits and their hard, round seeds ("good for the stomach", Jegela assured me) into my mouth.

One of the men, as we climbed higher, came across a wild bees' nest a little way up the slope from the narrow trail that we had been following. Jegela, knowing that I was after photographs, had scrambled up to join his colleague and called upon me to follow him to record the proceedings. I, knowing that the Hadzabe are relatively happy to be stung as long as they acquire the honey-combs that they crave, pretended to take a keener interest than I otherwise would in the activities of two of the women, who were half-sitting, half-kneeling on the path, legs outstretched, using digging sticks to unearth edible tubers.

But Jegela insisted. By the time I got to the site of the nest (making sure I didn't break any speed records) all the other men were there. They had, in no time, created a tiny fire at the foot of the paper-bark tree in the trunk of which the nest was situated. One of the men picked a smoking brand from the fire and thrust it deep into the natural hive. As I focused my camera I became aware of a dark patch of dazed bees clustered by the opening. And with rather more alarm I saw, and heard, a lot of their less dopey nest-mates buzzing around seeking retribution.

Expecting to be stung into a blistered red pulp I quickly took several photographs, as the man with his arm in the tree trunk withdrew a handful of golden combs. And then I beat it down to the path, astonishingly untouched. By the time the men rejoined us they had eaten most of the honey, including the combs and the grubs, but pleasingly had saved some for the women, who immediately left their digging to share the sticky-fingered feast.

The women had already dug out several small, dark-coloured tubers. When peeled they were like fat white radishes, 12 or 15 cm. long. I was handed one to eat. It had a faint, earthy taste and the crunchy texture you would expect, without threatening to take the world's vegetable markets by storm. Its value was in its high water content. If I was lost in the semi-desert bush by Lake Eyasi I would be glad to know how to find and dig out such wild radishes.

Once the honey and tubers were disposed of (the Hadzabe don't hang about mouthing click language "Bon appetit's!") the group set off once more, again quite spontaneously, along the path. We had now rounded the hill and were walking along a level stretch of the route, affording, in one or two places, open views across the dry flats of northern Eyasi to the Rift wall beyond, panoramas otherwise obscured by stunted trees and shrubs.

The hunter-gatherers knew these trees and shrubs intimately. Various species were pointed out, including a shrub that provides a cure for malaria and another that helps prevent malaria in the first place. All hopes of hunting now seemed gone, if any had ever been entertained, but the man who had found the bees' nest soon left the path yet again, this time returning with the nest of a bird.

The nest was small and reasonably well constructed, with a guinea-fowl's breast-feather adorning its interior, in which three tiny eggs rested neatly, white and fragile and translucent. He showed me the nest proudly, and carried it back to camp. I never found out what happened to it. I assume, probably romantically, that he would have given it to a sweetheart or perhaps a child, as a token. Whatever the case, the little eggs, I am sure, would have been quickly devoured rather than admired for their aesthetic qualities; the concept of intrinsic beauty, I would guess, evolved long after the human stomach.

And so we all trooped back to camp in single file and at the same steady pace, one man carrying a heavy branch of firewood over one shoulder. The morning had passed, and how many tens of thousands of years? For I had, in effect, been walking with my ancestors. An unassuming, unaggressive and utterly fascinating people.

Meanwhile I had unfinished business with their pastoralist neighbours the Datoga, or at least with their young "warriors", whom I had never met, let alone photographed. Their reputation, however, had gone before them. When I first went to live in Tanzania in 1977 the *Daily News*, then the country's only local English language newspaper, sometimes featured them in its editorials. It always referred to them as the Barabaig, who in fact are just one of various clans who make up the Datoga tribal group. The young "warriors" were in the habit, it seems, of committing ritual murders and cutting bits from their victims' bodies to impress their girl-friends. Not surprisingly the Tanzanian government disapproved, which is why its official mouth-piece, the *Daily News*, would announce from time to time that the "BARABAIG MURDERS MUST END!" As if repeating such directives was consonant with carrying them out.

I always imagined President Nyerere ordering his Minister for Home Affairs to "do something about these killings", causing the Minister to pass this on down a line of subordinates to the Chief of Police in Arusha or Babati. Who would then, through another line of subordinates, order some unfortunate, low-ranking constable to cycle out to the Datoga settlement in question on a Chinese "Flying Pigeon" to apprehend the offenders and bring them to justice.

The murders and mutilations went on regardless. Which might explain why I never sought out the Datoga until the mid-1990s, by which time the atrocities were far less frequent. By then the Datoga "warriors", who in the old days would have worked off their youthful belligerence by fighting their old enemies the Maasai, had been persuaded to kill animals rather than humans. Lions were the obvious substitute. Lion killing was already a cult and "lion killers" attracted the same kind of following that certain pop stars and other "celebs" attract among impressionable young girls in western societies. The Datoga girls, it is said, get "very excited" when an established "lion-killer" visits their *gheida*, sometimes offering him a favourite piece of jewellery (and, it seems, much else – "the hero's sexual prowess is discussed after his departure, with much jocularity"). The young men, with such incentives, would also spear elephants to win the girls' attentions, though these days this too is frowned upon.

For years I had wanted to photograph such 'lion killers' but whenever we had visited Momoya's uncle's *gheida* the "warriors" had always been "out in the bush". In the early 2000s, however, when I was camping alone by the Chem-Chem, I struck lucky. Momoya was away somewhere but a local school-teacher had offered to act as guide. He assured me that the young men attached to Momoya's uncle's *boma* were "at home". "They came for a ceremony", he said. "The ceremony is finished but the men are still there". And so we drove out to photograph them.

It was a dehydratingly hot morning, as it always seemed to be at the *gheida* in the dry season. We parked close to the huts and got out. The small family settlement seemed deserted but for a few women and girls who had recently finished the morning milking. My guide, whom out of respect I referred to as "Mwalimu" (teacher), went over to talk to one of the older women before returning to the car where I sat waiting. "The *vijana, the morani* ("The young men, the warriors") are here", he announced. "But they are sleeping. It is not good to wake them. We will wait".

They were sleeping on the floor of a nearby hut, "wasted", as the modern idiom has it, after partying all night. "Mwalimu" and I waited as the sun got hotter and hotter and the morning passed. Just as I was about to suggest coming back in the afternoon "Mwalimu" said "Wait. They are coming". And sure enough a young man soon staggered from the doorway of the hut, blinking in the sun. "Mwalimu" went to talk with him. When he came back he again said "Wait. They will come".

And one by one they did. About twelve of them. Unsteadily, like wild animals recovering after being darted. They were dressed in simple toga-like *khangas* or red-plaid Maasai blankets. The one who had first emerged began to talk to the others and soon they drifted over to the car, where "Mwalimu" and I were waiting. I greeted them in Swahili and "Mwalimu" began to talk to them in the indirect African manner, before getting down to business. Money was eventually discussed but I could see that they were not interested in what I could afford. "Wait", said "Mwalimu" in Swahili, "the *Mzungu*, the white man, has brought some clothes". Feeling uncomfortable, I took the clothes, second-hand jeans and t-shirts and a few other odds and ends, from the car boot and laid them on the bonnet. One or two of the young men fingered the jeans, briefly and with little enthusiasm.

I had been wanting for years to photograph Datoga "warriors" and now, just when I had caught up with some, the opportunity seemed to be slipping away. Until one of them, looking into the car boot, saw a half bottle of "Famous Grouse" whisky. Since being arrested by the Tanzanian army many years earlier for camping (inadvertently) on army land, and resolving the dispute over a similar half-bottle of whisky, I had always carried a bottle or two with me on safari for such emergencies. The young man in question spoke to his friends in his own language and then to "Mwalimu" in Swahili. And a deal was done. For the whisky and a certain sum of money the "warriors" would let me photograph them.

To avoid unfairness I doled out the whisky in small measures from the cap of the bottle, one measure to each man. They quickly gulped down this "hair of the dog" and after being promised more after the photography disappeared inside their hut. On re-emerging they were carrying spears and sporting whatever bits of Datoga "bling" they had found within. One was even wearing a headdress of fine brass chains that I had last seen on one of the girls. Two others, somewhat incongruously, were wearing American-type baseball caps, one orange, one red.

I attempted to shepherd them all into the open space in front of the huts for the photo-session but the young men demurred and spoke with "Mwalimu". "They will not let you take photographs here", he told me quietly. "We have to move into the forest [the bush], away from the women". And so, with my tripod and camera, I walked off into the bush with "Mwalimu", followed by a gang of groggy, male-supremacist "warriors". When we were some distance from the *gheida* we all stopped as if by common consent. At my request Mwalimu lined them up while I set up my tripod and camera nearby. Then one by one, and with much laughter and banter from their friends, I guided them into the open and photographed them.

I asked "Mwalimu" if any of the young men were celebrated "lion killers". He spoke to one of them then said "They have all killed lions". How true this was I will never know though they all looked capable. One of them, strongly built, muscular and unsmiling, looked particularly imposing. For some reason he was armed not just with one leaf-bladed spear but with two. When his turn came to be photographed he was so unbalanced that I had to manhandle him into position. In order to make him look even more imposing I unscrewed my camera from the tripod and knelt down in front of him. As I focused on his face Mwalimu, who was standing behind me, whispered "*Bwana*, be careful!"

"Why?" I asked.

"This man is dangerous".

With his sullen expression and a spear in either hand he looked dangerous enough but I clicked away while his friends enjoyed his discomfort. Later three other young men offered to pose, according to "Mwalimu", as they would have done when confronting their traditional enemies the Maasai, crouching in a semi-kneeling position, spears in one hand, cattle sticks in the other, against a background of spiky wild sisal and dry, distant hills. The Maasai know them as *Mangati*, from a word meaning "the enemy" that also implies respect. Had I been Maasai, facing up to these three, I might well have understood why.

After the photo-session we walked back to the *gheida* and I doled out the rest of the whisky. I felt a little like the white traders who had corrupted the north American Indians with "fire-water" but to have gone home without photographs of these fine young men after years of trying would have been hugely disappointing. As for the men themselves, they seemed quite happy with the deal and soon disappeared into their hut to resume sleeping it all off.

CHAPTER IXX

Farewell to the North

After bidding goodbye to David and Jeanette Anjum and I left Mang'ola and headed for the Serengeti, where we based ourselves in the National Park''s rest house at Seronera. The main purpose of the trip was to photograph some of the tribes-people (the Ikoma, Nata and Kuria) along the park's northern boundary but after accomplishing this objective we settled down to spend a few enjoyable days in the park itself. The highlight of the trip, however, and the highlight of our many visits to the Serengeti, came as we were leaving.

It was yet another head-over-heels-in-love-with-the-bush morning, the wide-angle plains confirming the curvature of the Earth and the skies terraced with clumps of cumulous that looked as if they had been cut and pasted from a graphics library, underbellies conforming to the flatness of the land. Behind us to the north, however, the sky was beginning to curdle, with distant parallelograms of rain slanting down amidst the paler grey and whey-coloured clouds. These dark shafts, and the sheet lightning that constantly flickered through them, had not escaped the notice of many other, more welcoming eyes...

Later I saw the first humps of the Simba Kopjes shimmering in the haze ahead. As we drew near and the granite outcrops sharpened into focus Anjum called out "Lion!". She cannot see to thread a needle but she can pick out a sleeping lion furlongs away. Over the years her cry of "Lion!", its eastern vibrancy defying my western ideas of propriety (behaviour gutted of all spontaneity and passion) still has me stiffening expectantly in my seat. As I did now.

When lying on their sides, as this one was, the big cats have scarcely more profile than deep-pile rugs. I marvelled yet again at Anjum's eyesight, for all she had seen were tufts of rufous mane among tufts of rufous grass. There were in fact seven lions, the other six concealed, even from Anjum, among shallow concavities of granite. The sub-adult whose scant mane had betrayed him raised his head, regarding us over his shoulder as we approached. Soon after I had stopped he turned to scan the deserted northern plains, before melting into the stone again. His pride-mates had surrendered to sleep or somnolence. Their bellies, if only they had known it, would soon be as big as beer kegs.

For almost as soon as we left them we saw, beyond the first high kopje to the south, more meat-on-the-hoof than the Serengeti's estimated 2,800 lions could collectively dream of. I stopped and raised my binoculars, doubting my own eyes, or more accurately my brain, for the human brain, especially mine, has problems with big numbers. And these numbers were very, very big. Anjum, rarely lost for words, was lost for words. When she did speak it was to murmur, slowly and twice over, "I can't *believe* it!".

I too was overwhelmed, not by the spectacle alone but by its mathematics. I clunked the Toyota into gear and drove quickly towards the apparition before it faded. Peeling off on to the track that half-encircled the kopje I cruised to a point closest to the nearest animals. From the base of the kopje the plains lifted, like a slowly rising sea, towards the skyline. Across that tilted perpetuity of grass were scattered thousands of zebras and wildebeeste, with uncountable thousands more, compressed by distance into a grainy band of grey.

I had seen the Serengeti migration many times but this was something else. It was like seeing the Milky Way in negative. Or, for those who feel uncomfortable with hyperbole, the equivalent of seeing the entire population of Philadelphia streaming from the city in unison. As we rounded the kopje and rejoined the main track more and more animals came into view, straddling the track and moving towards us, not so much like fleeing Philadelphians as four-legged extras in a dream-like Exodus, in which all roles were confused. For as we approached, the wandering hordes became the flood itself and I was transformed into an unlikely, motor-borne Moses, before whom the waters parted as the Land Cruiser land-cruised into them and was engulfed.

The nearest animals were no more than twenty metres away. Ahead, the track was blocked by who-knows-how-many others, unhurriedly moving aside as we advanced. We passed between small rocky outcrops, among which sprang woody clumps of wild sage, which the passing wildebeeste briefly nibbled, trampling them into a mash and releasing a pungent incense into the still air. An air discordant with the persistent croaking of the wildebeeste and the intermittent, pneumatic whinnying of zebras.

Some way into this incoming tide we stopped, as if becalmed, opened our doors and stood outside. The animals edged outwards a little. We leaned against the car, spellbound, and I took a few pointless photographs; there was no hope, from ground level, of capturing anything but a token of what we were witnessing. In my futility I turned to the Englishman's last hope of comfort short of petitioning God. I asked Anjum to make tea.

And so, in the midst of this miracle of evolution, she made tea, and we stood sipping it as the pageant passed by. And then we walked a little way, still with our mugs of tea, among the animals, to be at one with them. Not wishing to be at one with us they edged away again, but only slightly. All their instincts told them that two out-of-condition bipeds, encumbered as we were by mugs of hot tea, were hardly likely to rush at any of them, wrestle them to the ground and gnaw them into skin and bone. They tolerated our presence, albeit cautiously, and we settled for that, toleration being the next best thing to acceptance. And we rejoiced in the privilege of being part, however briefly, of the greatest wildlife show on Earth. Then, our mugs empty, we wandered back to the car, put away our tea-making things and drove on.

For six-and-a-half kilometres we pressed through the last of the herds. At the latter end were many wildebeeste calves, bleating out their oral identity cards, and an increasing number of weary-looking adults. Some must have made the 800 kilometre round-trip many times, cantered close to death year after year. Not, for many, for much longer. We saw no following predators but they would have been around, and the lions we had seen lolling among the rocks a little way back would soon be up and moving.

As we pulled away from the last stragglers and congratulated ourselves on our good fortune, Anjum broke off to cry "Look!" There, where grassland and sky coincided, was a dark line of wildebeeste, as if sketched in charcoal, relieved, here and there, by the paler grey of distant zebras. When I stopped and followed the line through binoculars, from the leading animals backwards, the line blurred to a point where reality and mirage overlapped. We discovered, as we drove on, that the line stretched back to Lake Ndutu, thirty-five kilometres away. A single line of large herbivores almost as long as a marathon course.

The following morning the plains below Naabi and along Oldupai and under the soft folds of Lemagrut were empty of wildebeeste and zebras, as if they had never been invented. Thanks to the quickly diminishing surface water to the south and the tempting rainstorms to the north, the migration had been deceived into leaving the short-grass weeks too early. Long after we had gone we heard that fresh rain had fallen by Ndutu, enticing the herds back. It did not matter; we had not only seen the great migration, we had seen it at its most awesome.

It was an entirely unexpected climax to what I had imagined to be our last safari in the Serengeti, and I remember thinking, as we passed through the Naabi Hill gate and over the boundary into the Ngorongoro Conservation Area, that we couldn't have asked for a more spectacular farewell. On reaching Ngorongoro Crater we stopped at the view-point at the southern extremity of the rim to say goodbye to the crater floor, where I had spent so many memorable days. But as it turned out we would soon be back.

Two years later, after being asked to write guide books to Ngorongoro and to the Serengeti, we returned to the Crater in our own Land Cruiser to do some research. A few months later, thanks to my publisher, we flew up to Arusha where we were met by representatives of Sunny Safaris and whisked off by one of their top driver-guides to spend time in three different Serengeti lodges.

These safaris, our last to these two famous venues, were as different from our old safaris in the Renault as can be imagined. En route to Ngorongoro, for example, Anjum and I were booked into Gibbs Farm at Karatu, beneath the eastern crater wall. Established in German colonial times the farm was taken over, after the Second World War, by James Gibbs, a British war veteran, and his wife Margaret, who had been born to British parents in Tanganyika. It quickly became a popular – and quite beautiful – stopping off place for settlers and expatriates, and later for tourists travelling to and from the Serengeti.

Compared with living in a tiny tent and on a diet based on corned beef our complimentary stay at Gibbs, with its "English country garden" atmosphere, its log fires and its comfortable armchairs, was a whole new experience in a new, very Anglicised, Africa. Not to mention a much more punctual, less scorching one, for even the sun had a set routine. It came out, we were assured, "at 2 pm each day". But "the real", haphazard Africa was just beyond the garden fence, on the forested outer slopes of Ngorongoro Crater. Here, among other creatures, roamed elephants and buffaloes, as we discovered when we took a little foot safari with an old Iraqw guide, appropriately, in this heavenly place, named Gabriel.

And despite the roses round the multi-paned window of our little cottage, the birds I saw whilst lying on the bed after a huge, debilitating breakfast were definitely African. They included a Bronze Sunbird, a Yellow-vented Bulbul, a group of Speckled Mousebirds, a Reichenow's Weaver and a Tropical Boubou, this last species attacking its own reflection in one of the panes. This was my type of birding.

And my type of routine, with that most civilized of British colonial legacies, afternoon tea, among its many attractions. Margaret joined us one day, out on the lawn in front of the old farmhouse. She talked of her first husband, James (now long dead), and of her "feeling of kinship" with the local people, the Iraqw, who "are very much like us". And of the old British aristocracy that "regained its vitality in the late 1800s by marrying 'the Gaiety girls'". This kind of thing, she added, had helped "to keep the British social system mobile" though "the enterprise and knowledge of the 1800s has now gone" and the "British education system has stifled people's natural curiosity".

It hadn't stifled mine. I found her company as edifying as it was enjoyable. And I blessed her for what she had contributed to "Gibbs" over the years, not least for teaching her Iraqw chef,

Reggie, how to make his classic rice pudding – and much else; lunch on the first day began with spinach soup followed by two kinds of quiche, pork and cabbage pie, beef and pasta pie, cottage pie, boiled ham on the bone and salad, with rhubarb crumble, crème caramel, fruit salad and the afore-mentioned rice pudding comprising the dessert course). In the old days lunch would have been a chunk of peanut brittle and a mug of tea.

Food was to be a major feature at our next port-of-call also, the "Ngorongoro Farmhouse", another one-time German colonial coffee farm. This new resort was situated just 5 km. from the main Ngorongoro Conservation Area gate, at the foot of the Crater's southern outer wall. It was owned by a Spanish couple and a youngish gentleman, half-German, half-Maasai, by the name of Willie (his email address began with "wildwillie").

The receptionist was another intriguing mixture, half-Chagga, half-Pare, called Veronica. Petite, vivacious and attractive, she also had a cheerfully unflurried temperament – every demand of mine was met with a "Don't *worry*, Mr Mer-cer!" She seemed to pop up everywhere for as well as acting as receptionist she also doubled, or more accurately trebled, as waitress and chamber-maid. And excelled at all three.

When I told her that we hoped to leave for the Crater at dawn the next morning and to stay down there all day she smiled and said "No problem, Mr Mer-cer". And when I asked if we could be provided with a packed lunch ("something simple") and maybe some kind of packed breakfast she again exhorted me not to worry. With another reassuring smile she promised to meet us at the car park at 6 am the next day. "With the food".

At the appointed time we were waiting by the car when I saw, against the lightening sky and at the top of the path that led down to the car park, what seemed to be a huge, four-legged laundry basket. The basket made its way slowly towards us and came to rest by the Toyota's rear door. "Good morning!" beamed

Veronica as she and a male colleague lowered the wicker basket to the ground, "This is your hamper".

I stared in astonishment. "Veronica", I said eventually, "We're just going for the day, not for a week!"

"Don't *worry*, Mr Mer-cer!" she replied, "Open your car". Still flabbergasted I opened the Toyota's rear doors and she and her colleague, with my assistance, lifted the hamper and manoeuvred it into the vehicle. It was like loading a small freighter. As we drove off soon afterwards Veronica waved and beamed her "Don't worry" smile.

And so, on this day and the next, we climbed, with the hamper, from the Farmhouse to the Crater rim in persistent mist, and then, still in mist, travelled around the rim of the eastern Crater wall to the Lemala Descent. This gentle track leads down into the Crater's northern sector, where the slopes of Ol Moti fall in graceful curves to the Munge River. It was the Munge that we would slowly follow, looking primarily for lions. We found them, in prides and in pairs, and also saw spotted hyenas and jackals on a kill, large herds of wildebeeste and zebras, elands, buffalos, warthogs and over in the Mandusi Swamp several elephants and a serval.

As a final goodbye to the Crater it could hardly have been better, but when I think about it now it is Veronica's hamper that comes to mind. For two consecutive days, at breakfast and lunchtime, I would park by the track or Ngoitokitok Lake and risk a rupture by hauling out the "laundry basket" and transferring it to the bonnet of the car, where it quickly became a tourist attraction. Passengers in passing safari vehicles would stare longingly at it, wondering why their own breakfast or lunch boxes were so relatively puny.

When I first opened the hamper at Ngoitokitok it was like opening Captain Kidd's treasure chest, crammed with edible goodies instead of Spanish doubloons. Breakfast consisted of water melon, two boiled eggs each, with brown bread, chunks of fresh local cheese and pancakes with butter and home-made jam. And a large flask of hot water for coffee or tea, with powdered milk.

Lunch was even more sumptuous. Omelette-like "patties", a cold pasta dish with herbs, thick cheese sandwiches, more pancakes and jam, a bar of chocolate, biscuits and a tangerine, with coffee or tea. Each day we gave food away to passing members of the anti-poaching unit yet we still had more than enough for ourselves. We were still eating left-overs from the Farmhouse hamper long after we left Ngorongoro.

Not that the hamper was the sole attraction. The truth is that I had never seen the Crater looking so beautiful. Partly because we were there at the height of the rains, when the grasses are at their greenest and most vibrant, but primarily because we had coincided with an occasional phenomenon known as floral synchrony, when tropical flowers, not bound by the constrictions of northern seasons, burst into simultaneous blossom. And as so many flowers in and around the Crater are of the *bidens* species of the *Compositae* family (which includes dandelions, daisies and sunflowers), this synchronized blooming can be spectacular in its golden profusion. As it was then.

On that first morning the mists that often hang around the Crater rim had been pouring over its eastern lip like a vapourised version of the Victoria Falls. But as the mists began to lift a few shafts of sunlight burst through the clouds like laser-guided missiles, to explode in showers of incandescent shrapnel on the rounded volcanic hills that grace the foot of northern Crater walls, and on the floor itself ahead of us. Struck by their impact I stopped. Through binoculars I saw scatterings of burning gold, on the hillsides and across the plains, brilliant where the slowly shifting sunlight fell. And amid the fields of gold a dark lava flow of wildebeeste and zebras.

I drove towards this molten mass of animals as it oozed through the resplendent fields, along the margins of the Mandusi Swamp where several bull elephants (cows rarely come down into the Crater) were feeding among the tall green reeds. Soon we were in the midst of the wildebeeste and zebras and the hock-high, golden flowers, where the northern Crater wall rises beyond the Munge in an upsweep of conical hills and curves towards Olmoti, high above the rim. As we motored through the swathes of daisies, like a boat on a gilded sea, the wildebeeste and zebras hardly bothered to move aside. I stopped amongst them and switched off the engine.

The superabundance of flowers and animals was enthralling. The flowers are in fact intrusive but the most pedantic of botanists would surely have stopped in wonder. Vincent van Gogh would have painted them into posterity. With rather less talent I tried to capture the scene on film, knowing that it was futile, for what you capture with a camera is mostly to do with seeing rather than feeling. But what I had really hoped to photograph was a black-maned lion, which are sometimes found in Ngorongoro or on the Serengeti plains, where the open landscapes and cool climate encourages larger and sometimes darker manes than those found on lions elsewhere. So giving up on the great herds and the golden daisies I turned east, to follow the Munge upstream.

Almost opposite the ruins of the old Siedentopf Farm we saw lions out on the short-grass to the south. And there, in the midst of several adult females, was one of the finest males I have ever seen. One of the lionesses obviously found him as handsome as I did, for in the next two or three hours she seduced him time after time. Like all female cats lionesses need repeated sex to stimulate ovulation (one male in the Serengeti mated 145 times within 55 hours with one lioness, and 12 times with another). And researchers have apparently discovered that size matters, at least in terms of the lion itself, and of its mane. Darker manes are more attractive than others, it seems, so this big male had a lot going for him, including libido and stamina. Which is why we now had to wait three hours before he decided to leave his concubine and plod towards the Munge for a much-needed drink. And, I suspect, a bit of peace, allowing me to take my long-anticipated photograph.

Grateful for such an opportunity I realized, with some prompting from Anjum, that we had not eaten since breakfast, and suggested that we turn back to enjoy our packed lunch among the flowers and the big herds. Some of the wildebeeste and zebras were now moving slowly towards the hills north-east of Engitate, so I drove to intercept them and parked by the track, in the midst of yet another vast sweep of golden flowers. As we sat, with not another vehicle in sight, enjoying lunch and mugs of steaming tea, the wildebeeste and zebras took us in their slow stride, bypassing the car in their hundreds.

One male wildebeest set up a temporary territory right by the Toyota, bleating in his strange wildebeestian way, like some ancient South Sea Island priest blowing on a conch shell. Despite their reputation for not being very bright, and for looking like "something designed by a committee", I find wildebeeste appealing, not only because of their absurdities but because of their shining, brindled flanks and subtle colours. Of course their huge, "roman-nosed" heads do look disproportionate, and their tiny eyes don't exactly sparkle with high intelligence, but I like them. And I noticed, for the first time, that wildebeeste have the most dainty hooves, like patent leather shoes with pointed toes.

In the late afternoon we drove south to leave the Crater by the formidable ascent track, seeing a quartet of cheetahs in the rough grasslands by the Lake Koitokitok turn-off, and when passing the Gorgor Swamp, on a white stone by the track, one of the loveliest of birds, a Rosy-breasted Longclaw. Whilst on the other side of the track, in the damp grasslands east of the Lerai, we saw an elegance (I have just coined the collective noun) of 74 Crowned Cranes. But soon my spirits sank and I lapsed into silence as we climbed out of the crater for what would surely be the last time. On emerging from the steep ascent we stopped at the nearby View Point to say a last goodbye and take a last few photographs. I told Anjum, melodramatically, that I never wanted to come back. And I never have been. For no subsequent visit could have lived up to that one.

When we finally drove off it was in a more gladsome mind and with a deep sense of privilege. Anjum, as is her habit, insisted on me turning around and looking back, "so that one day you will return". I looked back, despite never wanting to return, and saw, just for a moment, the sheen of Lake Magadi far below, in that most extraordinary of settings.

We did in fact return the following year, though only in passing, not to go down into the crater. For once the guide-book to Ngorongoro was finished my publisher sent us north again to research a similar book on the adjacent Serengeti. This time he had arranged for us to travel in a long wheel-base Toyota Land Cruiser with an experienced driver-guide, Pius. And to stay, among other places – and thanks to the generosity of Serena Hotels – at the company's luxurious Kirawira Camp by the Grumeti River.

The Grumeti flows through the Serengeti's Western Corridor, a rumpled, relatively little-visited wilderness that tapers like a leg of lamb towards Lake Victoria. An area that I had only passed through once before, and that I now needed to get to know. But there was another reason for wanting to go there. For ever since seeing the National Geographic's film "Here be Dragons" some years before I had been intrigued by the subjects of that astonishing documentary, the giant crocodiles that lurk in the Grumeti's mud-clouded waters, lying in wait for the annual crossing of the river by the great migration, usually in June.

Kirawira Camp itself was a small, discreet scattering of luxury tents on the northern slopes of the Simiti Hills, elegantly furnished in Edwardian style. With plush, leather-upholstered armchairs, leather-topped tables and a writing desk where John Galsworthy would have felt at home, all subtly illuminated by period-piece wall lamps. It brought to mind a film set for a production of *The Forsyte Saga*. Except that the main action took place a few kilometres away and had nothing to do with sophisticated early 20th Century English society. But everything to do with reptilian monsters that have evolved over 65 million years. The Grumeti's enormous crocodiles.

The crocodiles grow up to five metres in length and weigh as much as three-quarters of a tonne or more. They make "regular" crocodiles look like geckos. So much so that they seem like a different species. In fact, despite being much bigger and broader-snouted than most of their specific relatives elsewhere in Africa they are, like them, Nile Crocodiles (*Crocodylus niloticus*). At first sight, when only the head of one of these monsters is visible above the turbid waters, its jaws closed, it has the bizarre appearance of a giant's discarded shoe, covered in dry, lumpy mud, with a few discoloured nails showing where the uppers are beginning to come away from the sole. What impresses you is the breadth of this grotesque, shoe-like head, for the jaws taper only slightly towards the nose.

These jaws can snap open in 1/25th of a second. And when clamping shut again can crush a wildebeest's skull like a water melon. And it is wildebeeste (up to one-and-a-half million of them, plus something like 200,000 zebras), which make up the crowd scenes in this annual drama. For in June each year the Serengeti migration reaches the Grumeti and a month or so later crosses it. Except for the wretched individuals that drown, or are intercepted by the crocodiles. For the giant reptiles are capable of leaping explosively from the shallows to grab a 200 kg. wildebeest, and with a sideways sweep of the head, flicking it into the water like a rag doll. And then, by twisting their own bodies over and over like a rapidly rolling log, capable of ripping their victims to bloody rags.

Even the name Kirawira has a gory origin. It is said to be a corruption of "Kwehahura", an infamous poacher who had eluded the park rangers for years, but who was eventually cornered, in the mid-20th Century, close to this stretch of the Grumeti. To escape he is said to have leapt into the river, never to be seen again, though his belt buckle was apparently found the following dry season. It is a most unlikely story, for it would take a very desperate poacher to prefer swimming across this stretch of the Grumeti to spending a few years in prison. However, no safari is complete without its stories and unlikely things happen in Africa. And crocodiles do kill people (over 500 between 1986 and 1998, almost all outside the national parks).

Crocodiles are often described as "sinister" (certain rural Africans call them "the animals that kill while smiling"), and although such clichés are essentially anthropomorphic, few people who have spent time by the Grumeti at Kirawira would protest. The river itself, especially on an overcast day or as dusk falls, is ominous enough, its murky waters still and silent and shadowed by overhanging foliage. In places a hippo might break the surface and the silence with a puff of spray, or a heron or marabou might stab at a frog, small forewarnings of the greater menace that lies beneath the surface.

It was this air of foreboding that dominated my own brief visits to the banks of the Grumeti. For we were there in April, two months or so before the migration and the annual slaughter that its arrival inspires. There were a few wildebeeste around, as some opt out of the annual trek and remain resident on the Ndabaka and Ruana Plains, the eastern and southern extremes of which extend into the Kirawira vicinity. But none ventured to drink from the Grumeti while we were around. Yet it was difficult, as I focused my binoculars or camera lenses on the narrowed, watchful eyes of those crocodiles that were visible, not to see in their yellow slits an air of expectation, difficult not to imagine the ear-drums in the hidden ears tautened in anticipation of the faint vibrations of 8 million approaching hooves.

Reptiles can live without food for long periods and though the Grumeti giants, like other crocs, would take whatever opportunities arise, the annual arrival of the wildebeeste marks the beginning of a crocodilian Roman orgy. The great reptiles kill zebras also, though relatively few. Some researchers believe that the brief period when the migration passes through represents the breaking of a ten or eleven month fast for the crocodiles. If so, no wonder they lunge from the water, or from under bank-side bushes, with such passion, or fall upon swimming or drowned wildebeeste like starving savages.

There is more to Kirawira than crocodiles. During our first night we heard the familiar, strangely imploring call of lions from the plains below the camp, and although we didn't find them the following morning we encountered them in the evening, in rather strange circumstances. There were five, all adult but for one large juvenile, and including a full-grown male, lying precariously (and with obvious discomfort) among the foliage of a remarkably small bush. I have seen lions in trees many times but never so many in such an absurd situation. It was like seeing five tabby cats curled up among the leaves of a potted geranium.

There was another pride of lions in the Kirawira area that I wanted to see and photograph. It was said to include an adult male and female with only six legs between them. The three-legged lioness was apparently still capable of hunting successfully, the three-legged male rather less so, though he seemed to survive. There is much poaching for game meat along the fringes of the Western Corridor so perhaps the lions lost their legs in wire snares.

We didn't find this unusual pride but after crossing the Grumeti via a causeway we found some unusual trees. After winding through a swathe of whistling thorn we entered an area of short-grass fringed by other acacias, prominent among them *A mellifera*. Innocuous from a distance, *A. mellifera* was originally named (as *A. detinens* – the "acacia which holds back or detains") by the early botanist William John Burchell. Anyone who has made the mistake of trying to brush their way through *A. mellifera* country in anything less than an armoured car would smile wryly at Burchell's explanation: "I determined", he wrote (perhaps on blood-speckled pages) "to give the tree a name which should serve to caution future travelers against allowing themselves to venture within its clutches".

To be fore-warned is to be fore-armed and although I wandered among the *mellifera* to take a few photos, I didn't take too many risks. These were reserved for the journey back, when we stopped off by a sketchy-looking footbridge across a deep sector of the Grumeti. Our driver Pius told us that the place was "good for crocodiles" and that the footbridge had been erected to allow access to Grumeti Camp when the causeway was submerged. When I walked on to the bridge with my camera, to get photos from mid-stream, it was with some misgivings. And with a doom-laden warning from Anjum.

The bridge, for all its flimsy appearance, was suspended by wire cables, not rotting rope, and I'm sure it was safe enough as such bridges go. But the wooden planking that formed its narrow footway was heavily spattered with slippery baboon droppings and the wire supports that linked the upper and lower suspension cables were few and far between. There was a lot of opportunity, it seemed to me, to go skidding into the void on either side.

The bridge, as if responding to my uncertainty, began to sway. With one hand on the nearest suspension cable and the other hanging on to my camera I edged towards the centre as the bridge swung to my every movement. Below, too far down for comfort, lay the Grumeti, still and dark. There was no sign of crocodiles but I knew that they were there, watching and waiting. Unwilling to let go of the bridge's cable with one hand and to try to take photographs with the other, I slowly, and gratefully, edged my way back.

After re-crossing the causeway we drove slowly along the river's southern bank. Its associated woodland is said to be good for birds, among them the skulking but strikingly photogenic Black-headed Gonolek (*Laniarius erythrogaster*), jet-black above with brilliant red underparts. The website that informed me of this also told me that "All bird species at the study site were recorded whilst walking slowly through the forest". Keen as I was to see a Gonolek I wasn't quite so keen to "walk slowly through the forest". For the Kirawira crocodiles sometimes resort to ambushing prey, and the ambush speed of a croc has been estimated at 40 kph.

I did leave the safety of the car from time to time (with the reluctant consent of Pius and a groan of protest from Anjum). At one point I found myself on my hands and knees, using a riverside bush as cover whilst "stalking" a huge crocodile that was lying in the nearby shallows, to try to get a few photographic close-ups. But after a large monitor lizard suddenly shot from some rocks across my path, frightening the life out of me, I decided that discretion was the better part of valour and retreated to the Land Cruiser. "You do some stupid things!" remarked Anjum.

There are large pythons along the river also – we had seen a 4 metre one crossing the track ahead of us as we had approached Kirawira – though pythons would not attack a full-grown man without provocation. Buffaloes and elephants sometimes lie up or feed in the gallery forest, or come down to drink from the Grumeti. And the Kirawira hippos often feed by daylight in the riverside grasslands. It is not a place in which to take too much for granted.

It is mostly the great crocodiles that concentrate the mind. Yet they inspire admiration as well as fear. They are survivors in terms of their own individual lifespan as well as evolutionary survivors from the age of the dinosaurs. For crocodile eggs are relished by monitor lizards, mongooses and other creatures, and so are baby crocodiles. Yet the daunting odds against them achieving adulthood are lessened slightly by the instinctive but touching behaviour on the part of their mothers, who guard the eggs as much as possible and who protect their young for as long as two years. A devotion often unexpected of reptiles, whose "cold blooded" nature is much misunderstood.

When the time came to leave Kirawira I tried to keep this in mind. The great killing machines might have faces like a giant's discarded shoe, faces that only a mother could love, but some of them, against tremendous odds, might attain the age of fifty. And I told myself that an animal that has hardly changed in 65 million years has got to be pretty well-adjusted. Perhaps the Crocodile's reputation, like that of snakes, hyenas, wild dogs or sharks, is badly in need of revision.

We stayed in other parts of the Serengeti and saw lots of other fascinating creatures, including 48 lions and 10 cheetahs, but the greatest pleasure was in just being there, with Anjum, in this "great extended place". Visiting or passing through places that I had first seen almost 30 years before, where I and my various safari partners had spent so many memorable days. Places that I would never see again. But I left, as I had left Ngorongoro Crater, with a glad heart and with immense gratitude.

After a short diversion to the Gol Kopjes, where we saw three cheetahs and a three-legged lion on a zebra kill, we drove out via

Naabi Hill. I was standing up in the Land Cruiser, looking out from the roof hatch across the short-grass plains towards the familiar slopes of Lemagrut. And singing into the steady wind with joy. Just as we were passing under the overhead sign-board that marks the Serengeti/Ngorongoro boundary I saw a lioness walking down the track towards us. A symbol of the Africa we had known and loved; the old Africa, the wild Africa, going one way, and we going the other, each to a different world.

A few months later, in the dry season, we also said goodbye to the park where my safari companions and I had always felt relaxed and at home, Tarangire. Again I was there to do some research. My publisher had arranged for us to stay at the Tarangire Safari Lodge, the old "Tented Camp" as Barry, Kevin and I had known it. We were given a tent overlooking the river in this loveliest of locations, and our four days in the park, poignantly nostalgic as they were for me, were as pleasant as any I had known.

The trip stands out in my mind not because it was our last safari to a much-loved sanctuary but because we saw three leopards, on three different occasions. For experienced driver-guides, who communicate by radio as well as word-of-mouth, a "hat trick" of leopards is not so unusual, but for us, driving our own Land Cruiser and relying entirely on our own eyes and our own bushcraft, it was unique.

The last of the leopard sightings was unusual in itself. We were in our tent waiting to go to dinner when a young Dutch tourist, whose acquaintance we had made, came to call us out. "Come quickly! There's a leopard sitting on the wall outside the dining room!" We hurried off with him and sure enough, on the high wall surrounding the lodge's off-loading yard, was an adult male leopard, lying full length and staring down at us. Or rather, staring down at the skewers of beef, chicken and whatever else was cooking on the three barbecues that were set out on the walkway between the restaurant and the adjacent bush.

Twice a week the lodge put on a barbecue and twice a week, we heard later, the leopard came to lie on the wall and salivate. Suddenly realizing that I had left my camera in our tent I ran back to get it. Predictably, when I got back, the leopard had gone. One of the lodge chefs said it had jumped down and vanished into the bush beyond the barbecues. He and one or two colleagues, plus a crowd of excited tourists, were standing by the edge of the walkway peering into the undergrowth. Anjum and I joined them.

Suddenly the chef said "There it is!". We looked but in the semi-darkness beyond the lights of the restaurant could see nothing but vegetation and shadows. Then one of the shadows detached itself and walked towards us. The chef motioned us all back and everyone but Anjum and I, who were mesmerized by the leopard's behaviour, withdrew into the restaurant doorway. The leopard padded slowly towards us and I edged back, ordering Anjum to follow suit.

But Anjum is Anjum and stood her ground, the leopard no more than three metres away. This is a woman who is often frightened of dogs and always frightened of lizards. The chef called out to her and at last she moved back a little, but slowly, as if hypnotized by the nearness of the big cat. The leopard was intent only on the smoking meat and only deterred from grabbing some by the intense heat. After a minute or two, perhaps becoming nervous of the crowd, some of whom were shining torches at him or taking flash photographs, it turned and walked back into the undergrowth.

Eventually the three lodge chefs, with more than a few glances behind them, took up their positions behind the barbecues, their backs to the bush. We clients, still talking excitedly about the leopard, queued up to be served. The attractive young Tanzanian lady who was dishing out the chicken told me that one evening, whilst standing by her barbecue, she had felt something rubbing against her bare leg, and had looked down to see the leopard. She had, she said "Screamed and jumped away!" She also told me that at the end of the staff party some months earlier, one of the waiters, after sinking a few beers on the terrace and eating his food with his fingers, had fallen asleep in his chair. "He was woken up by the leopard. It was licking his hand".

Annette Simonson, the lovely co-owner/manager of Tarangire Safari Lodge, later told me more. Another leopard, a female, had found her way into the lodge kitchen one night, accompanied by her young cub. She had managed to open the huge fridge door and drag out all the bacon, but in doing so had pulled the fridge down on to the cub. In panic she had clawed at the fridge, stripping its electric wiring from the wall and rendering the fridge inoperative. The cub had eventually wriggled free and the two of them had then focused their attention upon the slowly defrosting bacon. Raising, no doubt, a few complaints at the breakfast table next morning.

Incidents involving leopards, which are normally shy and elusive, are uncommon in camps and lodges and can be dangerous. At the same time they provide much excitement for the guests in residence. Leopard sightings on safari are relatively few and far between and much sought after. So in the early 2000s Annette and her husband John were faced with a dilemma. Should they continue to allow a wild leopard to visit their lodge's barbecue or get the park authorities to discourage the animal?

The Simonsons, two decent, generous and well-meaning people, opted as I would have done. By accepting the risks. A decision that was to cause them much grief. And greater grief to two of their guests, an expatriate French couple. For three months after Anjum and I had come within a few metres of the leopard it killed the French couple's 6-year-old son. He had finished dinner with his parents and gone outside to play. The leopard had grabbed him and dragged him into the bush. The alarm was raised and the boy rescued and rushed to hospital but was declared dead on arrival.

During our stay, Anjum, no bigger than many young children, had walked to the restaurant area and back several times at night whilst I was busy writing notes in our tent. Almost certainly she would have sometimes passed within striking distance of the leopard. Our last visit to Tarangire, the park where I had always felt at home and secure, could so easily have ended in tragedy. As it happened we left Tarangire as we had always left it, with great reluctance and a sense of privilege.

CHAPTER XX

Farewell to the South, and to my "Second Wife"

After saying goodbye to the North we did likewise to the south. First to the Selous and then to Ruaha. And, thirty-four years after sitting in a café in Liverpool, staring at a ridiculously simplified map of Mikumi in John Williams' *Field Guide to the National Parks of East Africa*, we said goodbye to that underrated sanctuary. The park in which Anjum and I were to spend so much time, with so much pleasure. Where we had enjoyed our first "dates" and much of our married lives, the park that Anjum always called my "second wife". That even now, in my late seventies and back in England, I sometimes "drive" around via Google maps. Recalling every curve and camber of the tracks, every watercourse, every patch of woodland or bush or open plain. In an effort to somehow "bring back those hours "of splendour in the grass". And "find strength in what remains behind" Let us hope that Wordsworth was right.

Over the years, as we had left Mikumi to return to Dar, I would sometimes think, as we passed the huge roadside signs that mark the park's western border, "One day we will do this for the last time". And, in melancholy mood, wonder how I would feel when that time came. When it did come I forced myself to look back at the signs as we drove by. Not through a film of tears or with great heartache, only an achingly empty inevitability. An acknowledgement that something that I had loved had gone forever.

We were leaving the park after the annual school orientation trip, with two buses full of newly-hired teachers. Anjum and I had been invited along, as we had been for year after year, as "guides". We had stayed, as always on the school trip, at the Mikumi Safari Camp, known in the old days only as "The Tented Camp". And as always, the evening before we left the park, I had given my traditional slide show. It had been a pleasant-enough mini-safari. And as always the incoming teachers had enjoyed it. But for us it had been unsettling.

There was, for one thing, no time for poignant reflection. Except when sleeping we were always surrounded mostly by people we did not know and would never know, asking question after question. No privacy, no opportunity to say goodbye to many places that had meant so much to us. Campsite No. 1, the old Mikumi Lodge, Chamgore and Mwanambogo waterholes, the lovely glade at Choga Wale, the big baobab at Mbuyuni, the Ikoya Loop and so many others. We saw the familiar flood plains just north of the camp and the black cotton *mbugas* on the Kisungura Circuit further west, and we drove to the Millennium Dam, and each evening towards sunset to the Hippo Pool for the now traditional "sundowners". And we saw all the animals that we had expected to see.

The incoming teachers, most of whom had never been on safari, were always thrilled by their first experiences, as of course I had once been. They would sit in admiring near-silence watching and photographing herds of impala, marvelling, as I did and still do, at these exquisite antelopes. Antelopes that have hardly changed in five million years, for you cannot improve upon perfection. And the teachers would laugh as sounders of wart-hogs ran off in line ahead, tails stuck up in rod-like radio antennae mode, each piglet (or wartlet as I like to call them) assuming its own specific place in the line as they followed their mother.

Giraffes, so plentiful in Mikumi, were always the favourites among the women, who, already enthralled by the creature's slender, feminine beauty and dark, deliquescent eyes, would gasp with delight when the animals broke into a graceful, slow-seeming canter. Predictably, elephants, especially those with young, were also a major attraction, as much for their gentle, civilized social interactions as for their size and strength.

After the first one or two game drives, however, I could always sense, as a "guide", sitting on the leading bus alongside the school's head driver "Jeddo", the unspoken but growing desire to see lions. The pressure from behind, characterised by increasingly long silences, would build inexorably. I knew from long experience where the local lions were often to be found but they were never guaranteed. Fortunately "Jeddo", whom I knew as "*Bwana Simba*" had become something of an expert, over the years, and had much better eyes than me. Anjum, usually on the second bus, was just as keen-sighted, if a little more excitable. So between us we almost always succeeded in finding the big cats.

But on this occasion the first day passed without a sighting and the early hours of the second, when realistically we had to find lions by 9 a.m. or not at all, had almost slipped by without success. It was almost time to return to camp for breakfast before leaving when, out of desperation, I asked "Jeddo" to head up the main track to a secondary waterhole just south of the popular Hippo Pool. There, on a shelf of land above a dry channel of the Mkata, we found our lions.

Three mature and one adolescent females, lying together on the raised bank, one adult with a blind and clouded right eye. The teachers were thrilled and I greatly relieved. For once

Anjum was on the same bus, as animated as ever though she had seen lions a thousand times. "Take some photos!" she urged me. But somehow I didn't feel motivated. The school buses, for one thing, were not designed with photography in mind. The windows were slightly smoked and each one only opened a little way. And besides, everyone else was crowded against our side of the bus, clicking away. I felt suddenly redundant, a figure from the past.

One teacher, a young and attractive English girl, had a camera with a huge lens. And the self-confidence that I had always lacked. She was trying to squeeze her camera lens into the nearest window opening through a small scrum of other teachers so I called her over and invited her to shoot through the adjacent window. She immediately came and knelt alongside me, leaned one elbow on my knee, as my old safari partner Kevin would have done, and started firing away. "Firing" being appropriate as her camera was obviously set to continuous shooting mode. It sounded like a light machine gun on the Somme.

I couldn't help thinking how different it all was. In all my years in Africa, on hundreds of safaris, I had never used a camera in this way. Out of inertia rather than choice, though I like to think that I had always opted for the bolt-action rifle, as it were, to the machine gun. And I had never been able to afford such a large lens. I didn't feel envious, I was genuinely pleased for the girl, and for her new colleagues. My era, of modest camera equipment, battered old cars, independent travel and living in small tents, was over. Even teachers could now afford to fly to distant national parks or to travel in convoy in large and reliable 4WDs. And to stay in lodges or "luxury" camps. And, if they chose, to shoot several frames a second through expensive lenses without worrying, as we had once done, about the cost of developing the films. Such is progress and I hope I accepted it with good grace.

Yet somehow I was glad when the lions, disturbed by all the attention and noise and camera flashes, stood and stretched and slowly moved off. The girl with the classy camera thanked me and returned to her seat, as all the other teachers had done, buzzing with excitement. "Jeddo" started the bus and turned to follow the lions. They, anxious to get away, headed off-track and across the plains towards Marker Stone No. 7, that stands at the start of the "Sungura Circuit", the "Circuit of the Hare". The marker stone that had always, for me, represented the centre of the local lion pride's home range.

"Jeddo" parked the bus side-on to the lions and switched off the engine. And we watched the four predators amble across the grassland, stopping and flopping here and there in typical leonine fashion. Midway across the grassland they flopped again, one of the adults sitting upright, looking out towards the eastern hills. I watched her through my binoculars, seeing that familiar facial profile and the amber eyes gleaming in the sunlight, and wanting to commit that last, lingering look to my memory. And then she stood. And her companions stood with her. And followed in line ahead as she led them off towards the Sungura. "Jeddo" started the bus. And that was that.

As we left the park the next morning and drove past the boundary signs, Anjum ordered me to look back "...then we will come back again one day"... And to please her I looked back. Knowing, half a century after my first safari, that I would never see those signs again. Never again look into the eyes of lions in the African wild. Never again hear their imploring calls, at night, from within a tiny tent, under the Southern Cross.

Acknowledgements

Books might be written by one person but are the products of support and encouragement from many others. In my case my wife Anjum and my other main safari partners Barry Whittemore, Kevin Bartlett and John Boyce. Together with Hamid Bharmal, Arshad, Sameena and Zia Hussain, Patricia Barrett, Adele Whittemore, Sati Gadhvi, Arzoo and Anmol Rajpar, Carole "Pippi" Bird, Neil Baker, Bill and Anthea Dalton, Hasina, Kabir, Khalid and Shaheen Hyderali, Ernest and Pat Polack, Kathy Dawson, Ruth Wickham, Irene Hendries and Chanel Croker, with all of whom I have shared memorable safaris.

Thanks also to everyone at the International School of Tanganyika, Dar es Salaam who supported us during our 34 years there, all relatives and friends in Karachi and to Mohamed Amin, Urmila Waive, Roy Ramsey, Margaret Garner, Barbara Munnings, Gloria Mawji, Zeenat Thawer and family, Nisha Sanghvi and Amin Kurji, who all helped in their different, much-appreciated ways. And to Nicola and Caroline Colangelo and staff at their Coastal Aviation Company in Dar, the Tanzania-based Fox family, Iain Douglas Hamilton CBE and his old mentor Desmond Vesey Fitzgerald, Kim Howell, David Bygott and Jeannette Hanby, Karl Jaehn and former wife Christine; Karen Oakes, Peter Moscrop, Areta Williams, Nigel and Shelly, "Jeddo" Luwumba and colleagues at IST and Mamoya Bashgei Merus.

Thanks also to all wardens, rangers and game scouts in Tanzania and Kenya who welcomed and assisted us on our many safaris. And to the owners, managers and staffs of the old Mikumi Wildlife Lodge, Mikumi Wildlife Camp and Stanley's Kopje in Mikumi NP; Rufiji River, Lake Manze and Beho-Beho Tented Camps in the Selous Game Reserve; Ruaha River Lodge, Mwagusi Sand River Camp and Mdonya Old River Camp in Ruaha NP; Katavi Wildlife Camp in Katavi Plains NP; Oliver's Camp and Tarangire Tented Camp (now Lodge) in Tarangire NP; Gibbs Farm, Ngorongoro Farmhouse and Forest Hostel (now Rhino Lodge) by Ngorongoro Crater, all Serena lodges in the northern Tanzanian parks and "Sunny Safaris" tour operators, Arusha, and everyone at Matador Publishing Leicester, UK who have helped bring this book into print.